The Politics of Panem

CRITICAL LITERACY TEACHING SERIES: CHALLENGING AUTHORS AND GENRE

Volume 6

This series explores in separate volumes major authors and genres through a critical literacy lens that seeks to offer students opportunities as readers and writers to embrace and act upon their own empowerment. Each volume will challenge authors (along with examining authors that are themselves challenging) and genres as well as challenging norms and assumptions associated with those authors' works and genres themselves. Further, each volume will confront teachers, students, and scholars by exploring all texts as politically charged mediums of communication. The work of critical educators and scholars will guide each volume, including concerns about silenced voices and texts, marginalized people and perspectives, and normalized ways of being and teaching that ultimately dehumanize students and educators.

The Politics of Panem
Challenging Genres

Edited by

Sean P. Connors
University of Arkansas, Fayetteville, USA

SENSE PUBLISHERS
ROTTERDAM / BOSTON / TAIPEI

A C.I.P. record for this book is available from the Library of Congress.

ISBN 978-94-6209-804-6 (paperback)
ISBN 978-94-6209-805-3 (hardback)
ISBN 978-94-6209-806-0 (e-book)

Published by: Sense Publishers,
P.O. Box 21858, 3001 AW Rotterdam, The Netherlands
https://www.sensepublishers.com/

Cover picture by Mike Moon

Printed on acid-free paper

For my parents, who introduced me to the magic of story

TABLE OF CONTENTS

ACKNOWLEDGEMENTS

I would like to thank the authors who contributed to this volume. It has been a pleasure to read and respond to their work. Thanks to Mike Moon for contributing the cover image, and Karen Connors for sharing her artwork. I would like to acknowledge Peter de Liefde, the editorial staff at Sense Publishers, and the editorial board of the *Challenging Authors and Genres* series. Thanks to the students I've taught at the University of Arkansas. Not a day goes by that I don't appreciate how fortunate I am to work with them. Thanks to my colleagues, Chris Goering and David Jolliffe, for helping me carve out a space to pursue my interests in literature for adolescents. I could not ask for better colleagues. I am indebted to Paul Thomas, whose support and guidance were invaluable in helping me bring this project to fruition. I would like to thank Suzanne Collins, whose Hunger Games books continue to capture my imagination, and all those who read and responded to early drafts of this book.

Most of all, I would like to thank Brenda Connors, my wife and friend. Without her love, patience, and support, this book would not be possible. With her in my life, the odds are always in my favour.

SEAN P. CONNORS

INTRODUCTION

Challenging the Politics of Text Complexity

We shall not cease from exploration
And the end of all our exploring
Will be to arrive where we started
And know the place for the first time.
(T. S. Eliot, *Four Quartets*)

My first encounter with Katniss Everdeen occurred in 2008 after a student in a young adult literature course I was teaching at the time approached me after class and recommended that I read a then newly published novel by Suzanne Collins (2008) titled *The Hunger Games*. Influenced by the work of Anna Soter (1999) and Deborah Appleman (2009), I was experimenting with teaching young adult literature from the perspective of literary theory for the first time that semester. While this might seem like an odd pairing, my decision to ask students to apply theory to the texts they read was influenced by a number of factors, including what I experienced as reluctance of the part of many students to acknowledge young adult literature as a complex form of literature.

This isn't to say the undergraduates who took my course didn't enjoy reading young adult novels. They did. For some, the opportunity to do so constituted a welcome "break" from reading for other English classes. For others, it offered a chance to reconnect with beloved characters and stories they recalled from childhood. Still, I found that their experiences studying literature in high school and college English classes often seemed to lead students to differentiate between "Literature" with a capital "L"—which they defined as exploring universal themes, evincing a level of artistry, and inspiring deep, critical thinking (e.g., canonical literature)—and "literature" with a small "l"—which they associated with crass commercialism, but which they also embraced as "guilty pleasure" reading (e.g., young adult literature and other forms of popular culture texts). By inviting students who took the course to read young adult novels from the standpoint of theory, and by encouraging them to ask how these texts function to construct race, power, gender, class, and so on, my objective was (and continues to be) two-fold: first, to challenge students' often unexamined definitions of "Literature"; and second, to create an environment in which they are supported as they work together to critically investigate the complex, and often times thorny, issues and questions that a growing number of contemporary young adult authors explore in their writing.

S. P. Connors (ed.), The Politics of Panem, 1–12.

Following the advice of my student, I read *The Hunger Games* (Collins, 2008) for the first time that summer. In retrospect, I recall being taken by the character of Katniss immediately, and I enjoyed the novel as a fast-paced action adventure story. Collins's critique of reality television and her indictment of an oppressive class system intrigued me, but beyond that, I don't recall being particularly impressed with the book upon first reading it. Still, it had begun to attract a following, and so I chose to include it on my syllabus for the first time the following fall. In doing so, I asked the students who took the course to consider whether a feminist reading of the text supported (or undermined) arguments that depicted Katniss as a strong female protagonist. Impressed by the quality of our discussion and the depth of the ideas we explored, I chose to teach the novel again a year later. This time my students and I asked what an ecofeminist reading of the novel revealed about connections between the subjugation of nature and the oppression of women and minorities in patriarchal societies. Since then we have gone on to experiment with applying other critical lenses (Appleman, 2009) to *The Hunger Games* (Collins, 2008), and its companion volumes in the trilogy. With each passing year my appreciation for what Collins's accomplished as a writer has deepened. As this book attests, her dystopian narrative about a teenage girl unwittingly caught between competing political ideologies continues to capture my imagination. It also informs my efforts to characterize young adult literature as a complex body of literature capable of challenging readers of all ages (see, for example, Connors, 2013).

NAVIGATING THE DIVIDE BETWEEN HIGH AND LOW ART

In seeking a test case to examine young adult literature as a "challenging genre," the Hunger Games trilogy, which has proven immensely popular with mainstream audiences, might not seem to constitute the most logical choice. In 2012, the publisher Scholastic announced that 36.5 million copies of the novels were available in print in the United States alone (Lee, 2012). In the same year, the trilogy surpassed J. K. Rowling's seven-volume Harry Potter series to become the all-time best-selling books on Amazon (Haq, 2012). As of January 2014, the first two films—*The Hunger Games* and *Catching Fire*—in a planned four-film adaptation had broken a box office record, grossing over $800 million domestically (Busch, 2014). By any measure, the trilogy is a commercial success.

The popularity of the Hunger Games trilogy accompanies an increase in sales of young adult literature. According to Courtney Martin (2012), "[t]he number of [young adult] novels published each year has quadrupled in 12 years—from 3,000 in 1997 to 12,000 in 2009, when total sales exceeded $3 billion" (para. 5). In the same period of time young adult literature has garnered an adult readership. A report by one marketing research group determined that 55 percent of those purchasing young adult novels today are over the age of 18, with the majority between 33 and 44 years old (Bowker, 2012, para. 1). One might conclude that these adults are simply purchasing books for younger readers who lack the resources to do so for themselves. Yet when they were asked who they bought young adult novels for, survey respondents indicated "that 78 percent of the time they are purchasing books for their own reading" (para. 1). Nearly a third (30 percent) reported having read at least one book in Collins's Hunger Games trilogy (para. 3).

Popularity can be a double-edged sword, however, especially in academic settings where the study of children's literature can sometimes languish as a result of a distinction between so-called high and low art. Cindy Daniels (2006), for example, observes that there remain critics in secondary and higher education who believe that young adult literature does not warrant serious "attention because it doesn't offer enough substance to be included within the traditional literary canon" (p. 78). Similarly, Juliet McKenna (2014) argues that a "common assumption that 'kids' stuff' or 'commercially popular' means simplistic or inferior helps perpetuate [a] prejudice against science fiction and fantasy" (para. 13). One might assume that prejudices against young adult dystopias (and the adults who read them) are especially virulent. Responding to an increase in the number of adults who express an affinity for young adult literature, Ruth Graham (2014) unabashedly states, "Adults *should* feel embarrassed about reading literature written for children" (para. 3, emphasis in original). She continues:

> Let's set aside the transparently trashy stuff like *Divergent* and *Twilight*, which no one defends as serious literature. I'm talking about the genre the publishing industry calls "realistic fiction." These are the books, like *The Fault in Our Stars,* that are about real teens doing real things, and that rise and fall not only on the strength of their stories but, theoretically, on the quality of their writing. These are the books that could plausibly be said to be replacing *literary fiction* in the lives of their adult readers. And that's a shame. (para. 4, my emphasis)

It is possible to take exception to Graham's argument for a number of reasons, but her characterization of *Divergent* and *Twilight* as "trashy" and her coupling of realistic fiction and "literary" fiction are of particular interest to me here. I cannot help but sense that Graham's argument is in some ways a dismissal of speculative fiction—a category broadly defined as including dystopias, science fiction, steampunk, fantasy, and paranormal fiction, amongst others—as much as it is a criticism of the aforementioned texts. Realistic narratives may focus on "real teens doing real things," but that alone doesn't ensure their superiority to stories about teenage vampires and post-apocalyptic warriors. Likewise, it would seem that works of speculative fiction could also be said to "rise and fall on the quality of their writing." Indeed, McKenna (2014), a science fiction writer, postulates that speculative fiction may be more difficult to write than literary fiction:

> I can tell you from experience, as an author, as a reviewer, and after spending two years as a judge for the Arthur C Clarke Award and reading around 150 novels, that when readers are paying that much close attention to every hint and clue, the writer needs to have their internal logic, consistency of character and scene-setting absolutely nailed down. Readers have to be convinced that this unfamiliar world is solidly real if they're ever going to

suspend disbelief and accept the unreal, whether that's magic and dragons or faster-than-light travel. (para. 6)

McKenna (2014) concludes, "Speculative fiction may not imitate real life but it uses its magic mirror to reflect on the world around us" (para. 9). In doing so, it shares a goal of literary fiction.

Despite (or perhaps because of) its popularity with fans, there is a history of prejudice against dystopias in the field of literary criticism (see, for example, Milner, 2009). Nevertheless, Keith Booker (1994), like McKenna (2014), defends its literary value by pointing to the important work that the genre performs in holding up a mirror to society. Booker (1994) states:

> If dystopian literature functions in a sense as social criticism, it is also true that such literature gains its principal energies precisely from its literariness, from its ability to illuminate social and political issues from an angle not available to conventional critics. (p. 175)

He continues, "If the main value of literature in general is its ability to make us see the world in new ways, to make us capable of entertaining new and different perspectives on reality, then dystopian fiction is not a marginal genre" (Booker, 1994, p. 176). The same can be said of young adult literature, and of young adult dystopias in particular. By examining the Hunger Games trilogy critically, this collection of essays invites readers to reflect on how Collins's novels challenge us to see the world anew, and how they function to expose social and political inequities that are attributable to constructs such as race, gender, class, power, and so on.

THE HUNGER GAMES AND THE ISSUE OF TEXT COMPLEXITY

A host of blogs and websites attest to the popularity of young adult fiction with individual teachers and librarians. Many teacher education programs now require preservice teachers to take a course on young adult literature, and arguments for the value of teaching it abound. Wendy Glenn and her colleagues (2009) argue that young adult literature lends itself to promoting the sort of close reading that English educators have historically valued, while Soter (1999) recommends creating opportunities for students to apply literary theory to young adult novels as an exercise in thinking. Most importantly, research consistently suggests that students *enjoy* reading young adult literature (Dozier, Johnston, & Rogers, 2006; Miller, 2014; Sturm & Michel, 2009). Yet if some educators are excited about its educational value, the place of young adult literature in the secondary English curriculum is far from guaranteed in the current education reform context.

Stotsky's (2010) national study of the literature curriculum in public high schools identified a single young adult novel—*Speak* by Laurie Halse Anderson (1999)—among the 20 most frequently assigned book-length works in grades 9, 10, and 11. In terms of what students are required to read, Stotsky's (2010) study suggests that relatively little has changed in the approximately twenty years or so since Applebee (1993) determined that the 10 most frequently assigned book-length works in high school English classes were canonical.

Stotsky's (2010) finding is more disconcerting when one considers the appeal that young adult speculative fiction holds for adolescent readers. Citing statistics provided by Renaissance Learning, she explains that in 2008-2009 young adult fantasies accounted for 10 of the 16 books students in the top 10 percent of reading achievement in grades 9-12 read most frequently. More recently, a 2014 report issued by Renaissance Learning concluded that the Hunger Games trilogy—which is comprised of *The Hunger Games* (Collins, 2008), *Catching Fire* (Collins, 2009), and *Mockingjay* (Collins, 2010)—accounted for three of the 10 book that students in grades 9, 10, 11, and 12 reported reading most frequently in 2012-2013. These findings point to a discrepancy between the literary texts that adolescents self-select, many of which appear to fall under the umbrella of young adult literature and belong to the category of speculative fiction, and those that they are required to read for high school English classes, which are predominantly canonical and examples of realistic fiction. This divide is likely to widen as American schools implement the Common Core State Standards (CCSS).

Arguing that "the complexity of what students read matters," the architects of the CCSS have disseminated lists of "exemplar texts" that are said to reflect the level of complexity that students ought to experience in school to ensure that they are "college- and career-ready" (National Governors Association, 2010, p. 2). Although advocates of the CCSS use qualitative and quantitative measures to determine complexity, the general absence of young adult novels on these lists would seem to suggest that literature for adolescents lacks complexity and is therefore incapable of withstanding close, rigorous study. Unfounded assumptions of this sort have real world implications. Miller (2014), for example, explains that when students elect to write about young adult novels in response to an open question on the Advanced Placement English Literature and Composition exam, their essays "tend to be poorly evaluated by some readers because of their text selections, not on the quality of their essays, often receiving a 4 or lower (not a passing score)" (p. 46).

Anecdotal evidence from my own experiences as an educator at a university in the American South point to additional challenges that an emphasis on text complexity poses for secondary teachers interested in teaching young adult literature. Each year, as part of a course I teach on young adult fiction, I require students to interview a middle school or high school librarian about the role that young adult literature plays in both their school and its English department. A common thread in the papers I have read in the past few years suggests that while secondary students continue to check out young adult novels for independent reading assignments, these books are disappearing from the grade 8-12 English curriculum. Almost without exception, the librarians that my students interview attribute this to the emphasis that the CCSS place on rigor and complexity. Again, the implications for students are troubling.

In one school near the university where I work, English teachers chose to prohibit students from reading young adult speculative fiction and series books for independent reading assignments—this despite the librarian's reporting that dystopias and series books were among the most frequently checked out items in the library collection! The teachers defended their decision by pointing out that such books lack the complexity that they had been led to believe is necessary to prepare students to successfully complete the standardized assessments that will eventually be tied to the CCSS. A year ago I participated in a public panel on the CCSS. During the panel discussion, one school leader assured members of the audience that children's books that had traditionally been read at the fourth grade level were no longer being taught given that their readability scores indicated that they were not rigorous enough!

Such thinking, even if well intentioned, mistakes difficulty for complexity. Clarifying these terms, Jim Phelan (1999), in the foreword to Soter's (1999) *Young Adult Literature and the New Literary Theories,* states, "Difficulty is a measure of a text's accessibility, while sophistication is a measure of its skill in bending means to ends" (p. xi). Young adult dystopias like the Hunger Games novels may have lower readability scores, but so, too, do classics such as Camus's *The Stranger,* which has a readability score roughly equivalent to the novels in J. K. Rowling's Harry Potter series. Would anyone argue that *The Stranger,* which explores Camus's burgeoning philosophy about the absurdity of the human condition, lacks complexity?

Elsewhere, I have argued that the expectations and assumptions that readers bring to a work of literature contribute to their sense of its complexity (see, for example, Connors, 2013). The same can be said of the questions that readers ask of the texts they read. When I taught senior high school English, students who read Camus's *The Stranger* invariably characterized it as "easy" to read. Indeed, many of them regarded it as a relatively straightforward story about a man who (strangely) is put to death as a result of his refusal to cry at his mother's funeral. Asked to recall events from the story or to identify symbols and themes (that is, the sort of practices that standardized assessments tend to value and reward), these college-bound students would have had little difficulty doing so. Asked to consider how Camus's novel functions to illustrate tenets of existential philosophy, however, the same students found the text decidedly more challenging. In much the same way, when I invite undergraduates in the courses that I teach to ask how children's picture books function to reinforce racist, sexist, nationalist, or classist ideologies, they are often surprised to discover interpretive possibilities they hadn't previously recognized. In each instance, the invitation to read critically, and to draw on questions that theory makes available to them, deepens students' appreciation for the complexity of narratives that, upon first inspection, otherwise appear straightforward and simple.

That this should be the case isn't surprising. In Alan Purves's (1991) *The Idea of Difficulty in Literature,* Martin Nystrand (1991) argues that "curriculum and instruction—*what teachers ask students to do*—are themselves significant factors in the difficulty of any work of literature studied in school" (p. 143, my emphasis). In short, the questions that teachers invite students to ask of a text, coupled with the activities they invite them to take part in around it and the opportunities they create for them to share their interpretations of it with others, are crucial in determining the extent of the challenge that reading the text poses for them. In the case of literature, "difficulty is," as Nystrand (1991) concludes, "*more than a matter of which texts are taught; it is also a matter of how they are taught—that is, instruction*" (p. 152, my emphasis).

Nystrand's (1991) argument indirectly points to the importance of creating opportunities for readers of all ages to interrogate their definitions of "Literature" (with a capital "L"). Each semester, an essential question that I invite my students to explore as they read the assigned young adult novels, including those in the Hunger Games trilogy, asks: "What are the defining characteristics of "Literature?" As we progress through the semester, and as we read the assigned young adult novels and theoretical essays, we continually revisit that question. After much debate, students invariably conclude that the category of "Literature" is socially constructed, and, as such, subject to change. Along the way they also discover that, in many instances, they have inherited their definitions of literature from institutions and people in positions of authority without thinking to question those definitions. As fissures gradually begin to appear in students' ideas about what constitutes literature, and as they are given opportunities to read young adult texts such as Collins's Hunger Games trilogy from the standpoint of theory, their appreciation for their potential complexity and sophistication deepens.

This book was written with an audience of educators and advocates of young adult literature in mind. It does not, however, offer strategies for teaching literary theory. Likewise, it does not present ideas and activities that educators can use to teach Collins's Hunger Games trilogy. Rather, by bringing together a group of scholars in the humanities and social sciences whose work has led them to examine the Hunger Games trilogy critically, *The Politics of Panem*, in keeping with the aims of the *Challenging Authors and Genres* series, invites readers to view Collins's novels through fresh eyes, and to consider how both the books and the subsequent film adaptations, when examined from the standpoint of theory, can be used to initiate critical conversations about gender, class, identify, race, power, and perhaps even about adolescence itself. In doing so, this book takes as its guide T. S. Eliot's (1943) expectation that "the end of all our exploring/Will be to arrive where we started/And know the place for the first time" (p. 39).

THE HUNGER GAMES TRILOGY: CHALLENGING GENRES

In *Literary Theory*, Jonathan Culler (1997) eloquently argues that the goal of theory is "to show that what we take for granted as 'common sense' is in fact a historical construction, a particular theory that has come to seem so natural to us that we don't even see it as a theory" (p. 5). I would suggest that this includes "common sense" ideas about literature for adolescents, and about young adult dystopias in particular. *The Politics of Panem: Challenging Genres* is premised on an assumption that when readers approach young adult dystopias such as Suzanne Collins's Hunger Games trilogy critically, it is possible to see them in a new light and make visible the complex questions and problems that they invite us to explore. In this sense, it shares Pharr and Clark's (2012) observation that texts such as the Hunger Games novels stand as evidence of young adult literature's ability to "transcend the 'adolescent' label that so often limits its critical reception among scholars and mature readers" (p. 9).

The origins of this book are located in a series of questions that I posed at the outset of this project to the authors whose work appears in the pages to follow. A sample of my questions included:

- Read from a feminist perspective, how does Collins's trilogy illuminate power relations between men and women?
- In what ways does the trilogy instantiate, or subvert, dystopian genre conventions, and to what effect does it do so?
- How might examining the trilogy from the perspective of different philosophic frameworks deepen our appreciation for the issues it raises?
- What does reading the Hunger Games trilogy from a Marxist perspective reveal about the material basis of culture?
- How might adapting the trilogy for film complicate its ability to participate in sharp-edged social criticism?
- What do we stand to learn from considering fan responses to the Hunger Games trilogy?

Above all else, I encouraged the authors to consider what reading the Hunger Games trilogy from the standpoint of theory potentially reveals about its complexity and sophistication.

For organizational purposes, this book is divided into four parts. The essays that are featured in Part One, "'It's All How You're Perceived': Deconstructing Adolescence in Panem," share a broad interest in understanding what Collins's novels tell us about how society constructs adolescence. In chapter 1, "Some Walks You Have to Take Alone," Roberta Seelinger Trites argues that while the Hunger Games trilogy can be read as an example of anti-war literature, its intertextual connections also invite readers to consider how Collins manipulates ideology "to exploit and frighten her young readership into a distrust of government" (p. 15). For Trites, underlying the Hunger Games trilogy "is an implication that *only* adolescents can save the world because once they become adults they will be too corrupt to do so any longer" (p. 25). In chapter 2, "Worse Games to Play," Susan Tan challenges readings that regard the resolution to *Mockingjay* (Collins, 2010) as offering readers a "happy ending" that is at odds with the dystopian tenor of the series. In doing so, she argues that Katniss, like adolescence, can be read as "a powerfully destabilizing force" that continually challenges the "fixed boundaries of her world" (p. 41). For Tan, this raises questions about how society constructs adolescence, including a concern "that the rebellious teenager will become the rebellious adult" (p. 42). In chapter 3, "Hungering for Middle Ground," Meghann Meehusen examines how the Hunger Games, like other popular young adult dystopias, erodes binaries between a constructed and embodied self. In doing so, she argues that Katniss and Peeta exemplify social anxieties about the forces that construct a person's sense of self, as well as the power that "individuals have to affect or even recognize those influences" (p. 59).

The essays that make up Part Two, "'I Have a Kind of Power I Never Knew I Possessed': What Philosophy Tells Us about Life in Panem," examine the Hunger Games trilogy through the lens of philosophical criticism (Gillespie, 2010). In Chapter 4, "The Three Faces of Evil," Brian McDonald argues that the Hunger Games trilogy can be read as exemplifying Socrates' observation that the unexamined life is not worth living. Drawing on the work of Socrates, as well as Augustine of Hippo and the political philosopher Hannah Arendt, McDonald examines Katniss's evolution from warrior to philosopher. In doing so he argues that, in the end, her ability to stand against the evil she faces is directly attributable to her taking time to understand it. In chapter 5, "I Was Watching You, Mockingjay," Sean Connors examines how Collins's novels problematize philosopher Michel Foucault's deterministic view of surveillance as a mode of social control. Drawing on the work of Michel de Certeau, Connors argues that characters in Collins's trilogy use an array of tactics to subvert the gaze of the Capitol and, in some cases, even manage to turn it back on itself. Throughout his argument Connors invites readers to consider the tactics that are available to adolescents as they move between spaces (including school) in which the practice of surveillance is increasingly common. In chapter 6, "Exploiting the Gaps in the Fence," Michael Macaluso and Cori McKenzie draw on Foucault's analytics of power to contest arguments that characterize the power the Capitol wields in Collins's novels as absolute. In doing so, Macaluso and McKenzie persuasively demonstrate how Katniss and other characters exploit various modes of power to accomplish their ends. For Macaluso and McKenzie, the Hunger Games trilogy serves as a reminder to readers that "the possibility and potential for freedom and liberation are always present" (p. 122).

As the title suggests, the essays in Part Three, "'Look at the State They Left Us In': The Hunger Games as Social Criticism," share an interest in understanding how Collins's novels function as a form of social critique. Examining the trilogy through the lens of cultural criticism in chapter 7, "It's Great to Have Allies as Long as You Don't Have to Kill Them," Anna Soter considers how the world that Collins constructs exemplifies the sort of blurred ethics and moral ambiguity that one senses are increasingly characteristic of modern life. Nevertheless, Soter concludes that, in holding up a mirror to society, Collins's novels offer readers "the possibility of overcoming 'institutionalized' moral and ethical expediency and inertia" (p. 137). In chapter 8, "I Try to Remember Who I Am and Who I Am Not," Sean Connors offers an ecofeminist reading of *The Hunger Games* (Collins, 2008). In doing so, he argues that the novel can be read as a metaphor for the "damage that patriarchal institutions inflict on young females by inundating them with a steady stream of messages that function to actively limit the subject positions they recognize as available to them" (p. 141). In chapter 9, "We End Our Hunger for Justice," Rodrigo Joseph Rodríguez invites readers to consider how the Hunger Games trilogy, when paired with critical literacy, can awaken in readers a sense of social responsibility. For Rodríguez, equipping adolescents with critical reading skills is tantamount to empowering them. He consequently advocates reading "young adult dystopias critically with the goal of examining not only how they chronicle the human struggle, but also how they advocate liberating people from otherwise disempowering social conditions" (p. 159).

The essays in Part Four, "'That's a Wrap': Films, Fandom, and the Politics of Social Media," move the conversation about the Hunger Games trilogy from page to screen. In doing so, they explore a series of questions and issues that arise when Collins's novels are adapted for film. In chapter 10, "She Has No Idea. The Effect She Can Have," Hilary Brewster uses rhetorical narrative theory to demonstrate (or explore) how Collins (2008), through her use of a first person focalizer and present tense narration, complicates issues such as reader judgment and engagement in *The Hunger Games*. Having done so, Brewster then examines how adapting the story for film—a medium that, due to certain constraints, limits (if not eliminates) the possibility of narration and homodiegetic focalization—compounds issues such as ethics and audience. In chapter 11, "Are the -Isms Ever in Your Favor?," Iris Shepard and Ian Wojcik-Andrews argue for the value of examining film adaptations of young adult novels through the lens of critical theory. Applying Marxist theory, feminist theory, and multiculturalism to Ross's (2012) *The Hunger Games,* Shepard and Wojcik-Andrews demonstrate how the film works to perpetuate socioeconomic, political, and cultural inequities. For them, "Historical materialist readings of dystopian movies such as *The Hunger Games* (Ross, 2012) make important contributions to discussions about the representation of history and social class in film" (p. 201). Rounding out this set of essays, Antero Garcia and Marcell Haddix, in chapter 12, "The Revolution Starts Here," provocatively argue that Rue, not Katniss, is the real symbol of the revolution. In doing so, they examine the racial identities that fans of the Hunger Games books and films construct as they interact with one another on social media. For Garcia and Haddix, "Not seeing and naming race in novels such as Collins' (2008) *The Hunger Games* ... limits readers' comprehension of the text" (p. 216).

To conclude this book, P. L. Thomas, in the "Afterword," identifies a troubling pattern that he recognizes in adaptations of texts such as Collins's Hunger Games trilogy and Stieg Larsson's Millennium trilogy (*The Girl with the Dragon Tattoo*, *The Girl Who Played with Fire*, and *The Girl Who Kicked the Hornet's Nest*). Specifically, Thomas wonders why Hollywood studios feel compelled to transform already strong female protagonists such as Katniss Everdeen and Lisbeth Salander into figures of nearly superheroic proportions. For Thomas, this raises an important question, one that he envisions himself exploring with students: "Why are strong female characters not enough?" (p. 222). Echoing an assumption that I have emphasized throughout my introduction, Thomas writes:

> It is here, among the problems and questions raised by texts of all sort among genre, medium, and form, that I believe we must bring students. Our texts do not have to be pure or perfect—as is often the case with how women, minorities, and many "others" are portrayed—but nearly all texts can serve well our critical purposes to unpack art as it unpacks the real world captured in that imagined world. (p. 224)

Thomas's observation that virtually "all texts can serve well our critical purposes to unpack art as it unpacks the real world" provides a basis for contesting the politics of text complexity. It also offers a rationale for examining young adult literature, and young adult dystopias in particular, as a challenging genre. With these goals in mind, *The Politics of Panem* aims to highlight some of the problems and questions that teachers and students are capable of exploring together when they elect to read Collins's novels critically.

REFERENCES

Anderson, L. H. (1999). *Speak.* New York: Farrar, Straus and Giroux.

Applebee, A. N. (1993). *Literature in the secondary school: Studies of curriculum and instruction in the United States.* Urbana, IL: National Council of Teachers of English.

Appleman, D. (2009). *Critical encounters in high school English classrooms* (2nd ed.). New York: Teachers College Press.

Booker, K. (1994). *The dystopian impulse in modern literature: Fiction as social criticism.* Westport, CT: Greenwood.

Bowker. (2012). Young adult books attract growing numbers of adult fans. *Bowker.* Retrieved from http://www.bowker.com/en-US/aboutus/press_room/2012/pr_09132012.shtml

Busch, A. (2014). 'Hunger Games: Catching Fire' passes $409M domestically; Franchise hits record books. *Deadline Hollywood* [Blog post]. Retrieved from http://www.deadline.com/2014/01/hunger-games-catching-fire-becomes-highest-grossing-film-released-in-2013-passes-409m-domestically/

Collins, S. (2008). *The hunger games.* New York: Scholastic.

Collins, S. (2009). *Catching fire.* New York: Scholastic.

Collins, S. (2010). *Mockingjay.* New York: Scholastic.

Connors, S.P. (2013). Challenging perspectives on young adult literature. *English Journal, 102*(5), 69-73.

Culler, J. (1997). *Literary theory.* New York: Sterling.

Daniels, C. L. (2006). Literary theory and young adult literature: The open frontier in critical studies. *The ALAN Review, 33*(2), 78-82.

Dozier, C., Johnston, P., & Rodgers, R. (2006). *Critical literacy/critical teaching: Tools for preparing responsive teachers.* New York: Teachers College Press.

Eliot, T. S. (1943). *Four quartets.* New York: Harcourt, Brace & World.

Gillespie, T. (2010). *Doing literary criticism: Helping students engage with challenging texts.* Portland, ME: Stenhouse Publishers.

Glenn, W. J., King, D., Heintz, K., Lapatch, L., & Berg, E. (2009). Finding space and place for young adult literature. *The ALAN Review, 36*(2), 6-16.

Graham, R. (2014). Against YA. *Slate.* Retrieved from http://www.slate.com/articles/arts/books/2014/06/against_ya_adults_should_be_embarrassed_to_read_children_s_books.html

Haq, H. (2012). 'Hunger Games' passes 'Harry Potter' as bestselling Amazon series. *The Christian Science Monitor.* Retrieved February 28 from http://www.csmonitor.com/Books/chapter-and-verse/2012/0821/Hunger-Games-passes-Harry-Potter-as-bestselling-Amazon-series

Lee, S. (2012). Updated figures for 'The Hunger Games' books: More than 36.5M in print in the US alone. *Entertainment Weekly* [Blog post]. Retrieved from http://shelf-life.ew.com/2012/03/28/hunger-games-updated-sales/

Martin, C. E. (2012). From young adult book fans to wizards of change. *The New York Times.* Retrieved from http://opinionator.blogs.nytimes.com/2012/03/21/from-young-adult-book-fans-to-wizards-of-change/?_php=true&_type=blogs&_r=0

McKenna, J. (2014). The genre debate: Science fiction travels farther than literary fiction. *The Guardian*. Retrieved from http://www.theguardian.com/books/2014/apr/18/genre-debate-science-fiction-speculative-literary

Miller, s. (2014). Text complexity and 'comparable literary merit' in young adult literature. *The ALAN Review*, 41(2), 44-55.

Milner, A. (2009). Changing the climate: The politics of dystopia. *Continuum: Journal of Media & Cultural Studies*, 23(6), 827-838.

National Governors Association Center for Best Practices & Council of Chief State School Officers. (2010). *Common Core State Standards for English language arts & literacy in history/social studies, science, and technical subjects: Appendix A*. Washington, D.C.

Nystrand, M. (1991). Making it hard: Curriculum and instruction as factors in the difficulty of literature. In A. Purves (Ed.), *The idea of difficulty in literature* (pp. 141-156). Albany: State University of New York Press.

Pharr, M. F., & Clark, L. A. (2012). Introduction. In M. F. Pharr & L. A. Clark (Eds.), *Of bread, blood and The Hunger Games: Critical essays on the Suzanne Collins trilogy* (pp. 5-18). Jefferson, NC: McFarland & Company.

Phelan, J. (1999). Foreword. In Anna O. Soter, *Young adult literature and new literary theories* (pp. ix-xi). New York: Teachers College Press.

Purves, A. C. (1991). *The idea of difficulty in literature*. Albany, NY: State University of New York Press.

Renaissance Learning. (2014). *What kids are reading: The book reading habits of students in American schools*. Wisconsin: Renaissance Learning, Inc.

Ross, G. (Director). (2012). *The hunger games*. United States: Lionsgate.

Soter, A. O. (1999). *Young adult literature & the new literary theories*. New York: Teachers College Press.

Stotsky, S. (2010). *FORUM 4: Literary study in grades 9, 10, and 11: A national survey*. Boston: Association of Literary Scholars, Critics, and Writers.

Sturm, B. W., & Michel, K. (2009). The structure of power in young adult novels. *Young Adult Library Services*, 7(2), 39-47.

PART ONE

"It's All How You're Perceived": Deconstructing Adolescence in Panem

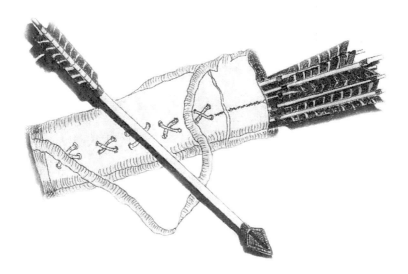

ROBERTA SEELINGER TRITES

1. "SOME WALKS YOU HAVE TO TAKE ALONE"

Ideology, Intertextuality, and the Fall of the Empire in
The Hunger Games *Trilogy*

In a rare interview with *Time* magazine, Suzanne Collins openly asserted in 2013
that she considers the Hunger Games trilogy to be an extended anti-war
commentary, and she admits that she was influenced by a variety of sources. "I
think that it's very uncomfortable for people to talk to children about war I
think we put our children at an enormous disadvantage by not educating them in
war, by not letting them understand about it from a very early age .... It's
something we should be having dialogues about a lot earlier with our children"
(Grossman, 2013a, para. 4 and 6). She then explains which stories about war
influenced her writing of the trilogy:

> In terms of the initial impulse for the story, I was a Greek mythology fanatic
> as a child, so you'll definitely see elements of that, from Theseus and the
> [M]inotaur and the oppression of Crete by Athens, the lottery and the calling
> of the youths and the maidens to be thrown into the labyrinth in Crete. Also
> *Spartacus*. (Grossman, 2013a, para. 12)

Collins thus acknowledges that she relies on many literary influences as she
advances what she perceives to be the anti-war message of the Hunger Games
trilogy.

Some of Collins' literary allusions serve simply as references that help readers
anticipate the plot of the Hunger Games books in terms of anti-violence. For
example, Katniss' and Peeta's unfulfilled threat of double-suicide evokes the
tragedy that concludes *Romeo and Juliet*, and the idea of people hunting people
leads logically to the same type of ending that Richard Connell's short story "The
Most Dangerous Game" implies: nefarious things will happen when people hunt
each other. But most of the literary allusions in the Hunger Games trilogy evoke
complex ideological dialogues between these three novels and their literary
predecessors.

In *Desire and Language*, Kristeva (1980) borrows from Saussure to clarify
Bakhtin's concept of dialogism when she defines "intertextuality" in these terms:
"any text is constructed as a mosaic of quotations; any text is the absorption and
transformation of another. The notion of intertextuality replaces that of
intersubjectivity, and poetic language is read as at least double" (p. 66). At its
heart, this definition of intertextuality is invested in what Kristeva refers to as the
"ideologeme" (p. 37), implying that intertextuality is always already implicated in

S. P. Connors (ed.), The Politics of Panem, 15–28.

ideology. Frederic Jameson (1982) defines an "ideologeme" as "the smallest intelligible unit of the essentially antagonistic collective discourses of social classes" (p. 76). Moreover, John Stephens (1992) argues that intertextuality in children's literature has the potential to encourage readers' "self-conscious subjectivity" for two reasons: "because it keeps visible the processes of narrative discourse and representation and because its play of differences functions as a critique of social values" (p. 6). It is the latter of these two functions that interests me most. Collins relies heavily on intertextuality in the Hunger Games series to establish a "critique of social values" that does far more intricate work than the anti-war agenda she acknowledges. The intertextual ideologemes on which she relies are largely invested in issues of power and its corruption, and the ideologemes are sometimes so conservative as to be reactionary. In this chapter, I will explore some of Collins' intended anti-war ideology; then I will turn to an examination of the relationship between intertextuality and ideology in her trilogy. Ultimately, this essay deconstructs Suzanne Collins' intertextual references in the Hunger Games trilogy to demonstrate how one author manipulates ideology in order to exploit and frighten her young readership into a distrust of government.

ANTI-WAR IDEOLOGIES IN THE HUNGER GAMES TRILOGY

Collins believes that she is writing about war in an effort to teach teenagers about its violence and the problem with being a voyeur during times of war. She believes it is a message necessary for adolescents to hear because "if we wait too long" to tell them about the horrors of war, "what kind of expectation can we have?" She then adds, "I don't write about adolescence .... I write about war. For adolescents" (Dominus, 2011, para. 15 and 17). The novels that comprise the Hunger Games trilogy were published from 2008-2010 when the United States was engaged in wars in both Iraq and Afghanistan and when conversations about reinstating the draft emerged. Collins' father served in Vietnam; during World War I, her grandfather was gassed, and his uncle was wounded in battle in World War II (Dominus, 2011). In many senses, then, the reapings in the Hunger Games stand in for the unfairness of a wartime draft.

As played in the arena of Panem, the Hunger Games themselves are both an aftermath and deterrent to war: after a war that almost destroyed Panem, the Capitol demands tributes from each of the districts as a reminder to the people of the futility of rebellion (Collins, 2008). The government's blatant betrayal of its people occurs in *Catching Fire* (Collins, 2009), when the Capitol demands that only survivors of previous Hunger Games, victors from past Games, will serve as tributes in the seventy-fifth Hunger Games (p. 250). After the rebels penetrate that arena and rescue Katniss and some of the other rebel-tributes, the Capitol shows its power by destroying Katniss' home region, District 12. The rebels then engage in total warfare in *Mockingjay* (Collins, 2010). The destruction is brutal and often senseless, which Peeta especially emphasizes. He discusses fighting in the arena as a metaphor for war: "It costs a lot more than your life. To murder innocent people ... [i]t costs everything you are" (p. 23). Later, in the same novel, Katniss talks to

16

Gale about what it means to kill someone in the type of hand-to-hand combat the arena requires: "I don't know what to tell him about the aftermath of killing a person. About how they never leave you" (p. 69). Both Peeta and Katniss subsequently grapple with the ethics of warfare, as when, for example, a military leader named Boggs asks Katniss, "If we engage in that type of war with the Capitol, would there be any human life left?" (p. 81). Peeta insists that the ethical costs of war are too high when he urges Katniss not to act as the symbolic leader of the rebellion: "They've turned you into a weapon that could be instrumental in the destruction of humanity. If you've got any real influence, use it to put the brakes on this thing. Use it to stop the war before it's too late" (p. 113). War, these comments imply, always comes at too high of a cost.

Katniss' awareness of the ethical stakes increases when, in *Mockingjay,* she realizes that Gale is using human nature against itself to design brutally lethal weapons: "This is what they've been doing. Taking the fundamental ideas behind Gale's traps and adapting them into weapons against humans" (Collins, 2010, p. 186). She then realizes, "It's less about the mechanics of the traps than the psychology behind them …. Like compassion. A bomb explodes. Time is allowed for people to rush to the aid of the wounded. Then a second, more powerful bomb kills them as well"—which is exactly what happens when the rebels' own bombs first kill a large group of children and then explode to kill an even larger group, including the medics who have swept in to help the children (p. 186). Katniss is also horrified at the thought of trapping people in a mountain called the Nut, but she does not have the language to argue "why it is so wrong to be exchanging fire when people, any people, are trying to claw their way out of the mountain" (pp. 211-212). She then immediately raises an ideological question about the ethics of war: "Or is my own history making me too sensitive? Aren't we at war? Isn't this just another way to kill our enemies?" (p. 212). She asks a man who has escaped from that burning mountain, "It just goes around and around, and who wins? Not us. Not the districts. Always the Capitol" (p. 215). People die in war. Citizens die. Even children die. But Katniss is making clear to all who are listening that soldiers never win; only governments do, which is what makes me question the underlying ideological implications of the trilogy. Under the leadership of President Alma Coin, the rebels, after all, have proven to be as corrupt and insensitive to basic humanity during warfare as the Capitol and President Snow have been. This leads me to interrogate the competing ideologemes in these novels. Are they *really* anti-war novels? Examining the novels' intertextuality provides one way for us to perceive an even clearer distinction between Collins' ideologemes about pacifism and those about abuses of government power.

DYSTOPIC INTERTEXTUALITY

The Hunger Games trilogy clearly belongs to a long literary tradition of dystopic novels. Literally defined as a "hard or bad landscape," the first use of the term *dystopia* in English occurred in England in 1868 when John Stuart Mill created a neologism from Thomas More's 1551 term "utopia" to describe how ill-conceived the British government's Irish land policy was ("Dystopia, n.," 2013). Hintz and Ostry (2003) link the utopian tradition to the dystopian tradition. "We use the term 'utopia' ...," they write:

> to signify a nonexistent society that is posited as significantly better than that of the reader. It strives toward perfection, has a delineated social system, and is described in reasonably specific detail. Dystopias are likewise precise descriptions of societies, ones in which the ideals for improvement have gone tragically amok. (p. 3)

Joseph W. Campbell (2010) argues that dystopian novels ask readers to "look critically at the power structures that envelop and seek to construct them" (p. 2); moreover, "[d]ystopian literature ... is concerned with making the often-seemingly invisible cycle of ideological subject formation clear," he writes (p. 6). Dystopian fiction, as Jack Zipes (2003) observes, "often includes a critique of 'postmodern,' advanced technological society gone awry" (p. xi).

George Orwell's *1984* (1949) is perhaps the English language's most famous dystopia. As in Panem, the government of Oceania manipulates language and does not hesitate to torture its citizens to remind them where social power lies. Mark Mills (2013) traces the following intertextual connections between the two novels: both novels depict violent brutality, the use of nuclear weapons, impersonalized place-names, and a government that manipulates people to hate those whom they originally loved; and both novels involve a concept that Mills refers to as "The Tarnished Revolution." I would add to that list "the panoptic presence of surveillance," whether by Big Brother or the government of Panem. But it is Mills' last point, specifically, his reference to "The Tarnished Revolution," that interests me most as an intertextual connection between *1984* and the Hunger Games trilogy because that is the ideologeme that reflects Collins' ideas about the impossibility of government reform, a point I expand on later in this chapter.

Collins acknowledges that dystopias such as *1984* and *Brave New World* "directly influenced" the writing of *The Hunger Games* (Grossman, 2013a, para. 14). The trilogy shares with *Brave New World* an emphasis on a government-manipulated caste-system and the idea of a tarnished (or in the case of *Brave New World*, failed) revolution. In a reference to another major dystopia, Katniss Everdeen serves in *Mockingjay* in squad 451—a clear reference to Ray Bradbury's *Fahrenheit 451*. (As with the books in Bradbury's dystopia, the soldiers in squad 451 experience more than one form of flame and toxic, burning gas.) Moreover, Collins acknowledges that she can't "pretend" she has not been influenced by Shirley Jackson's dystopian story, "The Lottery": "[I]t's a lottery in which you draw a name and people die. That's a short story, but it's such an incredible short story" (Collins, qtd. in Grossman, 2013a, para. 14). That story is set in an abstractly agrarian future, and the people there hold an annual lottery every June for reasons no one quite understands. The random selection of the black spot gets one stoned to death in "The Lottery," which is as arbitrary as being selected in the evocatively agrarian lottery called "the reaping" in the Hunger Games. The plot device shared by these stories underscores two ideologemes: governments can hold absolute power over people, but that power nonetheless resides in the people themselves. The agrarian people of "The Lottery," like the citizens of Panem, are complicit with a government that allows citizens to destroy each other.

A specifically recurring feature of adolescent dystopias is their tendency to insert teenagers into a dystopic future in which they are held responsible for fixing their culture's current corruption. One adolescent dystopia that shares both intertextual plot and ideologeme similarities is Takami's (1999/2003) *Battle Royale*—which Collins denies ever having read, although speculation about the possibility that she borrowed heavily from either the novel's or the film's plot abounds in the blogosphere. In 2011, Collins told *The New York Times*, "I had never heard of that book or that author until my book was turned in" (Dominus, 2011, para. 18). Nevertheless, in both stories, teenagers are pitted against each other to the death as a sort of cautionary tale for their nation's young citizenry. *Battle Royale* comments on widespread youth violence and corruption in Japan in the 1990s; *The Hunger Games*, on the other hand, presents adolescents as the potential saviors of the culture, rather than as a source of corruption. In this sense, *Battle Royale* might have more in common with *The Lord of the Flies* than *The Hunger Games* does with Golding's novel. But it should be noted that Collins calls *The Lord of the Flies* "one of my favorite books. That was a big influence on me as a teenager; I still read it every couple of years" (Grossman, 2013a, para. 11). In all of these novels, however—*Lord of the Flies*, *Battle Royale*, and *Mockingjay*, in particular—teenagers ultimately prove either unable to implement a new government or unable to prevent corruption in a newly established government. Collins' intertextuality is thus heavily invested in the ideologeme that absolute power corrupts absolutely.

CLASSICAL CONNECTIONS

As I noted in my introduction, Collins openly acknowledges the influence of the story of Theseus and the Minotaur in crafting the reaping in *The Hunger Games* (Dominus, 2011). In various versions of the ancient myth, seven young warriors and seven beautiful virgins are chosen by lottery to be sacrificed to the half-man, half-bull created by Daedelus to protect the labyrinth in Crete. Both stories thus share such concepts as the idea of a lottery and an elaborate setting (labyrinth or arena) for a hunt to the death, as well as ideologemes about a corrupt leadership that sacrifices its young for malevolent purposes.

Moreover, Collins also pays direct tribute to Stanley Kubrick's (1960) film *Spartacus*. Multiple parallels exist, since Spartacus is the name of a slave who leads an extended uprising against the troubled Roman Empire in the years when Julius Caesar was still only a senator. The film has an almost dystopic setting in the way that a totalitarian government controls every aspect of daily life. One character even acknowledges that "there are more slaves in Rome than Romans" (Kubrick, 1960), just as the citizens of the districts in Panem outnumber the citizens of the Capitol. Spartacus is trained to be a gladiator by an unctuous slave-trader named Lentulus Batiatus, a man as expedient and status-conscious as Effie Trinket.

Batiatus even speaks a phrase that prefigures Effie Trinket's much-parodied adage, "May the odds be ever in your favor" (Collins, 2008, p. 19) when he says to the gladiators-in-training with saccharine insincerity, "And may fortune smile on most of you" (Kubrick, 1960).

Collins herself provides a clear summary of the influence of *Spartacus* on her trilogy:

> There's a basis for the war, historically, in the *Hunger Games*, which would be the third servile war, which was Spartacus's war, where you have a man who is a slave who is then turned into a gladiator who broke out of the gladiator school and led a rebellion and then became the face of the war. So there is a historical precedent for that arc for a character. (Grossman, 2013a, para. 7)

In the Kubrick (1960) film, under the leadership of Crassus (one of the First Triumvirate, the three leaders who were instrumental in bringing down the Roman Republic to establish the Roman Empire), the slave rebellion fails, but the Romans promise clemency to all the slaves if they will identify their leader. Instead of doing so, one man after another loyally stands to make the false claim, "I am Spartacus" (Kubrick, 1960). To punish their loyalty, Crassus has all 6,000 men crucified—Spartacus last of all. He has led his men in a doomed rebellion because he believes that the only form of freedom available to a slave is death. He says, "[A]ll men die, but a slave and a free man lose different things .... When a free man dies, he loses the pleasure of life. A slave loses his pain. Death is the only freedom a slave knows .... That's why we'll win" (Kubrick, 1960). Later, Spartacus redefines what he means: "Just by fighting them we won something. When just one man says, 'No, I won't,' Rome begins to fear. We were tens of thousands who said 'no'" (Kubrick, 1960). In other words, *Spartacus* is not a pacifist, anti-war film; on the contrary, it advocates violence when revolt against a corrupt government is justified. But like the character Spartacus, Katniss in *Catching Fire* (Collins, 2009) also recognizes the power—and the problem—inherent in one person having the strength to rebel against an entire government: "All I was doing was trying to keep Peeta and myself alive. Any act of rebellion was purely coincidental. But when the Capitol decrees that only one tribute can live and you have the audacity to challenge it, I guess that's a rebellion in itself" (p. 18). She also perceives the rebellion in Panem in terms of a slave-revolt when she hears herself described as the leader who "turned a country of slaves into an army of freedom fighters" (Collins, 2009, p. 294).

Whereas the rebels in Panem succeed in overthrowing the government, and Katniss, the face of that rebellion, is allowed to live, Spartacus is killed in the Kubrick (1960) film. As he hangs dying on the cross, however, he has a personal victory when he sees his wife and infant son; Spartacus dies aware that at least his son will grow up no longer living as a slave. Like the rebellion in the Hunger Games trilogy, then, the revolt in *Spartacus* has a compromised ending that leads the plot to an ambiguous ending, one in which the terms of success are contingent upon each character's personal view of events. Although Crassus thinks he has won the rebellion, Spartacus dies knowing that the institution of slavery has been undermined in the Roman Empire. And just as history tells us that Crassus and the First Triumvirate were all in some way betrayed and ultimately defeated, Katniss betrays President Coin, the corrupt leader of Panem's rebellion; Katniss herself assassinates Coin.

In an additional reference to classicism, Collins names one of the major rebel leaders in the trilogy "Plutarch" in a clear nod to the historian who wrote *The Life of Caesar*—one of the Roman leaders instrumental in fighting Spartacus. Collins' father routinely read to her from Plutarch's biographies of Roman leaders (Grossman, 2013a), and she identifies Plutarch Heavensbee as the character who is most like herself: "Plutarch masterminds the rebellion, so he's thinking in many ways about the story and how the story is unfolding in the same way I am as an author when I'm telling it" (Grossman, 2013b, para. 16). Collins may well share with Plutarch a metanarrative sense of gamesmanship and showmanship, but it should be noted that the Roman historian Plutarch was more likely to glorify war than condemn it. Indeed, the Kubrick (1960) film *Spartacus* also condones war as a means of ending oppression. *Spartacus* implies that although rebellion and war have a cost, that cost is well worth the loss of human life.

In another bellicose reference to Rome, Collins names one character after an orator, Cato, who opposed Caesar and killed himself in 46 B.C. when he realized that Caesar would triumph in the Civil War. Cato tried to commit suicide by piercing himself with his own sword. According to the Roman historian Plutarch (1919):

> Cato drew his sword from its sheath and stabbed himself below the breast. His thrust, however, was somewhat feeble, owing to the inflammation in his hand, and so he did not at once dispatch himself, but in his death struggle fell from the couch and made a loud noise by overturning a geometrical abacus that stood near. His servants heard the noise and cried out, and his son at once ran in, together with his friends. They saw that he was smeared with blood, and that most of his bowels were protruding, but that he still had his eyes open and was alive; and they were terribly shocked. But the physician went to him and tried to replace his bowels, which remained uninjured, and to sew up the wound. Accordingly, when Cato recovered and became aware of this, he pushed the physician away, tore his bowels with his hands, rent the wound still more, and so died. (para. 107)

Readers know from his very name that Cato, the Tribute in *The Hunger Games* from District 2, will be a formidable opponent, one who will die violently from wounds that are in some ways connected with his own self-destruction and martial nature.

There are, of course, additional references to classical era history and literature about it in the Hunger Games trilogy, some of which have ideological import, others of which do not. The brothers with linked fates, Castor and Pollux, are named for the twins in classical mythology who constitute the constellation Gemini. Claudius Templesmith, the announcer of the Hunger Games, evokes the

ROBERTA SEELINGER TRITES

misunderstood but basically good Roman Emperor Claudius—celebrated in Robert Graves' (1934) novel *I, Claudius*—but Claudius also shared the consulship of Rome for two years with his infamous, brutal, and corrupt nephew, Caligula.

An intertextual reference with more militaristic overtones includes *Ben-Hur*, which was written by Lew Wallace (1880), one of the Civil War's Union generals. The novel justifies the use of violence to overthrow usurping forces—such as the Romans in biblical times or the Confederacy in 1861. With the Holocaust and the founding of Israel fresh in American minds in 1959, the movie *Ben-Hur*, directed by William Wyler, is far more direct about justifying the Jews' use of military force to defend a nation from those who would claim dominion over the land, as the Romans had 2,000 years earlier. Although the similarities of narrative arc and dialogue are not as pronounced as those between the film *Spartacus* and the Hunger Games trilogy, the film *Ben-Hur* nonetheless advocates the necessity of military force, just as *Spartacus* does. Moreover, Messalla in *The Hunger Games* (Collins, 2008) appears to be named for Ben-Hur's best friend growing up, Messala—a friend who ultimately betrays Ben-Hur's earlier trust and dies because of it. Like Messalla, Cressida is also a member of squad 451 in *Mockingjay*. Her name evokes Cressida, the untrue woman in Shakespeare's *Troilus and Cressida* who utters the lines, "Ah, poor our sex"—although in *Mockingjay*, neither Messalla nor Cressida show such perfidy.

Other intertexts contain ideologemes that are even more closely linked to those of Collins' trilogy. For example, President Coriolanus Snow's name links him ideologically to Shakespeare's play *Coriolanus*, in which the title figure is despised for withholding grain—one thinks of the tessareae of grain in Panem—from commoners; Brutus is one of the leaders who schemes against him; Coriolanus is eventually killed by conspirators angry that he has betrayed them to Rome. Additionally, in Roman history, Seneca the Younger was forced to kill himself because he allegedly plotted to assassinate Nero. While in the film adaptation of *The Hunger Games* (Ross, 2012) Gamemaker Seneca Crane is assassinated for allowing Katniss and Peeta to live, his sympathy for Katniss and Peeta has perhaps suicidal implications, since President Snow holds Seneca responsible for allowing these tributes to live. Snow actually tells Katniss, "If the Head Gamemaker, Seneca Crane, had had any brains, he'd have blown you to dust" (Collins, 2009, p. 20). Most of the intertextually-inspired names in the Hunger Games trilogy thus evoke not pacifism but gross misuses of power. Cato's, Claudius', Messala's, Coriolanus', and Seneca's stories are not really cautionary anti-war tales. All of them reference the lengths political leaders will take to ensure their continued hold on political power, including violence. Several of these stories even justify war as a political necessity. In other words, most of Collins' intertextual references contain ideologemes about power and who wields it. The intertextual references to the corrupt nature of politics and governments play a far more prominent role in the Hunger Games trilogy than Collins' putative anti-war ideologies.

JULIUS CAESAR, JUVENAL, AND THE FALL OF THE EMPIRE

Collins has clearly set the Hunger Games trilogy up as a parable for the fall of the Roman Empire. Just as Romans were too focused on "bread and circuses"—in Latin, *panem et circenses*—Collins implies that American citizens are too focused on free government hand-outs and entertainment-as-spectacle. As all readers of this volume are aware, in Collins' dystopias, the U.S. has itself been renamed "Panem" and the country is ruled from a capital, not unlike Rome, which is divided into districts, just as the Romans divided their provinces and ruled from afar. Indeed, at least seven characters from *The Hunger Games* (Collins, 2008) have their names borrowed directly from *Julius Caesar*: Portia, Flavius, Octavia (instead of Octavius), Cato, Cinna, Brutus, and Caesar. And of course, the Hunger Games themselves involve the loss of human life and are held in arenas and watched by the citizenry, just as Roman gladiatorial games were.

In other words, Collins is not just writing a speculative novel about the future; she is writing a cautionary tale about contemporary U.S. life based on ancient history. While she claims she is writing anti-war novels, she also seems to be warning adolescents not to rely on the government for handouts and Hollywood for entertainment—because otherwise, the populous will become too corrupt and the Empire will fall. Indeed, Juvenal's original words written in 128 C.E. speak to his belief that the Roman Empire fell because of the corruption that followed too heavily from a reliance on "*panem et circenses*": "Now that no one buys our votes, the public has long since cast off its cares; the people that once bestowed commands, consulships, legions and all else, now meddles no more and longs eagerly for just two things: Bread and Games!" (Juvenal, 1918, para. 5). Referencing this line in *Mockingjay*, Plutarch states, "The writer was saying that in return for full bellies and entertainment, his people had given up their political responsibilities and therefore power" (Collins, 2010, p. 223). Katniss responds, "So that's what the districts are for. To provide the bread and circuses" (pp. 223-224). Plutarch is then as ideologically direct in his response as any passage in all three of the novels: "Yes. And as long as that kept rolling in, the Capitol could control its little empire. Right now, it can provide neither, at least at the standard the people are accustomed to" (p. 224). This accounts for the willingness of some citizens in Panem to join the rebellion.

Katniss knows that she is only the face of a rebellion; she is, quite literally, the actor put in front of cameras to inspire other people's rebellions. A rebel leader tells her, "[Y]ou're the mockingjay, Katniss .... While you live, the revolution lives" (Collins, 2009, p. 386). Her role is not to be a military leader; it is to be propaganda. Her self-description of this awareness emphasizes her embodiment, particularly her face, as an emblem of rebellion rather than the brains behind it: "I must now become the actual leader, the face, the voice, the embodiment of the revolution .... They have a whole team of people to make me over, dress me, write my speeches, orchestrate my appearances ... and all I have to do is play my part" (Collins, 2010, pp. 10-11). She knows she can trust almost no one, "[c]ertainly not that crew in [District]13" who are the real leaders of the rebellion (p. 13); she knows also that she and Peeta have been used by the rebels "as pawns" (p. 21). Her doubts about the rebels mount throughout *Mockingjay*: "In some ways, District 13 is even more controlling than the Capitol" (p. 36). Later, she tells her prep team to be wary of President Coin: "If you had any delusions about having power, I'd let them go now" (p. 50).

Katniss directly identifies the four "forces" that have manipulated her: the Gamemakers, President Snow, President Coin, and the rebels "ensnaring me in the metal claw that lifted me from the arena, designating me to be their Mockingjay" (Collins, 2010, p. 59). Katniss recognizes that she has "[p]ower. I have a kind of power I never knew I possessed"—and she knows that Coin feels so threatened by that power that the president of District 13 "must publicly remind her people that I am not in control" (p. 91). Katniss does not "trust the rebels or Plutarch or Coin. I'm not confident that they tell me the truth"—and she's right: they don't (p. 114). Peeta also openly says that no one is immune from power and its corrupting force: "No one is safe. Not in the Capitol. Not in the districts" (p. 133). And when Boggs, the military leader whom Katniss trusts most, lies dying, he tells her, "Don't trust them. Don't go back" (p. 280). He is warning her not to trust the rebel government.

Plutarch tells Katniss in *Mockingjay* that if the rebels win, "everyone" will "be in charge of the government" because "[w]e're going to form a republic where the people of each district and the Capitol can elect their own representatives to be their voice in a centralized government .... And if our ancestors could do it, then we can, too" (Collins, 2010, pp. 83-84). Katniss' voice grows distinctly ideological in response:

> Frankly, our ancestors don't seem much to brag about. I mean, look at the state they left us in, with the wars and the broken planet. Clearly, they didn't care about what would happen to the people who came after them. But this republic idea sounds like an improvement over our current government. (p. 84)

Katniss, of course, has to kill the first leader of the new republic in order for representative democracy to have any chance at all of working.

IDEOLOGEMES OF POWER AND TRAUMA

By the end of the trilogy, Katniss is an adult woman who has managed to have a family, despite her post-traumatic stress disorder (PTSD). Predictably, the clichéd love triangle that overdetermines much of the plot has been resolved. Although it has taken Katniss far too long to decide whether she loves the emotionally unavailable man or the one who is emotionally available, she finally realizes that she cannot choose Gale because he will forever be implicated in her mind in the corrupt mechanisms of war, particularly those that killed her sister. Moreover, he has become a successful political operative in the new regime, with "some fancy job" (Collins, 2010, p. 384). Political power has corrupted Gale, just as it has ruined Katniss' world. Her traumatization is complete; for years, she "wake[s] screaming from nightmares of mutts and lost children" (p. 388) and she dreads having to explain her nightmares to her children: "Why they [the dreams] came.

Why they won't ever really go away" (p. 390). She wonders how she can ever explain about the governments that did this to her and Peeta and their children: "How can I tell them about that world without frightening them to death? ... My children, who don't know they play on a graveyard?" (pp. 389-390). One wonders, then, how young readers of this novel are supposed to be anything other than frightened "to death" of their own futures.

Significantly, Katniss seems largely disempowered by the end of the novels. She ends the trilogy as a sad and traumatized adult: "It's been a long time since I've been considered a child in this war," she says when she contemplates whether the rebels or the Capitol have intentionally killed children, including her sister (Collins, 2010, p. 360). Moreover, she insists: "I no longer feel any allegiance to these monsters called human beings, despite being one myself .... Because something is significantly wrong with a creature that sacrifices its children's lives to settle its differences" (p. 377). After Katniss has assassinated Coin, Plutarch cynically comments on the unlikelihood of peace enduring: "collective thinking is usually short-lived. We're fickle, stupid beings with poor memories and a great gift for self-destruction" (p. 379). He doubts that this government will be able to sustain its temporary goodness. Ideologically, the message to teen readers is bleak and potentially disempowering: Never trust peace. Never trust government.

As an adult, Katniss herself rejects the internal strength that has empowered her all along:

> [W]hat I need to survive is not Gale's fire, kindled with rage and hatred. I have plenty of fire myself. What I need is the dandelion in the spring. The bright yellow that means rebirth instead of destruction. The promise that life can go on, no matter how bad our losses. That it can be good again. (Collins, 2010, p. 388)

She rejects public leadership and power and defines happiness only in personal, individual terms, no longer caring to inspire others. She resents that she has been a tool of the rebels: "I was a piece ... [u]sed without consent, without knowledge" (p. 383). As a result, she ultimately cares only about herself and her family unit, so she seems more repressed as an adult than empowered. Perhaps one could argue that Katniss is empowered because she has come to accept a more gentle way of living. Or perhaps she has achieved maturity in recognizing that adults always already live in a repressed condition that is largely disempowered. But either way, she has had far more social and political power as a teenager than she has as an adult. And she has proven a point that she makes early in *Mockingjay* when she claims, "Some walks you have to take alone" (Collins, 2010, p. 5). As an ideologeme, the statement implies the ultimate self-responsibility each individual must take for herself or himself. Again: trust no government.

Katniss has been betrayed by two different governments and by her first love, and the only way she has been able to heal is to isolate herself from others and have only limited contact with the few beings she trusts: Peeta, Haymitch, Greasy Sae, Dr. Aurelius—and Prim's cat. While many people are tempted to claim Katniss as a feminist hero, she ends the series in a role more evocative of the type of 1950s housewife against which second-wave feminists rebelled than as an adult self-actualized enough to employ her strength for the greater good of her society. She has become this shadow of herself because the corruption of two governments has succeeded in making her wish to self-efface her own potential power.

In portraying all government as corrupt and in having Katniss and Peeta live the lives of semi-recluses in what is effectively a bunkered compound, Collins reveals an ideological position very close to Libertarianism—the underlying ethics of which involves an inherent distrust of government. Collins is not writing about the future; she is teaching her contemporary readership never to trust *any* government—because if they do, they will still ultimately have to save themselves from the greed and corruption of the adults who comprise the government. But since maturation is largely inevitable for the majority of teens, the message seems to be a mixed one. The Hunger Games trilogy may be a metaphor for contemporary problems, one that implies that social decay is imminent. But underlying that message is an implication that *only* adolescents can save the world because once they become adults they will be too corrupt to do so any longer. These novels place great burdens on the shoulders of adolescents and imply a confusing message that not only *must* adolescents grow-up, but they *must* solve the world's problems *before* they grow up and become incapable of doing so (because once they are adults they will have become too corrupt or traumatized to reform anything anymore). It is possible that Collins is providing her reader with competing ideologemes and hoping that they will choose for themselves whether war is inevitable or to be avoided at all costs. But either way, it is governments that wage wars. And if all governments are corrupt, in what political system can the maturing teenager hope to find a stable future?

CONCLUSION

One wonders how an adolescent generation raised on a steady diet of dystopias and vampire books internalizes the metaphors of these genres. The vampire book, for example, gained its first traction at the end of the longest period of economic decline in nineteenth-century England, when Bram Stoker's *Dracula* (1897) invited people to begin thinking about a blood-sucking aristocracy in much the same way that the *Twilight* books invite readers to contemplate the blood-sucking "one percent" that dominated the U.S. economy in the era when Stephenie Meyer's books were published (2005-2008). Collins' novels became the next sensational series to dominate the market, in not only the same year but also the same month that the economy plummeted. The economic downturn sharpened severely in mid-September 2008, and *The Hunger Games* (Collins, 2008) hit the *New York Times* bestseller list on September 28, 2008 ("Bestseller"). For almost a century, dystopias have increased in popularity in times of political and/or economic instability: the first major dystopia of the twentieth-century, *Brave New World*, was published in 1932, three years after the second Great Depression gripped Europe and the Americas in another powerful time of economic contraction. Sales of dystopias also peaked during World War II, during the Cold War, and then not again until the Great Recession started in 2008 (Boog, 2012). Economic and political anxieties can thus be correlated with a surge in the publication of novels that express fears about people being held hostage by their own or other governments. Undoubtedly reflecting the economic *zeitgeist*, dystopias always rely on ideologemes that entail the corrupting nature of power, the untrustworthy nature of government, and the shared assumption that humans are cruel to one another.

Certainly, "man's inhumanity to man" is a theme shared by almost every intertextual reference that Collins includes in her novels, from classical mythology to twentieth-century dystopias. For example, *Adventures of Huckleberry Finn* is a novel in which the protagonist experiences man's inhumanity to man in multiple forms: slavery and its brutality; selling a free man into slavery and allowing teenagers to treat him like a play-thing; separating families via slave auction; abusive parenting; alcohol abuse; honor killings; double-crossing; murders; lies; scams; two characters tortured by being tarred and feathered; and incivility of every sort. Huck watches the Duke and King as their near-dead bodies are being run out of town on a rail, and he thinks the words that serve as the predominant theme of that novel: "People *can* be awful cruel to one another" (Twain, 1885/2002, p. 290, emphasis in the original). The same can be said of the Hunger Games—a series in which a character named Boggs is cut down in the prime of his life by man's inhumanity to man, just as Boggs, the victim of one of the murders in *Huck Finn*, is killed by a man clearly invested in retaining his social power in the status quo.

Huck lights out for the territories, rejecting human civilization—and by implication, its governments—as incurably corrupt. Katniss Everdeen does not have that choice, although she shares his *anagnorisis* about man's inhumanity in the moment that she recognizes: "The truth is, it benefits no one to live in a world where these things happen" (Collins, 2010, p. 377). One wonders then: if all humanity is as cruel and corrupt as Collins implies, how can a government of the people and by the people ever truly be for the people? With its many intertextual references and its bleak plot resolution, the Hunger Games trilogy implies that, while war is heinous, governments will never refrain from waging them and are therefore never to be trusted.

REFERENCES

Bestseller list: Children's books. (2008, Sept. 28). *New York Times*. Retrieved from
   http://www.nytimes.com/2008/09/28/books/bestseller/bestchildren.html
Boog, J. (2012). Dystopian fiction on Goodreads. *Galleycat*. Retrieved from
   http://www.mediabistro.com/galleycat/infographic-dystopian-fiction-on-goodreads_b48815
Campbell, J.W. (2010). The order and the other: Power and subjectivity in young adult literature.
   (Unpublished doctoral dissertation). Illinois State University, Normal, IL.
Collins, S. (2008). *The hunger games*. New York: Scholastic.
Collins, S. (2009). *Catching fire*. New York: Scholastic.
Collins, S. (2010). *Mockingjay*. New York: Scholastic.
Dominus, S. (2011, April 8). Suzanne Collins's war stories for kids. *New York Times*. Retrieved from
   http://www.nytimes.com/2011/04/10/magazine/mag-10collins-t.html

"Dystopia, n." (2013). *Oxford English Dictionary Online*. Retrieved from http://www.oed.com/view/Entry/58909?redirectedFrom=dystopia

Graves, R. (1934). *I, Claudius*. London: Arthur Barker.

Grossman, L. (2013a, Nov. 20). "I was destined to write a gladiator game": A conversation with Suzanne Collins and Francis Lawrence. *Time Entertainment*. Retrieved from http://entertainment.time.com/2013/11/20/i-was-destined-to-write-a-gladiator-game-a-conversation-with-suzanne-collins-and-francis-lawrence/

Grossman, L. (2013b, Nov. 21). "I'm more like Plutarch than Katniss": A conversation with Suzanne Collins and Francis Lawrence. *Time Entertainment*. Retrieved from http://entertainment.time.com/2013/11/21/im-more-like-plutarch-than-katniss-a-conversation-with-suzanne-collins-and-francis-lawrence/

Hintz, C., & Ostry, E. (2003). Introduction. In C. Hintz & E. Ostry (Eds.), *Utopian and dystopian writing for children and young adults* (pp. 1-20). New York: Routledge.

Jameson, F. (1982). *The political unconscious: Narrative as a socially symbolic act*. Ithaca, NY: Cornell UP.

Juvenal. (1918). Satire 10. *Satires*. (G. G. Ramsay, Trans.). Retrieved from http://www.tertullian.org/fathers/juvenal_satires_10.htm

Kristeva, J. (1980). *Desire in language: A semiotic approach to literature and art*. New York: Columbia University Press.

Kubrick, S. (Director). (1960). *Spartacus* [Motion picture]. United States: Universal.

Mills, M. (2013). Orwell in Panem: What the Hunger Games owes to *1984*. *Matter of Facts*. Retrieved from http://matteroffactsblog.wordpress.com/2013/11/26/orwell-in-panem-what-the-hunger-games-owes-to-1984/

Orwell, G. (1949). *1984*. London: Secker and Warburg.

Plutarch. (1919). The life of Cato the Younger. *Parallel lives*. Retrieved from http://penelope.uchicago.edu/Thayer/E/Roman/Texts/Plutarch/Lives/Cato_Minor*.html

Ross, G. (Director). (2012). *The hunger games* [Motion Picture]. United States.

Stephens, J. (1992). *Language and ideology in children's fiction*. New York: Longman.

Stoker, B. (1897). *Dracula*. New York: Archibald Constable and Company.

Takami, K. (1999/2003). *Battle royale*. (Y. Oniki, Trans.). San Francisco: Viz Media.

Twain, M. (1885/2002). *Adventures of Huckleberry Finn*. Berkeley: University of California Press.

Wallace, Lew. (1880). *Ben-Hur*. New York: Harper & Bros.

Wyler, W. (1959). *Ben-Hur* [Motion picture]. United States: Metro-Goldwyn-Mayer.

Zipes, J. (2003). Foreword: Utopia, dystopia, and the quest for hope. In C. Hintz & E. Ostry (Eds.), *Utopian and dystopian writing for children and young adults* (pp. ix-xi). New York: Routledge.

SUSAN S. M. TAN

2. WORSE GAMES TO PLAY?

Deconstructing Resolution in The Hunger Games

INTRODUCTION: BEGINNING AT THE END

At the conclusion of the Hunger Games trilogy, Katniss Everdeen watches her children at play. The previously inaccessible wilderness of District 12 has been opened up, and the once fenced-in meadow is now an open space where Katniss's children roam freely. Ignorant of the Hunger Games, or the violent history which their mother participated in, Katniss's children are privileged with an innocence impossible at the trilogy's beginning. They live without fear of Games and reapings and are spared the televised spectacle of violence and death which the Hunger Games once instituted.

This invocation of childhood innocence in the final pages of Collins' trilogy is striking, as a seminal and groundbreaking work in the Young Adult (YA) canon ends with this more classic vision of children at play. Nameless and faceless, the "dancing girl with the dark hair and blue eyes" and the "boy with blond curls and grey eyes, struggling to keep up with her on his chubby legs" stand in stark contrast with the gritty, violent, and haunted characters who have thus far populated the trilogy (Collins, 2010, p. 454). When compared to the vivid portrayals of arenas, war, and their gruesome human cost in the preceding narrative, this final scene reads more like a dream—hazy and distanced— reminiscent of Arkadia rather than dystopia.

The end of the Hunger Games trilogy is an ostensibly happy one. And yet, a sense of instability remains. One reviewer on Amazon writes, critically, "As for the 'fairytale ending' … I never needed one. At all" (mari, amazon.com). Another laments the lack of resolution, writing, "Collins tried to give us that in the epilogue, but is was forced and not sincere" (Lauren, Goodreads.com). For one reader, the "'[h]appy ending' scenario with Katniss and kid" is not "happy at all and I don't buy it. That felt empty and depressing (Wesker, Goodreads.com). And another writes, "It's baffling to me that this tacked-on ending is still fairy-tale-esque (that is, Katniss did settle down with her True Love and have children). But why bother giving her this semblance of a fairy-tale ending....? It's just empty" (Suzanne G., Goodreads.com). Two interesting strands emerge here. In these criticisms, either the ending is seen as "forced and not sincere," an unworthy conclusion for the fiery Katniss (Lauren, Goodreads.com), or it is read as straightforwardly happy, a "fairy tale ending." And yet, both are marked as unfulfilling.

S. P. Connors (ed.), The Politics of Panem, 29–43.

While this sample of reader response is in no way comprehensive or conclusive, it points towards an underlying tension in the finale of Collins's bestselling trilogy; these comments reveal a level of dissatisfaction with the trilogy's conclusion, and offer a nice jumping off point for my discussion here. Some of these comments point towards the false note which Katniss's tenuous happiness strikes; still others express disappointment because the ending seems so unabatedly happy as to be unbelievable. Critical discourse on the Hunger Games has equally pointed towards issues in the trilogy's conclusion, with Katherine R. Broad (2013) arguing that Katniss's resolution with Peeta, maternity, and domestic life undermines her standing as a feminist figure. For Broad, "Katniss's cop-out" ultimately "reframes the way we read the rest of the novels as it redirects the energies of the narrative from social upheaval to the maintenance of a reproductive status quo" (p. 125). The epilogue is enough to undercut the entirety of the radical narrative that has come before, and "Katniss's rebellion serves to keep her an appropriately gendered, reproductive, and ultimately docile subject" (p. 125).

This gendered reading of the Hunger Games trilogy is compelling, and suggests a cogent reason for the dissatisfaction surrounding the conclusion. Indeed, many readers echo this notion on Goodreads and Amazon, lamenting Katniss's easy subsumation into the role of "wife" and "mother." However, I would like to suggest here an alternate reading, though one no less centered on Katniss as mother, and her ultimate domesticity. Drawing on Derridean theorizations of language and representation, I will argue that Katniss's children are central to the uneasinesss which surrounds the trilogy's conclusion: Katniss's nameless, faceless offspring, who should suggest the continuation of life, point instead to its continual potential for disruption.

Indeed, what are we to make of the fact that the resolution of a watershed YA dystopia ends with children in a meadow—nameless, faceless children, whose ignorance of the historied ground they play upon evokes a distinct atemporality? The Hunger Games series ends with a vision of childhood evocative of the pastoral, Romantic child, and in doing so it raises a puzzle in their very presence. What are these children doing here? And how are we to read this contradiction, as Katniss's conclusion brings us back to a pastoral beginning that is jarring in comparison to the rest of the narrative? What are we to make of this enigma: of the presence of timeless figures at the end of dystopian time?

Drawing upon the many tensions implicit in Collin's epilogue, this chapter will examine the conclusion of the Hunger Games trilogy through the lens of deconstruction: a post-structuralist critical approach geared towards uncovering tensions and contradictions implicit within texts. Focusing specifically on Rue's death in *The Hunger Games* (Collins, 2008) and Katniss's nightmares in *Catching Fire* (Collins, 2009) and *Mockingjay* (Collins, 2010), I employ deconstruction to argue that the trilogy's resolution comes to resemble these episodes of trauma: its instabilities lying in its resuscitation of previously fraught binaries of child/adult, nature/society, and sleeping/waking. Reading the end of the series against its whole, I will demonstrate that the conclusion of the Hunger Games trilogy draws upon binaries it has already queried and destabilized, pointing towards continuing disruption in a resolution that in its elegiac, "dreamlike" quality emerges as highly problematic and deeply unsettling.

DECONSTRUCTION AND *THE HUNGER GAMES*

Deconstruction aims to demonstrate the contradictions and "disunity" which can be imagined to underly a text (Barry, 2002, p. 72). While the term itself suggests a destruction or disassembly of some kind, it "is in fact much closer to the original meaning of the word 'analysis,' which etymologically means 'to undo'" and which demands a "careful teasing out of warring forces of signification within the text" (Johnson, 1980, p. 5). Jonathan Culler (1993) writes that "to deconstruct a discourse is to show how it undermines the philosophy it asserts, or the hierarchical oppositions on which it relies" (p. 86).

Deconstruction is based on the works of Jacques Derrida (1997), who complicates structuralist notions of sign and signifier, or "word" and "referent" (Barry, 2002, p. 111). Derrida (1997) argues for the inability of signifiers to truly capture that which they represent. For Derrida:

> [t]he so-called "thing itself" is always already a *representamen* shielded from the simplicity of intuitive evidence. The *representamen* functions only by giving rise to an *interpretant* that itself becomes a sign and so on to infinity. The self-identity of the signified conceals itself unceasingly and is always on the move. (p. 49)

This idea lies at the heart of deconstruction. The notion of "moving" signification implicitly disrupts Saussurean binaries between signifier and signified, leaving room for constant play and subversion within basic acts of speech and representation. For Derrida (1997), to assign a link between sign and object is to fix it through a kind of violence: freezing the limitless play and potential of moving signification into a binary. However, as Derrida views all of language as a part of this signifying mechanism, he acknowledges that this violence cannot be escaped. Indeed, "[f]rom the moment that there is meaning there are nothing but signs. We *think only in signs*. Which amounts to ruining the notion of the sign at the very moment when ... its exigency is recognized in the absoluteness of its right" (p. 50, emphasis in original).

Derrida (1997) thus envisions all expression as enmeshed in the tension between sign, signifier, and a violence which affixes one to the other. Language is inescapable, and language is constantly evoking itself, but also contradicting and refuting its own stability and finite meaning. In the same way, the very act of deconstructionist reading demands that analysis "borrow[s] its resources from the logic it deconstructs" (p. 314). Deconstruction "finds its very foothold" in the parts of a text that seem the most stable—its hierarchies, its binaries, its absolutes—and by querying these elements, demonstrates an innate instability within seemingly stable unities (p. 314). Derrida's articulation of language and meaning thus maps the process of critical deconstruction itself. A deconstructionist reading involves identifying binaries asserted by a text and, in so doing, querying the stability of the dynamic established. To deconstruct a text is to pay attention to moments where the binary inverts or is troubled, where sign and signified are forced to acknowledge their own limitations in encompassing the other, as the text itself emerges as its own source of ontological tension.

GOOD AND SAFE?: SIGNIFYING CHILDHOOD IN RUE'S MEADOW

To bring a deconstructionist reading to bear on Collins' Hunger Games trilogy immediately points towards a series of oppositions which continually reappear throughout the series and order Katniss's world to a stark degree. The first, centrally, is an opposition established between child and adult, or, in the vocabulary of Collins's world, between those who are vulnerable to selection in the Hunger Games and those who are not. Of course, the fact of adolescence immediately complicates this framework, as it introduces a tension which itself is evident in the texts, and which lends itself to a Derridean reading. Katniss can be a sexually alluring adolescent in the initial pageantry of the Games, and yet, at its conclusion, be made to "look very simply, like a girl. A young one. Fourteen at the most. Innocent. Harmless" (Collins, 2008, p. 431). I will return to this point more fully in the conclusion.

Although Katniss herself demonstrates the potential for boundary-elision within the framework of "tribute," she nevertheless buys into binaries of child and adult, and it is her strictly delineated vision of childhood in opposition to adulthood which I will focus on in my discussion here. Centrally, Katniss does not seem to consider herself a child—instead, she reserves that label for characters such as Prim and Rue: the small, innocent, and ultimately, victimized characters who Katniss seeks to protect precisely because of their "childness." Indeed, both Prim and Rue align strikingly with Romantic, traditional visions of childhood, each standing as a figure closely aligned with the natural world—as their very names suggest—and each offering Katniss a link with her more nurturing, emotional side. Like the ahistoric children of the Gold Age (Nikolajeva, 2000), both Prim and Rue demonstrate an innate goodness which aligns with an innate vulnerability. This conception of youth, vulnerability, and innocence stands in direct contrast to Katniss's vision of the adult world: a brutal, harsh, and dystopian world where survival is paramount. Thus, Rue's death, which marks the moment when Katniss resolves to take a stand beyond simple survival in the first round of Games, acts as an elucidating moment when Katniss's worldview shifts and exposes instabilities in the framework that underlies it. This moment, I argue, provides the trilogy's first real glimpse into several strands which will intersect with increasing force throughout the series: troubling signifiers of awake/asleep, survival/death, child/adult, and nature/society.

Rue's last request—that Katniss sing to her—immediately demonstrates the power of the signifier of "child" in Katniss's worldview. Katniss, "throat....tight with tears, hoarse from smoke and fatigue," reflects that "if this is Prim's, I mean, Rue's last request, I have to at least try" (Collins, 2008, p. 283). This slippage is telling, as is Katniss's choice of song, "a simple lullaby, one we sing fretful, hungry babies to sleep with" (p. 283). Katniss's conflation of Prim and Rue demonstrates the solidity and power with which the signifier of "child" manifests itself for her, and the song she sings is equally revealing. It is a lullaby which promises safety and love in a pastoral meadow, one in which we could imagine that both Prim—the child who heals animals, raises goats, and tames strays—and Rue—who sings with the mockingjays and can "fly, birdlike, from tree to tree" (Collins, 2009, p. 49)—would make their natural home.

However, this natural imagery does not remain within the realm of Katniss's song, nor can it be contained within the framework of childhood innocence which Katniss asserts so strongly. As Katniss wreathes Rue's body in flowers, pastoral associations become blurred. With "blossoms in beautiful shades of violet and yellow and white," Katniss disguises the reality of Rue's wound and death with the trappings of the Arcadia her song has just evoked, "[c]overing the ugly wound. Wreathing her face. Weaving her hair with bright colours" (Collins, 2008, pp. 286-287). Of course, there is a highly positive valence to this action. As Katniss honors Rue, she lays claim to nature—made so deadly in the space of the arena—to assert Rue's humanity. Katniss wants to demonstrate that "Rue was more than a piece in their Games. And so am I," and in her act of care she disrupts the brutal mechanisms of the adult dystopian world with this evocation of the childhood which Katniss asserts that Rue should have had (p. 286).

At the same time, however, the appropriation of natural imagery, and its associations with childhood—and a sense of "safe," protected childhood at that—points towards a simultaneous disruption. The lullaby has eased the child towards death, rather than sleep, and as Katniss looks on Rue one last time, she reflects that "[s]he could really be asleep in that meadow after all" (Collins, 2008, p. 287). The meadow of Katniss's song—the space of perpetual security and love—has become Rue's grave, prefiguring the actual graveyard which Katniss's children will play in later in the trilogy's epilogue. As death is equated with inhabiting this space, the question of its attainability is raised. In Katniss's world, this scene seems to suggest, the child can only remain "good and safe," secure in the pastoral, natural world, through death.

Katniss's dream following Rue's death only seems to solidify this uneasy dynamic. Katniss reflects that:

> Sometimes when things are particularly bad, my brain will give me a happy dream .... Tonight it sends me Rue, still decked in her flowers, perched in a high sea of trees, trying to teach me to talk to the mockingjays. I see no sign of her wounds, no blood, just a bright, laughing girl. She sings songs .... On and on. Through the night. There's a drowsy in-between period when I can hear the last few strains of her music, although she's lost in the leaves. I try to hold on to the peaceful feeling of the dream, but it quickly slips away, leaving me sadder and lonelier than ever. (Collins, 2008, p. 290)

In Katniss's dream, Rue is alive and at peace with no "sign of her wounds" (p. 290). And yet, "decked in her flowers," Rue bears the trappings of her death, and indeed, as Rue is preserved and idealized in Katniss's dream, so too do these

33

shroud-like flowers become enmeshed in Katniss's vision of Rue. As Rue becomes the "bright, laughing girl," she is described with more vibrancy in Katniss's dream than she ever was in life (p. 290). In this way, the child is preserved in death, and she reaches the carefree, safe promise of Katniss's song only when the "tomorrow" that her lullaby promises brings *"dreams ... true"* is no longer possible (p. 284).

After Rue, the signifier of "child" will never be the same for Katniss, and indeed, this slippage between life and death will continually reemerge. Looking at Prim in later books, Katniss cannot help but violently evoke the specter of Rue, as the sight of the happy, bird-like Prim is cut off:

> *Bam!* It's like someone actually hits me in the chest ... the pain is so real I take a step back. I squeeze my eyes shut and don't see Prim—I see Rue ... Rue, who I didn't save. Who I let die. I picture her lying on the ground with the spear still wedged in her stomach. (Collins, 2009, p. 49)

Representation here blurs dangerously: for Katniss, the signifier of "child" evokes a Derridean (1993) "free play" (p. 224)—a slippage of signification—where to "read" the signifier of "child" which should yield "Prim" in fact evokes "Rue," and even further, Rue in the moment of death.

NIGHTMARES OF MUTTS AND LOST CHILDREN: SIGNIFYING TRAUMA

Katniss' dream of Rue points towards another central division within the Hunger Games trilogy: the waking and sleeping world. Indeed, Rue's appearance in Katniss's dreams prefigures what will become an increasing reality for Katniss, as death and visions of the dead come to continually invade her sleep. While these nightmares begin as the simple reliving of trauma, they gradually escalate as living and death, and sleeping and waking, blur in Katniss's almost perpetual stream of nightmares.

For Katniss, the arena of the Games is "the place of nightmares" (Collins, 2009, p. 211), a site of trauma which proves inescapable. Katniss relates that horrors from the Games "plague me whenever I sleep .... I relive versions of what happened in the arena. My worthless attempt to save Rue. Peeta bleeding to death .... Cato's horrific end with the mutations. These are the most frequent visitors" (p. 66). The notion of "visitors" is apt: like her dream of Rue, Katniss's dreams become a point of interaction with the dead where memories are resuscitated, warped, and take horrific physical form.

As Katniss's dreams force her to relive the Games, their inescapability gradually points to a larger reality. At the end of *The Hunger Games*, a desperate Katniss reflects, "[I]f [Peeta] dies, I'll never go home, not really. I'll spend the rest of my life in this arena, trying to think my way out" (Collins, 2008, p. 417). As she emerges with Peeta as a victor, in turn, she imagines, for the first time, the joys of returning home and leaving the Games behind her. However, even in *The Hunger Games*, Katniss finds herself "still half in the arena" (p. 432), easily startled, unable to fully inhabit the present of her safer, domestic life. Significantly, Katniss's nightmares reflect this idea. Katniss dreams of the past, her nightmares acting to anchor her unconscious mind in the arena, making manifest her fear that she will "spend the rest of [her] life" there (p. 417). Katniss's dreams, it seems, have always had this backward focus, and nightmares of the Games supplant dreams of older traumas, including Katniss's "old standby," a dream of her "father being blown to bits in the mines" (Collins, 2009, p. 66). Indeed, as she and Peeta begin to share a bed, to "manage the darkness as we did in the arena, wrapped in each other's arms, guarding against dangers that can descend at any moment" (p. 89), a striking dichotomy between past and present emerges. Nightmares resuscitate a horrific history, but one which is clearly delineated from the present; Peeta's companionship can ward off, or lessen the impact, of nightmarish past visitations.

However, as the trilogy continues, the boundaries between nightmare and reality begin to disintegrate. The creations which once dwelled in Katniss's dreams are made manifest in reality. In *Catching Fire*, reeling from the revelation that a person she knows has been turned into an Avox—a tongueless, voiceless servant of the Capitol—Katniss dreams of "someone with a flicking, wet tongue who…stalks me," and "when he catches me and pulls off his mask, it's President Snow, and his puffy lips are dripping in bloody saliva" (Collins, 2009, p. 266). This dream is brought to disturbing life later in *Mockingjay* when Katniss is hunted by humanoid mutts, "their faces a mess of conflicting features," pursuing her "with wide, lathered mouths, driven mad by their need to destroy" her (Collins, 2010, p. 363). Designed to resemble "[w]hatever Snow thinks will scare [Katniss] the most" (p. 357), the mutts reek with "[t]he smell of Snow's roses": his signature scent of saliva and blood which Katniss's initial dream stages (p. 364).

As if mapped alongside this, as the horrors of the arena are brought to life in the Capitol, and as the violence once reserved for the unreal space of the Games bursts forth into the "real" world, signifiers of dream and reality and waking and sleeping blur. Nightmares, which once preserved the horrors of the Games, and which Katniss battled in her domestic world, invert, and in the Capitol, Katniss recounts, "I have only one dream I remember. A long and wearying thing in which I'm trying to get to District 12. The home I'm seeking is intact, the people alive" (Collins, 2010, p. 377). Katniss now dreams of home as the "past," and her dream becomes a nightmare in its false hope—that is, it presents her with a home that is whole and safe, as opposed to the burnt-out ruin which District 12 has become. "Home" now stands as the site of trauma and loss which the Games once occupied; the violence of the Games have, in turn, invaded everyday life.

The element of the everyday, or a "real world" distinct from the performance and spectacle of the Games, is highlighted as reality—rather than the arena— becomes the site of greatest possible horror. As Katniss learns of Peeta's torture at the hands of the Capitol, she is told that the constant broadcasting of tortured screams "was part of it …. Like the jabberjays in the arena. Only it was real. And it didn't stop after an hour" (Collins, 2010, p. 286). In Katniss's subsequent nightmare, the living and dead, animals and objects, are all blurred in the horror of this revelation: "Roses. Wolf mutts. Tributes. Frosted dolphins. Friends. Mockingjays. Stylists. Me. Everything screams in my dreams tonight" (p. 286). The violence of the arena infiltrates the everyday world, and as it becomes "real"

Katniss's nightmares stage a breakdown of representation, signifiers jumbled together in a wordless stream of horror.

This breakdown between dreams and reality, sleeping and waking, correlates with a breakdown of self. Like my previous discussion of the resemblance between sleep and death, to be asleep, it is suggested, is to become a conduit towards death, and in the wake of revolution, Katniss becomes victim to just this: her dreams and nightmares staging her own fight for survival. As Katniss hovers between life and death, as her burnt and mutilated body must be literally regrown, she sees:

> The ones I loved fly as birds in the open sky above me .... I want so badly to follow them, but the seawater saturates my wings, making it impossible to lift them. The ones I hated have taken to the water .... Dragging me beneath the surface.

> The small white bird tinged in pink dives down, buries her claws in my chest, and tries to keep me afloat. *"No, Katniss! No! You can't go!"*

> But the ones I hated are winning, and if she clings to me, she'll be lost as well. *"Prim, let go!"* And finally she does. (Collins, 2010, p. 408, emphasis in original)

In a recapitulation of Katniss's initial foray into the Games, Katniss's dream becomes the only way to process the traumas of her loss and injury. Representing herself as a creature with wings in a literal evocation of a mockingjay, Katniss's dream signals a profound loss: both the loss of her sister and the loss of her physical human form. Katniss is now a self-described "fire-mutt," a mutation forged in the very trauma which killed her sister (Collins, 2010, p. 407). This vision of self is negotiated as Katniss's dreams stage a confrontation between life and death, and as she chooses to force dream-Prim to let go, much as she did in her initial reaping, she emerges once more as the consummate, unlikely, survivor.

With the warping of the world around her, Katniss takes refuge in her dreams, which now stage an unrelenting flow of hauntings, the present and the past, and reality and dreamed-visions, almost completely inseparable. Katniss recounts that "more visitors arrive," "open[ing] the door to the dead and alive alike. Haymitch, yellow and unsmiling. Cinna stitching a new wedding dress" (Collins, 2010, pp. 408-409). So porous are the boundaries between life and death that Katniss's parents are briefly reunited: her dead father "sings all four stanzas of 'The Hanging Tree' and reminds me that my mother—who sleeps in a chair between shifts—isn't to know about it" (pp. 409-410).

As *Mockingjay* draws to a close, Katniss must face the reality that she "will not be allowed to live in [her] dreamland" forever (Collins, 2010, p. 410), a space which now—far from the traumas of arenas, games, and violence—in fact signifies the traumatic loss of home, family, and friends. Unsurprisingly, resolution demands a re-balancing of representation. Katniss can no longer dwell in, or find companionship in, her dream world. And, as her closing arc requires a suturing of her visions of past, memory, family, and self, so too must dreaming assume its proper place: returning to its old, backwards-looking function as Katniss rejoins the waking world.

It is not incidental that Katniss finds peace through a book of memories, a physical site which fixes meaning, representation, and signification. Indeed, Katniss notes that there are "things you cannot trust to memory" (Collins, 2010, p. 387), perhaps one of the central lessons that she has taken from her experiences with the slippery, shifting implications of signification and Derridean play. Katniss's loved ones will no longer haunt her dreams. Rather, their representations are preserved here, codified in her memory book "begin[ning] with the person's picture" (p. 451), and followed by significations which:

> it would be a crime to forget. Lady licking Prim's cheek. My father's laugh .... Rue poised on her toes, arms slightly extended, like a bird about to take flight. On and on .... Additions become smaller. An old memory that surfaces. A late primrose preserved between the page. (pp. 451-452)

The slippage, it would seem, which characterized Katniss's initial conflation of children and childhood innocence, loss and sleep, nightmares and waking, is fixed within these pages; representations are pinned down and codified rather than left to the fluidity of freeplay.

And yet, of course, as Katniss re-establishes the boundaries which the violence of dystopia corroded, the re-establishing of her waking world and self necessitates a similar re-assertion of her nightmare-world. Katniss still "wake[s] screaming from nightmares of mutts and lost children" (Collins, 2010, p. 453). Resolution, it seems, can be found in the re-ordering of the world, the stopping up of porous boundaries and fluid realities. It does not, however, prefigure the end of dreaming or nightmares, nor does it negate the larger ontological questions of self raised by the destabilization of these boundaries. Katniss has ostensibly "woken up," the waking-dreams of trauma dispelled. And yet, as the epilogue of Collins's trilogy draws upon the many strands which I have discussed in this chapter thus far, profound questions are raised. As Katniss is exiled to District 12, relegated to a life outside of the political world she has played such a central role in winning, the very possibility of resolution, domesticity, and indeed the signifier of "ending" is itself queried.

REAL, NOT REAL, OR SOMEWHERE IN-BETWEEN?:
THE RETURN TO THE MEADOW

At the end of the Hunger Games trilogy Katniss's children seem to have stumbled in from the golden pastures of another genre and another era, and their presence poses a telling disruption. Are we to read them as a symbol of ultimate hope, a continuation that suggests that innocence can be reborn in even the most violent, apocalyptic of times? Or are we, like Katniss, to mourn the inherent transience of their innocent state, fearing the day they will learn the history of their world, and feeling a "terror ... as old as life itself" in the contemplation of their very existence (Collins, 2010, p. 454)?

Here, Katniss's own reflections of her children's state is telling, and points perhaps to the core of the profoundly unsettling strain within this final scene. Both Katniss and the reader know that this vision of a transient, treasured innocence is a fantasy in itself: an illusory scene of domestic paradise underlaid by death and violence. Katniss's children "don't know they play on a graveyard," their space of childhood literally built upon the bodies of victims of war (Collins, 2010, p. 455). That they play in the meadow at the edge of what was once a violently patrolled border only heightens this sense of uneasiness: Katniss's children now frolic where Katniss once risked her life daily to keep her family from starvation.

Indeed, of all the central signifying objects throughout the trilogy, the evocation of the meadow as a site of play emerges with the full force of its many fraught connotations. In one of her few moments of peaceful dreaming during her second round in the arena, Katniss "drift[s] off ... try[ing] to imagine that world, somewhere in the future, with no Games, no Capitol. A place like the meadow in the song [she] sang to Rue as she died. Where Peeta's child could be safe" (Collins, 2009, p. 427). And, as Katniss watches her children play, it seems that perhaps she has finally found a way to make her dreams physically manifest: her final victory lying in the achievement of the meadow promised in her song. And yet again, the meadow here, in all its connotations of nature and the pastoral, is inseparable from the dying child's body: the lullaby she sang to Rue. Once again, the dream is inseparable from the horrors of the arena, even when this world, "with no Games, no Capitol," emerges as the desirable, indeed, utopian conclusion to an otherwise brutally dystopian world.

This resolution, and the happiness which so many readers found so disappointing, points to a larger binary in-negotiation here: the split between utopia and dystopia itself. Indeed, Broad (2013) argues for an alignment of Peeta as a utopian figure who "dreams of a quiet and private home life as the end goal of utopia and the reason for social change" (p. 120). As a happy ending seems to demand the shedding of dystopia for the reclamation of utopia, the Hunger Games trilogy seems to indeed fit this model, the series itself engaging in generic unmooring to provide its characters with a resolution which would in fact be unthinkable in a strictly dystopian world.

And yet, as Katniss watches her children, much as she watched Rue and Prim in both lived-reality and in her ill-contained nightmares, she herself seems to disrupt and refute this fully utopian conclusion. Katniss's declaration of her children's innocence stands at odds with her acknowledgment that someday they will not simply be educated about their world, but will also demand to know why their mother is haunted by dreams of inescapable adolescent horror. There is an uneasiness in the ending of the Hunger Games trilogy, a sense of purgatorial limbo as the end of dystopian destruction is juxtaposed with pastoral beginning, and it is Katniss who stands as the fulcrum who unites, and yet disrupts, the full union of these worlds, refusing to lose herself—or allow readers to lose themselves—in the full joys of utopian conclusion.

Throughout, this chapter, my discussion has centered on Katniss's vision of the world: her sense of children and childhood, her relationship with nature, dreaming, and the past. Of course, this discussion draws attention to a central facet that has thus been only briefly touched upon: the fact of Katniss's adolescence. Katniss is neither child nor adult, and indeed, in her very presence she disrupts the binaries of child/adult which she herself ascribes to so powerfully. Arguably, it has been her status as adolescent, and her ability to defy the violence of binary codification, which has granted Katniss such power in her world, and which allows her to exact the degree of revolutionary change and signifying disruption that her presence inspires.

Indeed, Katniss's adolescence links her to larger discussions of adolescent change, ambiguity, and disruption. Even the etymological roots of the term "adolescence" points towards transition and movement, the term stemming from the Latin "*adolescere*," "to grow up" (Tucker, 2014, p. 82). This break-down is telling: Kerry Mallan and Sharyn Pierce (2003) write of the difficulties of defining "youth" or adolescence, stages which are "regarded as a state of becoming, as a necessary (and often tortuous) pathway to adulthood" (p. ix). Adolescence is defined through change, comprised of "uncertainties that characterize the transience of youth" (Mallan & Pierce, 2003, p. ix). This notion of "uncertainty" and the adolescent is central. Kimberley Reynolds (2007) notes the strong disruptive connotations of youth culture associated with a villainization of young people, and "institutional associations between youth culture (linked to sex, drugs, and popular music) and counter culture" (p. 84). Similarly, Lisa Sainsbury (2005) points to the link between the adolescent and the uncanny in the popular imagination. Addressing the presence of the uncanny in YA novels popular with adults and teenagers alike, Sainsbury posits that this link taps into a tension within conceptions of "adolescence" itself, as young people are ascribed a social power that is profoundly unnerving and threatening to the adult establishment. The representation of young people as potentially dangerous, unnatural or inhuman points to the "dichotomy that underpins contemporary thinking about childhood," one which envisions "childhood as a time of innocence" while simultaneously demanding that children be "cordoned off and made safe as if they were a social danger" (Reynolds, 2007, p. 125).

Little wonder, then, that Katniss has emerged as a figure of such force and power, one who possesses the capability to reach uncannily into suggested death, and whose presence can unleash the horrors of nightmares, arenas, and dystopian trauma upon the cities of the "real," waking world. As Romantic childhoods are resuscitated and recalled from another time and genre, we can perhaps point again to the destabilizing power of the adolescent—and through her, YA literature—in this vision of genre-crossing. Indeed, extrapolating from the phenomenon of "crossover" literature, this collusion of genre and age confusion seems in keeping with the ethos of the trilogy and genre thus far.

Within this dichotomy, however, the question of where Katniss herself fits emerges once more. Following the *bildungsroman* format so common to the YA novel (Trites, 2000), Katniss indeed grows up: her age, her achievements, and the fact of her motherhood pointing towards this inevitable maturation. At the same time, however, Katniss's growing up seems tenuous compared to the stark binaries which have thus far separated childhood from adulthood within the series. Just as Katniss has always inhabited the realm in-between the binaries and significations she so disrupts, so too does her very identity seem innately in-between.

It is here that we can perhaps locate an innate tension, if not irreconcilability, in any idea of conclusion for Katniss Everdeen. To return again to the site of her epilogue, Katniss has not taken her children to the woods beyond the meadow, her sanctuary throughout the trilogy. Rather, Katniss remains at the site of her old border-crossing from District 12 to wilderness, the space where she learned the deadly skill of hunting which she would later employ in the Hunger Games. And, as she sits at the space of her previous liminality, she ponders her own in-betweenness: gazing upon her children, protected by their ignorance, she considers her own distance from them. Evoking the song she sang to lull Prim to sleep and Rue to her death, Katniss herself points toward the impossibility of her children's maintained, pastoral innocence and play. Indeed, she knows all too well that literal continuation will demand that her children grow up, that they too will acknowledge and trouble the binaries of the world around them. Katniss's children indeed suggest hope and futurity. And yet, Katniss acknowledges that they stand at the boundaries of a highly fraught, porous border: the graveyard underlying the meadow making manifest the specters of Rue and Prim which inevitably saturate this Romantic vision of children at play.

Katniss's irresolvable, uncodifiable adolescence is particularly compelling when brought to bear on discussions of endings and conclusions in the YA context. Elaine Ostry (2013) writes that:

> young adult literature—like teenagers themselves—occupies an uneasy space between childhood and adulthood, resting on a spectrum that has children's literature on one end and literature for adults on the other. The amount of despair that books decide to end with depends on where writers place adolescents on the maturity spectrum. (p. 109)

In this configuration, a happy ending "can be seen as somewhat forced and infantilizing, a bone thrown to the young reader," in contrast to "despair and inconclusiveness" which "may encourage adolescents to face inconvenient truth, and ... be inspired to make sure ... doom like that of the novels never comes to pass" (p. 111). The Hunger Games trilogy's disruption of narrative resolution taps into this larger discussion of YA literature and the types of conclusions and—transitively—critiques it can offer.

Ultimately, Katniss emerges as a figure of innate liminality, and in her refusal of stable definition, she defies either option within the signification of "resolution" itself. Katniss carries scars and burdens, irreparable losses and nightmares which will never leave. And yet, even as her ending demonstrates the inescapability of her traumas, even as it places her in a position of political exile and potentially deprives her of voice and full self-determination, it cannot rob her of this defiance of the signifying chain. In her epilogue, Katniss situates herself in one of the most problematic spaces in all of the trilogy in an act which both reclaims and reminds, which asserts continuation and the possibility of childhood even as it actively refutes total resolution and the "happy endings" which the full assumption of utopia would seem to demand. It is here, perhaps, that dissatisfaction with Katniss's ending simultaneously lends itself to the power of the Hunger Games trilogy's critique. Katniss stands at the liminal space which she has always inhabited, with all its comforts and discomforts, its power and its danger. It is up to the reader to choose where they will similarly situate themselves. As strains of hope and despair are each proffered and denied, it is left to readers to negotiate a border-crossing of their own.

CODA

Suzanne Collins's Hunger Games trilogy draws to a strikingly neat resolution. After a bloodbath in the Capitol maims Katniss's body, kills the sister she fought for, and results in her assassination of President Coin, the prospect of a "happy" or "peaceful" ending seems bleak. And yet, the trilogy ends in an almost pastoral scene of family: Katniss looking out on her children, who play with the happy innocence that she was once denied. While trauma remains, resolution has—it seems—been reached. At the same time, however, this vision of resolution has been pointed to as a jarring one, disappointing in everything from its gender politics to its attempt at a resolution dubbed discordantly "fairy tale" and ineffectively "happy" in turn.

Drawing upon Katniss's past traumas—her moments of loss, the nightmares that torment her—I have argued that this denial of narrative resolution is, in fact, precisely in keeping with Katniss's experiences throughout the trilogy: both her experiences of violence and trauma, and perhaps more positively, her experiences of power and agency. A deconstructionist reading of the Hunger Games trilogy yields a vision of Katniss as a powerfully destabilizing force, one who queries, even if momentarily, the binaries and fixed boundaries of her world.

I would like to conclude by further considering the implications of this vision of Katniss. For indeed, it is possible to extend this reading of Derridean disruption to read the adolescent as a figure who, in herself, is innately disruptive, demanding new categories in the interstices of cultural binaries, reminiscent of Homi Bhabha's (1994) notion of third space.

In *The Location of Culture,* Bhabha (1994) writes that the "borderline work of culture demands an encounter with 'newness' that is not part of the continuum of past and present" (p. 10). Rather, "[i]t creates a sense of the new as an insurgent act of cultural translation," and "does not merely recall the past as social cause or aesthetic precedent" but "renews the past, refiguring it as a contingent 'in-between' space that innovates and interrupts the performance of the present. The 'past-present' becomes part of the necessity, not the nostalgia of living" (p. 10). This theorization of the past, present, and cultural innovation is aptly drawn upon when looking both at YA literature and the role which the adolescent-protagonist of YA dystopias is placed in. Here, cultural newness is inherently "insurgent" and hybrid. It both renews and threatens; it is innovative and interrupting as it forces confrontation with the pre-existing structures which make it possible. This is quite striking given Roberta Seelinger Trites's (2000) assertion that YA literature demands an introduction of, and capitulation to, existing adult social structures. YA literature, and the figure of the adolescent, demands the reification and affirmation of the adult world. Enmeshed in these institutional strands are profound questions about adolescent's incipient social and political power, which the adolescent seems to wield in the very fact of their "newness" and hybrid, liminal status—not child, not adult.

Similarly, Kimberley Reynolds (2007) has examined the interplay between popular culture and youth culture, as youth culture inhabits the fringes and periphery precisely because of its inherent "newness." Drawing from Reynolds, it is important, here, to distinguish this notion of "newness" from the more literal "newness" of the child, who is, of course, temporally "new" in the world. Adolescents are "radical" and sites of potential transformation not because they were recently children, but rather, because they are almost adults, what I would term "imminent adults." As adolescents move away from the status of "child" closer to adult agency, this shift is accompanied by real social influence, including political sway and economic spending-power. Teenagers are radical in their freedom, in the very fact of where they fall in the process of "becoming." The adolescent will soon take his or her place in the adult world, with the cultural capital and—ostensibly, though not necessarily—the agency of adulthood. What shape this adult identity will assume, however, is unknowable. Teenage rebellion becomes threatening less in its developmental existence, but rather, in the idea that the rebellious teenager will become the rebellious adult.

The adolescent subject is a subject in transit, moving between physical and emotional markers of place, their literal and figurative voices sounding mid-pitch. Indeed, an almost physical sense of ungrounding emerges here. To imagine adolescence is to unground the child. To be in the process of becoming is to be moving. To be initiated into a new subject position is to unmoor from a previous one. Little wonder, then, that Katniss is constantly engaged in an interplay of borders and boundaries, threatened and empowered in turn by the slippages she uncovers, the binaries she queries, the "newness" which she creates.

Indeed, perhaps readers well-versed in the trilogy should not be surprised that Katniss's ending so defies resolution, so resists the relinquishment of "becoming" for the fixed marker of adult identity. Katniss's emphasis has continually lain in her movement through her world, never her fixity or rigidity within it. Indeed, in another one of her rare, happy dreams, Katniss recounts, "I was following a mockingjay through the woods. For a long time. It was Rue, really. I mean, when it sang, it had her voice" (Collins, 2009, p. 104). When Peeta asks where dream-Rue took her, Katniss—the force of social newness and change, the rebel, the subject continually in-transit, the consummate adolescent—replies, simply, "I don't know. We never arrived … but I felt happy" (p. 104).

REFERENCES

Barry, P. (2002). *Beginning theory: An introduction to literary and cultural theory.* Manchester: Manchester UP.

Bhabha, H. (1994). *The location of culture*. London: Routledge.

Broad, K.R. (2013). The dandelion in the spring: Utopia as romance in Suzanne Collins's *The Hunger Games* trilogy. In B. Basu, K. R. Broad, & C. Hintz (Eds.), *Contemporary dystopian fiction for young adults: Brave new teenagers* (pp. 117-130) New York: Routledge.

Collins, S. (2008). *The hunger games*. London: Scholastic Children's Books.

Collins, S. (2009). *Catching fire*. London: Scholastic Children's Books.

Collins, S. (2010). *Mockingjay*. London: Scholastic Children's Books.

Culler, J. (1993). *On deconstruction: Theory and criticism after structuralism*. London: Routledge.

Derrida, J. (1993). Structure, sign, and play in the discourse of the human sciences. In J. Natoli & L. Hutcheon (Eds.), *A postmodern reader* (pp. 223-242). Albany, NY: State University of New York Press.

Derrida, J. (1997). *Of grammatology* (G. C. Spivak, Trans.). Baltimore: Johns Hopkins University Press.

Johnson, B. (1980). *The critical difference*. Baltimore: Johns Hopkins UP.

Mallan, K., & Pearce, S. (2003). Introduction: Tales of youth in postmodern culture. In K. Mallan & S. Pearce (Eds.), *Youth cultures: Texts, images, and identities* (pp. ix-xix). London: Praeger.

Nikolajeva, M. (2000). *From mythic to linear: Time in children's literature*. London: Scarecrow Press.

Ostry, E. (2013). On the brink: The role of young adult culture in environmental degradation. In B. Basu, K. R. Broad, & C. Hintz (Eds.), *Contemporary dystopian fiction for young adults: Brave new teenagers* (pp. 101-116). New York: Routledge.

Reynolds, K. (2007). *Radical children's literature*. New York: Palgrave MacMillan.

Sainsbury, L. (2005). Childhood, youth culture and the uncanny: Uncanny nights in contemporary adolescent fiction. In K. Reynolds (Ed.), *Modern children's literature: An introduction* (pp. 124-140). New York: Palgrave Macmillan.

Trites, R. S. (2000). *Disturbing the universe: Power and repression in adolescent literature*. Iowa City: University of Iowa Press.

Tucker, H. E. (2014). *A new companion to Victorian literature and culture*. Oxford: John Wiley.

MEGHANN MEEUSEN

3. HUNGERING FOR MIDDLE GROUND

Binaries of Self in Young Adult Dystopia

As this collection demonstrates, Suzanne Collins's Hunger Games trilogy offers a distinctive example of young adult dystopia for many reasons, including its engagement with a wide range of critical perspectives. Among these, the series is unique in the way it portrays social anxieties relating to the tension between a constructed or embodied self, a tension that seems a crucial element to many popular contemporary texts of this genre. The Hunger Games series foregrounds the nuance of this anxiety by emphasizing not only the issue of constructed self versus embodiment, but also society's fear of a future where external constructing forces become embodied. Collins's two central figures, Katniss Everdeen and Peeta Mellark, provide insight into this anxiety as it relates to gender and the self, an idea that is further explored in dystopian texts such as Patrick Ness's (2009) *The Knife of Never Letting Go* and M.T. Anderson's (2002) *Feed*. These YA dystopias demonstrate individuals who are shaped by their surroundings, and the texts also include frightening examples of how constructions could become embodied and internalized, thus revealing contemporary cultural fears of a constructed self. What is more, these texts often develop this concept in gendered examples, further complicating the binary of social construction and embodiment.

I would suggest that YA dystopia, a genre known for acting on cultural fears, explores social anxiety about breaking down binaries between constructed and embodied self by melding the cognitive with culturally constructed forces. This is especially evident in the Hunger Games series, which draws attention to the tensions between a culturally constructed self and individual subjectivity by setting up a binary between Katniss as a constructed figure and Peeta as an essentialized individual. Not only does the series highlight this binary, but it also disrupts it in ways dependent upon cognition, evidenced when Peeta is brainwashed. The Capitol's ability to alter Peeta's mind is perhaps the most frightening part of the story, with Collins playing on society's fear of the interaction between cultural forces and embodiment by describing a troubling future when social constraints might not simply affect the self, but become embodied. The way these constraints become embodied also places emphasis on cognition, thus interacting with theoretical models of the self in important ways.

My contention in this chapter is that contemporary YA dystopia like Collins's Hunger Games series problematizes the interactive nature of a constructed and embodied self and the role of cognition in this dynamic. Furthermore, in YA dystopias that feature the embodiment of cultural forces as the norm, cognition plays a vital role, especially in texts built on the idea that cognition has been

S. P. Connors (ed.), The Politics of Panem, 45–61.

altered to such a degree that individual consciousness and social forces bleed into each other. Texts like *Feed* and *The Knife of Never Letting Go* naturalize this state of being, such that everyone experiences the overlap of construction and embodiment. Additionally, the way that characters respond to this overlap breaks down along gender lines, revealing social anxieties over how gender contributes to a continual opposition of construction and embodiment, a point that is especially relevant within the context of feminist theory that seeks to break this binary.

BRIDGING DIVIDES—CONSTRUCTED AND EMBODIED SELF

In *Volatile Bodies: Toward a Corporeal Feminism*, Elizabeth Grosz (1994) contextualizes the concept of a mind/body split within its theoretical history, ending her chapter by contrasting the work of theorists she categorizes as social constructionists with the work of theorists such as Irigaray, Cixous, Spivak, Butler and others who consider questions of sexual difference. She notes how "instead of seeing sex as an essentialist and gender as a constructionist category, these thinkers are concerned to undermine the dichotomy" (Grosz, 1994, p. 18), and she continues by positing that "the binary opposition between the cultural and the natural—needs careful reconsideration" (p. 21). One way that contemporary theorists have complicated this binary is through a consideration of cognition and embodiment, drawing on criticism developed by such scholars as Raymond Gibbs (2006), who explores the way embodiment is "an essential part of the perceptual and cognitive processes by which we make sense of our experiences in the world" (p. 3). This concept that an individual's sense of self is impacted by his or her embodied experience sometimes seems contrary to the notion of a constructed self, and theorists continue to question to what extent a person's identity is constructed via the influence and constraint of social and cultural forces. Notions of embodiment that build especially from cognitive science suggest that the self might not be wholly constructed from these forces, but impacted by a range of complex factors related to the brain, body, and society. The role and balance of social and biological factors in determining selfhood is a complex question, and one with which writers of YA dystopia seem frequently to grapple.

Grosz (1994) contrasts social constructionist approaches in which "the distinction between the 'real' biological body and the body as object of representation is a fundamental presumption" (p. 17) with theories that back away from this split to figure the body as a "cultural interweaving and production of nature" (p. 18). She complicates the "binary opposition between the cultural and the natural," calling for a feminist philosophy where "both psychical and social dimensions must find their place ... not in opposition to each other but as necessarily interactive" (p. 23). I argue that characters in dystopian texts like the Hunger Games series problematize this kind of interactive relationship.

Complication of the binary between cultural and biological forces on the self in YA dystopia corresponds with critical dissatisfaction with the idea that culture entirely constructs identity. Critics question, as Paul Vitz (2006) does, whether studies of the "universal characteristics of the human nervous system ... put severe limits on the notion of an arbitrary social or self-constructed identity" (p. 111).[1] Scholars like N. Katherine Hales (1993), Nancy Easterlin (1999), and Elizabeth Hart (2001) also explore intersections between cognition and selfhood.[2] As Hart (2001) describes, in addition to social forces, "'cognitive predispositions' control at least some of what constitutes human knowledge and therefore human culture" (p. 325). Hart goes so far as to identify a paradigm shift in the cognitive sciences wherein scientists consider "the 'embodiment' of mind; that is, of the mind's substantive indebtedness to its bodily, social, and cultural contexts" (p. 315). Instead of an embodiment versus construction binary, she aligns with the notion of constrained constructivism, which "exemplifies the alternative epistemology defining the continuum between untenable extremes of realism and relativism" (Hart, 2001, p. 324).[3] According to Hart, theorizing cognition can be the key to understanding this continuum.

Whether called "constrained constructivism" or, as Paul Gross and Norman Levitt (1994) term it, "weak constructivism" (p. 131), the result is the same: when ideas about cognition are combined with theories of the self, neither embodied biological factors nor socially constructed forces bear the entire burden of constituting selfhood. My suggestion is that against this theoretical backdrop, contemporary YA dystopia illustrates and complicates notions of the self by offering a frightening future where such forces are not simply intertwined, but melded in disturbing and often very gendered ways.

KATNISS EVERDEEN—PRODUCT OF CULTURAL CONSTRAINT

Collins's Hunger Games trilogy opens up questions of selfhood as they relate to gender by presenting a seemingly progressive female protagonist who appears to break gender binaries. However, what makes Katniss a more intriguing character is the way she exists very clearly at one end of the constructivism versus essentialism binary. This binary is not a new one in contemporary dystopian fiction. As Bradford, Mallan, Stephens, and McCallum (2008) write, dystopia frequently explores the "tension between essential subjectivity and the intersubjectively formed self" (p. 20), a point they use to define these texts as transformative because they reveal "the ways in which human needs and agency are restrained by existing institutional, social, and cultural arrangements" (p. 16). This might seem to problematize constructivism, agency, and essentialism, and yet many of these texts feature characters who act against "society's propensity to represent itself as always already instituted," offering examples of "the possibility of creative action to individuals" (Bradford et al., 2008, p. 16).[4] Characters capable of creative action defy what these scholars term a "hard-line Foucauldian determinism" approach to subjectivity, a concept they describe as questioning whether "we have any choice in choosing the choice we choose" (Bradford et al., 2008, pp. 30-31). YA dystopia, they submit, figures protagonists as having choice and creative agency, for although society may influence or even construct these teenagers, they still claim individual power, especially in their rebellions.

Katniss, however, exists outside of this paradigm, personifying exactly the hard-line Foucauldian determinism that Bradford et al. (2008) describe. Katniss represents the epitome of a socially constructed self because her actions are responsive to a worldview developed under the constraints of a society that teaches her to survive and rebel at any cost. This construction exists on several levels, the most obvious of which is her continued performance to appease the Capitol, which she must maintain in order to save herself and the people she loves. She performs first for the viewers of the Hunger Games, relying on Haymitch's cues and noting, "If I want to keep Peeta alive, I've got to give the audience something more to care about. Star-crossed lovers desperate to get home together" (Collins, 2008, p. 261). Later, she must continue to enact this reality, as she realizes, "It's so much worse than being hunted in the arena. There, I could only die. End of story. But out here Prim, my mother, Gale, the people of District 12, everyone I care about back home could be punished if I can't pull off the girl-driven-crazy-by-love scenario" (p. 358).

The Capitol and its representatives dictate Katniss's actions through physical threat, as when President Snow notes her survival mentality by observing that "any girl who goes to such lengths to preserve her life isn't going to be interested in throwing it away with both hands. And then there's her family to think of" (Collins, 2009, p. 20). Katniss promises to do whatever Snow commands, but a simple show is not enough for him. When she vows to perform the romance with Peeta and "be in love with him just as I was" (p. 29), he tells her not just to convince the Capitol, but to make this performance so authentic that it convinces him. Even away from Capitol control, rebellion leader President Coin mirrors this sentiment by pardoning Katniss, Peeta, and the other tributes only if Katniss will become the Mockingjay. Coin tells Katniss, "[Y]ou'd better perform" (Collins, 2010, p. 41), creating a similar constraining paradigm to the Capitol's control, wherein as Katniss puts it, "I step out of line and we're all dead" (p. 58). Consistently, powerful forces in Katniss's life compel her to repetitively enact a perceived identity not of her own making, but dictated to her by external, socially motivated forces. In this way, Katniss is demonstrating the power of culture identified by such theorists as Judith Butler. Butler (1993) posits gender as "ritual reiterated under and through constraint, under and through the force of prohibition and taboo, with the threat of ostracism and even death controlling and compelling the shape of the production" (p. 95). I would suggest selfhood is similarly reiterated under such constraint, with individuals enacted into being by these cultural forces. Katniss represents just such a notion of selfhood, wherein the constant threat of death that controls and compels her is very real, dictating both her behavior and how she views herself and her society.

Additionally, the cultural norms imposed upon Katniss are often extraordinarily gendered. When Peeta professes his love for her in an interview aired to the entire Capitol, for example, viewers see Katniss as the feminine heroine, a persona they adore. Although her immediate reaction to this persona being chosen for her is profound anger at being made to look weak, Haymitch clarifies that she has been made "desirable," even if "It's all a big show. It's all how you're perceived"

(Collins, 2008, p. 135). Katniss molds herself to this persona, and her acquiescence to dictated gender performance is tangible; when she plays into what the viewers want, she receives food, medicine, and other survival necessities.

Furthermore, this perception of Katniss is constructed through language (Peeta's comments about her) and a commodity driven social order (Cinna's brilliant fashion make-overs). Much of Katniss's performance relies upon Peeta figuring her as an object of his desire, which he does primarily in grand and romantic speeches. Cinna reinforces this persona through very purposeful fashion choices, working within the constraints of a commercialized culture to create an identity for her. Collins emphasizes this point when Cinna tells Katniss to be herself, a concept she does not seem able to comprehend. Cinna tries to help define this "self" for her, and then uses fashion to display and reinforce it. Even when Katniss leaves the arena, Peeta and Cinna help her to continue this charade under the literal threat of violence issued by President Snow. Katniss may seem to internally resist this persona, but her actions consistently reinforce it until even she is uncertain whether components of this constructed self are real or unreal. Katniss must don, even embrace, this perceived notion of self to survive, leaving readers to question whether similar pressure exists in contemporary society.

Even when Katniss finally joins the rebellion, she immediately finds herself again thrust into the public eye, and although her role as an emblem of the resistance requires her to perform differently, her actions still respond to what others tell her she must do to survive. She recognizes her behavior as simply another performance, commenting that as the Mockingjay, she has "a whole team of people to make me over, dress me, write my speeches, orchestrate my appearances—as if that doesn't sound horribly familiar—and all I have to do is play my part" (Collins, 2010, p. 11). Katniss willingly gives herself over to this construction, for she knows no other way. When Peeta tells her of his desire to hold on to the idea that "there's still you, there's still me" even within this constraining framework, Katniss responds by saying she only understands this "A little" and asks "who cares," claiming that it is more important to focus on staying alive (Collins, 2008, p. 142). Katniss even more clearly recognizes the force of culture to construct and constrain in her comments about the citizens of the Capitol. She reflects, "Who knows who I would be or what I would talk about if I'd been raised in the Capitol?" (Collins, 2009, p. 38), indicating that although she abhors their attitudes, she believes that the Capitol citizens have not chosen their positionality any more than she has chosen hers.

Not only before the camera, but even in private spaces, Katniss's actions and conception of self are socially constrained by either the forces of the Capitol or those cultural factors that shape her life in the Seam. In the Seam, Katniss's central focus is survival, and the limitations of her poverty force the role of protector upon her. What is more, this constraint in the Seam influences her to internally reject traditionally feminine characteristics. Facing her father's death and her mother's incapacitating depression, Katniss has no choice but to become the provider for her family, which means taking on a role often scripted as masculine. Thus, Katniss performs femininity when necessary in front of the cameras, but her vehement internal displeasure at doing so also seems a construction built from a similar survival imperative.

Yet to really understand how much these forces influence Katniss's sense and presentation of self, it is most useful to examine those actions that other characters in the trilogy identify as completely "Katniss's." When filming promotional spots as the rebellion emblem Mockingjay, Katniss has a "jerky, disjointed quality, like a puppet being manipulated by unseen forces," prompting the deceptively wise Haymitch to ask the group to list moments where Katniss made them feel "something real" (Collins, 2010, p. 74). In articulating what all of these moments have in common, Gale identifies them using the possessive "Katniss's" to indicate her ownership over them, as if they were hers alone because "no one told her what to do or say" (p. 75). Despite the appearance that these instances exist outside of external influence, they too are the product of the constraining cultural forces under which she learns to live.

In the Seam, Katniss's actions are driven by two forces: a survival imperative imposed upon her when her father dies and the constant knowledge of the injustice of the Capitol, an ideology repeatedly reinforced by the attitudes of the members of District 12 and her best friend, Gale. Survival and rebellion, therefore, act as the two cultural norms that dictate almost all of her actions, both of which derive from the dominant cultural attitudes of her community, rather than some internally motivated source. When Katniss's comrades describe the inherently Katniss moments that "made them feel something real" (Collins, 2010, p. 74), they name seven instances, all of which demonstrate one of these two constructions. Four are motivated by a survival/protection response: taking Prim's place at the reaping, drugging Peeta to procure the medicine, allying with Rue, and attempting to carry Mags. In all of these cases, Katniss does not choose, but reacts automatically in the way her culture indoctrinates—to survive and protect the weak. Katniss is a protector because she has been trained over years of hardship to become one, which she expresses when evaluating the Champion Tributes in *Catching Fire*, musing that "a lot of them are so damaged that my natural instinct would be to protect them" (Collins, 2009, p. 234). Nevertheless, this response is not a natural instinct, but behavior built out of the influences of her culture.

While most members of the Seam community are likely influenced in similar ways that prioritize survival and rebellion, Katniss also experiences a unique set of circumstances resulting from the death of her father, which even more concretely instills these constructions into her identity and actions. This differentiates her from Peeta, for example, whose position as the son of a merchant limits the survival imperative in constructing his identity. Similarly, while Gale's behavior also reflects the influence of culture, Katniss's unique experience of being on the brink of starvation after her father dies makes the survival imperative the most critical component of her sense of self, while Gale's character is constructed more out of ideologies related to rebellion.

The other instances listed by Katniss's comrades to describe her are even more interesting, however, because although they appear to be acts of dissent, Katniss's rebellion is also the product of cultural forces. Katniss rebels when she sings to

Rue as a burial tribute, when she extends her hand to Chaff to signal solidarity among the Champion Tributes on interview night, and most importantly, when she suggests she and Peeta eat the poisoned berries rather than give the Capitol their victor. She claims that "[a]ny act of rebellion was purely coincidental" (Collins, 2009, p. 18) or "not intentional" (p. 62). However, her lack of intentionality reveals these actions as automatic responses to a deeply indoctrinated ideology, one made evident in the third book when the people she cares about dictate her acts of rebellion.

In this way, Collins depicts even rebellion as reactive, institutionalized, and part of what constructs Katniss's identity, an idea perhaps best exemplified in one of her first rebellious acts: when she proposes that she and Peeta kill themselves by eating the poisoned berries rather than give in to the Capitol's tyranny.[5] Not only is her act of agency prevented, in a way it was also never really a choice at all. Katniss thinks, "I know death right here, right now would be the easier of the two," referring to the choice between dying in the arena or killing Peeta and going home to "live with it" (Collins, 2008, p. 343). If she were to save herself at Peeta's expense, she believes her community would ostracize her—making the rebellious act of double suicide the only choice. Katniss's acts of rebellion align with a hatred of the Capitol ingrained in the people of Districts 12 and 13 for so long that it becomes one of their defining cultural markers. Fear of ostracization is not the only reason for Katniss's automatic response of rebellion, however. Her daily experience in the Seam has also taught her that survival necessitates rebellion, from forbidden hunting in the forest to acting as the Mockingjay. Thus, nearly everything Katniss does falls into one of three categories: performing for the cameras, attempting to survive/protect, and rebelling against the Capitol. In each case, her actions are responsive to external forces of constraint, aligning with what Bradford et al. (2008) call "hard-line Foucauldian determinism" (p. 31).

PROACTIVE PROTAGONISTS AND PEETA'S PURITY OF SELF

This representation of Katniss as a product of cultural constraint offers a striking difference from many YA dystopian texts. Responding to Lois Lowry's *The Giver*, for example, Don Latham (2004) writes, "Clearly, Lowry endorses the possibility of a proactive rather than a merely reactive subject" (p. 148). Critics like Carrie Hintz (2002) and Kay Sambell (2004) identify this idea in other YA dystopia, a pattern that characterizes many of the emerging and classic texts in this genre.[6] In contrast, Collins takes the opposite approach in developing Katniss as a reactive subject. If authors far more commonly depict proactively rebellious teens rather than reactive characters like Katniss, perhaps this reflects a continued investment in a humanist approach that believes individual "resistance to power structures is possible and even productive" (Latham, 2004, p. 150). This is certainly the sentiment exposed by Katniss's counterpart, Peeta, for much of the series, setting these two characters as strongly opposed to one another in the ways they represent institutional power and the self.

Instead of demonstrating qualities built on constraining social forces, Peeta is figured as "always so reliably good" (Collins, 2009, p. 66) and "truly, deep-down better than the rest of us" (Collins, 2010, p. 277). Katniss continually describes Peeta in these ways, so that he begins to represent an unchanging force of goodness and an unwavering pillar of strength, not solely enacted into being by outside forces, but able to maintain intrinsic qualities despite powerful constraint.[7] The difference between Peeta and Katniss rests in the fact that Peeta not only desires to resist these institutional forces and stay true to that which he believes to be his essential sense of self, but he repeatedly attempts to do so. In contrast, Katniss disregards this perspective as not even an option, a concept most clearly emphasized when Peeta confides in her that his one wish is to "die as myself" (Collins, 2008, p. 141). Katniss identifies the contrast between them: while she is "ruminating on the availability of trees, Peeta has been struggling with how to maintain his identity. His purity of self" (p. 142). She identifies that this makes her feel "inferior," for while she survives because she adapts as necessary and is consistently reactive, she recognizes Peeta as different, a proactive instead of reactive subject (p. 142).

This quality distinguishes the two characters, but also makes Peeta a powerful figure because "[n]o one needs to coach [him] on what to say" (Collins, 2009, p. 66). He is keenly aware of the social constraints that shape how he must navigate the world, but instead of succumbing to them in reactive, even automatic ways like Katniss, he strategizes to bend these forces to his own designs. More importantly, though Katniss sees herself as more powerful as a symbol, even a martyr, Peeta is a skilled performer, able to "use words ... And maybe it's because of that underlying goodness that he can move a crowd—no, a country—to his side with the turn of a simple sentence" (Collins, 2009, p. 338). Peeta's power rests in his ability to use language to enact his own ideas into the reality around him. This ability to manipulate and control language sets him up in a distinct binary against Katniss. Peeta appears more thoughtful and capable because of his ability to traverse social construction according to his desires, while Collins portrays Katniss as merely reactive, unable to navigate this space with the same kind of agency.

Butler (1997) discusses power in this regard, arguing that "power not only acts on a subject but, in a transitive sense, enacts the subject into being" (p. 13). This definition fits with Katniss's position within the power structures of her dystopia, where power both acts on and enacts her into being. Roberta Seelinger Trites (2000), however, suggests this definition also "allows for an internally motivated subject who can act proactively rather than solely in terms of taking action to prevent oppression," identifying language as the "marker of power" in these situations (p. 5). Peeta, not Katniss, wields language to assert this power, and his position as the male hero of the text makes this a key distinction. Collins portrays Katniss, a female protagonist, as the one more affected by social forces, setting her against a male character impacted by constraint to a lesser degree. This could reflect a belief that cultural forces have a greater impact in constructing subjectivity in women than in men.

Simply put, Katniss represents wholly constructed selfhood, where she does not make choices but only reacts based on those constraints that have enacted her into being. This places her at the far end of a spectrum that Robyn McCallum (1999) describes when contrasting "an individual's sense of a personal identity as a subject—in the sense of being subject to some measure of external coercion," versus a sense of one's identity "as an agent—that is, being capable of conscious and deliberate thought and action" (p. 4). Peeta views himself on both ends of this spectrum, both as subject to the Capitol to some degree, but also as a clear agent. Katniss, on the other hand, represents a different kind of agency. She instead fits with the way that Trites (2000) describes the postmodern adolescent subject, in which "awareness of the subject's inevitable construction as a product of language renders the construct of self-determination virtually obsolete" (p. 18). Herein lies the importance of two diametrically opposed primary characters; they emphasize the kind of binary that scholars debate at length when it comes to theorizing the self.

Furthermore, Collins also demonstrates the notion of embodiment as important to her depiction of these contrasting characters, especially when she overturns binaries of self in the final text of the series. If readers attribute an inherent "goodness" to Peeta for the first two books, the third text reveals this trait as an embodied characteristic, one dependent on cognitive faculties that provide Peeta with his perceptions. In *Mockingjay*, Peeta's fear of losing his true self is terrifyingly realized when the Capitol abducts him from the Quarter Quell arena and brainwashes him through a "type of fear conditioning" wherein memories are changed, "brought to the forefront of your mind, altered, and saved again in the revised form" (Collins, 2010, pp. 181-182). The Capitol irreversibly alters Peeta's brain chemistry in order to manipulate his memories, turning him into a weapon against Katniss. In doing so, everything about Peeta changes; he is no longer the same person and responds to situations in skewed ways. This proves one of the most striking twists of Collins's plot, whereby the character who was so solidly, even intrinsically, good becomes broken and dangerous through manipulation of neurochemistry.

What seems particularly important about this reversal of Peeta's perspectives and character is its emphasis on cognition. If Peeta's "goodness" can be taken away by altering his memory, then those qualities that constitute his self appear to reside within a cognitive, even embodied realm. This seems to support Gibbs's (2006) idea about embodiment as a crucial factor in how "we make sense of our experiences in the world" (p. 3). However, this additionally emphasizes the middle ground of constrained constructivism, for this textual move demonstrates the way the self is influenced by both culture and embodied cognitive forces. Peeta's brainwashing reveals that his selfhood does not reside in either mind or body, for his memory and cognitive faculties exist within a complex web, influenced by both cultural and natural forces. This complexity depicts a complication of binaries of self that theorists call for in scholarship exploring constrained constructivism. After setting up two divergent representations of the self, Collins strips away this binary by suggesting that cognition plays a crucially important role.

More important still is the idea that Peeta's brainwashing does not just problematize the binary, but offers a synthesis. Not only does this brainwashing constitute a physical change to Peeta's embodied cognitive structures, but the Capitol also does this with the purpose of imposing a new ideology upon him. This action represents a forced and violent blending of construction and embodiment to place constraining forces within an embodied self. When a distraught Peeta supports the Capitol in a national broadcast, Katniss and her fellow rebels believe Peeta has been made to make this statement by means of torture. Peeta's comments in this initial broadcast seem a product of constraint, but the rebels do not believe the Capitol can make Peeta adopt this construction because he is too inherently good. In response, the Capitol makes Peeta more useful to their cause by forcing this construction, not by social constraint, which has had little effect, but by making that construction embodied.

The leaders at the Capitol remove the self that up to this point has characterized Peeta as an individual, changing fundamental truths that act as the basis for his worldview at the cognitive level. They force a new construction not via externally constraining forces, but by making their ideologies part of his internalized and embodied cognitive structures. Thus, while the rebellion and Katniss's community in the Seam help to indoctrinate her into becoming a person who automatically reacts, the Capitol does the same to Peeta through cognitive alteration, a notion that seems to reflect society's fear that cultural constructs could become embodied by force.

If dystopia represents that which we fear from an unchecked society, then Peeta's brainwashing indicates a cultural anxiety over blending social constraint with an embodied self. Furthermore, this move suggests that Panem, as a dystopian nation, cannot tolerate an essentialized identity, so that the constraint that Katniss reacts to automatically must be forced upon Peeta, his sense of self biologically altered through a cruel advancement in technology. Again, gender plays an important role here: Katniss responds to cultural constraints without the need to alter her embodiment, while Collins figures Peeta as the one for whom social forces must become internalized in order to strip him of his inherent self. Collins's dystopia asks what might happen if technology grants cultural forces more power, so that they may be wielded to make social constraint not just part of one's experience, but part of the *embodied* experience. If the dystopian society of Panem will not allow for an essentialized identity, taking the idea of constraint so far that the line between construction and embodiment is lost, this represents contemporary culture's fear of the blurring of this line, despite the fact that theorists have responded positively to moves in this direction.

EMBODIED CONSTRUCTION—ADDING GENDER TO THE MIX

The Hunger Games series poignantly emphasizes this social anxiety by starting with two characters representing the binaries associated with ideas of the self, only to dismantle these binaries by inserting the role of cognition into the dynamic. However, two other male characters of YA dystopia demonstrate the same anxieties about embodied social construction as Peeta: Titus of M.T. Anderson's (2002) *Feed* and Todd of Patrick Ness's (2009) *The Knife of Never Letting Go*. If Peeta is an example of construction and constraint becoming embodied, then Titus and Todd represent what happens when this is naturalized—that is, when external constraint becomes internalized through the manipulation of cognition. Both exemplify the loss of the divide between a private, individual, embodied self and those external forces that construct selfhood. What is more, this kind of bleeding between external forces and internal self is depicted as profoundly negative.

In Anderson's (2002) text, Titus's selfhood is enacted into being by the influence of the Feed, a constant stream of commercialized and social networking opportunities implanted into his brain. Abbie Ventura (2011) describes this by writing that in *Feed*, "the brain has simply become an extension of the technology ... once attached to the Feed, the individual's experience of time and space negates human subjectivity and autonomy" (p. 93). Ventura explores *Feed* in terms of models of social change available or limited to adolescents, but I suggest that in addition to providing "commentary on the failure of the lone youth revolutionary" (p. 94), similar to Katniss's somewhat bleak end, *Feed's* use of technology to blend the line between subjectivity and social forces also aligns Titus with Peeta from the Hunger Games series.

The difference for Titus, however, is that this element is not a punishment. Instead, a merging of construction and embodiment is naturalized, a norm challenged not by the male protagonist, but by the female love interest in Titus's life. In fact, it is actually the relationship between Titus and Violet that moves him in the direction of recognizing those constraining forces that construct him. As Clare Bradford and Raffaella Baccolini (2011) describe, in the case of *Feed* as well as Philip Reeve's *Mortal Engines*, "the female characters represent the misfit citizens: displaced from the very beginning for different reasons, they are more aware and critical than their respective male companions" (p. 54). Violet can see the problematic nature of the Feed and resists it actively much like Peeta. In the Hunger Games series, at least at first, Bradford and Baccolini's dynamic is reversed, with Katniss always doing what is necessary to survive within society in contrast to Peeta, the seemingly more aware and critical rebel misfit. Like Violet, who dies when she tries to resist the Feed, Peeta is punished for his resistance.

Patrick Ness's (2009) *The Knife of Never Letting Go* similarly explores this dynamic of external factors becoming internalized within a gendered dichotomy. In the New World created by Ness, characters live in a dystopia where all men's thoughts—and only men's thoughts—are projected into the minds of others. Although the women do not broadcast what is termed the Noise, they can hear it, creating what becomes a very problematic power dynamic frequently exploited by the men of the text. The men often do not trust the women who are able to hear and not be heard, and either ostracize or, in Prentisstown, kill them.

Like the Feed, the Noise profoundly affects Todd. In fact, he recognizes that this force constructs, or at least influences, his sense of self, and he often tries to cling to something beyond this construction by repeating his name, age, and home in his mind, a trick he claims helps "settle my Noise. You close yer eyes and as clearly and calmly as you can you tell yerself who you are, cuz that's what gets lost in all that Noise" (Ness, 2009, p. 17). This individual self becomes difficult to separate when the Noise pervades Todd's mind at all moments, similar to the Feed in its influence on Titus's cognitive state. For Todd, the Noise creates his reality, much like how the Feed constitutes Titus's view of the world. The men of Todd's community consistently mandate Todd's actions and are able to do so because they share this cognitive connection. In this way, those social forces that might externally construct, constrain, or enact a subject into being have become internalized to horrifying results, much like the examples of the Feed and Peeta's brainwashing.

Again, the relation of gender to this dynamic offers a particularly unique part of the way Ness (2009) portrays the Noise's influence. Todd does not initially realize that this normative blurring of embodiment and construction exists as a reality for both men and women, who are both able to hear the thoughts of others. However, since men can only hear each other but cannot hear the women, the females of the society appear to have the advantage. Because the men's thoughts are always accessible to those around them, they cannot establish any sense of a separate, embodied, individual self. Any thought they form or action they consider always exists under the scrutiny of others, and thus the Noise affects the men far more than the women, whose cognitive processes are more private or unique to them. The women, because they have private lives and separate selves apart from the Noise, can see themselves as independent beings. In many cases, though, the men cannot tolerate the women having this private self, for as Todd says, "How can they be a person if they ain't got no Noise" (Ness, 2009, p. 71). This idea turns the women into threats who must be removed from the paradigm whether through ostracization or death.

Just as Titus cannot exist apart from the Feed, and just as Peeta can only see the world through the perspective imposed upon him through a similar cognitive mapping, an embodiment of cultural constraints profoundly influence Todd and the other men of Ness's (2009) New World in *The Knife of Never Letting Go*. In the works of Ness (2009) and Anderson (2002), the female characters are the ones to resist cultural construction, whereas the male characters are victim to the forced embodiment of cultural factors. Katniss, I would suggest, reverses this dynamic, and yet by the end of the series, she complicates it as well.

Bradford and Baccolini (2011) remark that *Feed* and Reeve's *Mortal Engines* present "dystopian settings that the male protagonists do not recognize as such at first; it is their interpersonal relations and the emotional and geographical journey undertaken with the female characters of the novels that will enable the young men, on different levels, to achieve a mild critical distance from their own society" (p. 49). Similarly, Viola fills this role in *The Knife of Never Letting Go*, acting as a moral guide in many instances and helping Todd to navigate and understand his world in order to rebel against it. In both Ness (2009) and Anderson's (2002) texts, the male protagonists contrast the female characters who resist (albeit somewhat unsuccessfully) external, constraining forces becoming internalized.

On the surface, this seems different from Katniss, who allows herself to become a symbol in accepting the self constructed for her by external forces. Still, despite the fact that she is herself constructed, when she sees those constraining forces embodied in Peeta, her role in the story changes. As a result, in all three dystopian texts, the women save their men by helping them to understand the nature of those influences that construct them. Violet opens Titus's eyes to the Feed; Viola helps Todd understand his experience with the Noise; and although Katniss does not seem to play this role at first, by the end of *Mockingjay* she saves Peeta by helping him find his way back by answering whether that which he experiences is "Real or Not Real" (Collins, 2010, p. 272).

At first, Katniss has difficulty relating with the changed Peeta because he has lost the essential goodness that previously characterizes him. Eventually, though, she attempts to help him and thinks, "I try to imagine not being able to tell illusion from reality…I suddenly want to tell Peeta everything about who he is, and who I am, and how we ended up here. But I don't know where to start" (Collins, 2010, p. 271). Perhaps Katniss has difficulty expressing to Peeta the complexity of what is real and not real because she does not always know for certain herself. Like him, people around Katniss often manipulate her, and her reality is constructed through the forces that act upon her. For her, "real or not real" is complex because, though not embodied, external constructing forces play a tremendous role in her reality.

This idea of "real or not real" takes on an even more important role in the final pages of the Hunger Games series, for although Katniss has been primarily interpreting this distinction for Peeta's benefit, she also uses this phrase when she comes to realize that the Rebellion may represent the same constraining, destructive force as the Capitol. When she sees what she later realizes was quite possibly a Rebellion hovercraft dropping parachutes that then explode as bombs, Katniss's reaction is this same idea—"real or not real?" (Collins, 2010, p. 348). For she now realizes that the distinction between the Rebellion and the Capitol, a distinction that symbolizes all those powerful forces that have influenced her every action, is one that she can no longer count on, one she cannot distinguish as "real or not real." In this way, she is actually very similar to the brainwashed Peeta. Neither knows the difference between real and not real because there is no "real," only that which has acted upon them and enacted them into being.

Katniss articulates recognition of this influence at the end of the series, reflecting how "every emotion I have has been taken or exploited by the Capitol or the rebels" (Collins, 2010, p. 330), and therefore deciding "I no longer feel any allegiance to these monsters called human beings, despite being one myself" (p. 377). This increased awareness fits with how Trites (2000) describes growth within power dynamics as a function of all adolescent literature: "Growth is possible in a postmodern world, especially if growth is defined as an increasing awareness of the institutions constructing the individual" (p. 19). In the end, Katniss is finally able to demonstrate growth by making her first fully proactive or individual choice. The decision to kill the newly appointed President Coin puts her on the same side of the binary as Viola and Violet—a female character who recognizes the danger of a constructed self and seeks to pull away from it, a move Katniss makes by choosing assassination and then leaving society to live in exile.

CONCLUSION: MORE THAN A STRONG FEMALE AND SENSITIVE MALE

Katniss and Peeta may originally seem to reverse the binary set up by other YA dystopia that deal with an embodiment of external forces such as *Feed* and *The Knife of Never Letting Go*, with Katniss more representative of a constructed self and Peeta offering a more humanist depiction of subjectivity. Yet when the emphasis shifts to consider cognition, this dynamic returns to one more traditionally held by YA dystopia, wherein the female character must save the male made victim to cognitive manipulation. Therefore, readers are left with several disconcerting ideas regarding gender binaries, making these efforts seem like a misguided feminism. These dystopias depict women as saviors of socially constructed men. Furthermore, for the men, the impact of such a social construction is not a natural state of being, but must be forced upon them by society through cognitive manipulation. Although the Hunger Games trilogy complicates this notion by positioning Katniss as always already socially constructed, even this dynamic must be reversed in order for Katniss to save Peeta and be saved, finally able to extract herself from those forces that construct her selfhood. Thus, if brainwashing Peeta to punish him shows our fears of constructing forces blending with an embodied self, perhaps first representing Katniss as socially constructed and then forcing her to reevaluate what is "real or not real" demonstrates a similar anxiety over a fully constructed self, and in this case, a constructed female self.

Dystopia shows us what we fear, what ills of society might look like if taken to their extreme. In these cases, two elements are revealed as truly frightening: the embodiment of constructing forces that would signal a merging of constructivism and an embodied self, and the notion of a fully constructed self—and in particular a constructed female self. Though these stories reflect some of the ways that critics consider cognition as crucially important to breaking down the dialogic of embodiment and constructivism, they also show this merging as a frightening eventuality. What is more, these texts reflect a gendered breakdown of constructivism, with men only forced into submission to such constraint by cognitive manipulation and women the saviors of those men. The Hunger Games series does unique work to complicate this, and yet in the end, Katniss reveals perhaps an even more frightening idea—that even without technological advancement, one might be so completely the product of construction that what is "real or not real" becomes arbitrary. Perhaps this is what we most fear—not that the social forces that constrain and construct individuals into existence could merge with an embodied experience, but that, especially for women, they already have.

Theorists have suggested the need to consider the self as both constructed through social forces and the product of an embodied experience, but while these dystopian YA texts reflect both of these influences, they are still kept separate, even binaries from one another. Rather than a synthesis of both elements, the technological advancements of *Feed*, *The Knife of Never Letting Go*, and the Hunger Games series result in a violent blending, wherein the male characters seemingly have no agency to resist the constraining forces that have become one with their embodied experience. In all three examples, male characters are the victims of this merging of social construction and embodiment, and while female characters have the ability to save their counterparts by illuminating the forces at work, they are able to do so because they have always already existed in a power position in which these forces are merged, even without technological advancement. Katniss exemplifies this, for she is perhaps best suited to help Peeta navigate the forced embodiment of social constraint because for her, these influences have always been intertwined and inseparable. While a feminist theoretical perspective that balances both embodiment and cultural construction would posit the influence of these elements on both men and women, it seems striking to note the ways these dystopian texts draw gender lines. The women of these stories are powerful heroes in part because they can identify the dangers of embodied social constraint, but in their ability to do so, they perhaps reflect the notion that those who bear the burden of a culturally constructed self can best see the problematics of a society wherein such forces are even more powerful if they become internalized.

The Hunger Games trilogy presents two dynamic characters that offer nuanced depictions of gender, and both Katniss and Peeta not only evade stereotypes, but also reflect a complexity of gender depiction certainly worthy of praise. However, if we dig deeper into the ways these characters interact with contemporary theoretical conceptions of the self, they also seem to follow a pattern in YA dystopia. More than simply a strong female or a sensitive male, Katniss and Peeta reflect society's concerns about what forces are at play in constructing a person's sense of self and what power individuals have to affect or even recognize those influences at work. In this way, Collins's series is not only critically complex, but it engages with contemporary questions about gender and selfhood in remarkable ways. In presenting Katniss as culturally constructed and stripping Peeta of his essential goodness through cognitive manipulation, Collins creates a society where men and women must traverse a treacherous social order that calls into question the balance between embodiment and constraining social forces. Yet perhaps most frightening of all, this element of her society bears a disturbing resemblance to our own.

NOTES

[1] Vitz (2006) writes against the idea of the "saturated self," a phrase Kenneth Gergen (1991) uses to express discontent with postmodern conceptions of the self as entirely constructed.

[2] Although these theorists' work highlights constructivism in terms of constructing knowledge more than selfhood, I draw on the connection Hart (2001) makes in noting that "the parallelism here between knowledge and subjectivity means that varying commitments to position along the realism/relativism continuum also imply certain commitments to subjectivity" (p. 328).

³ Katherine Hayles (1993) defines constrained constructivism as "species-specific, culturally determined, and context-dependent" relying on "active and complex engagements between reality and human beings" that require "cultural readings of science" (pp. 32, 34).

⁴ Like Bradford and her contemporaries, I would not dismiss the notion of agency, rather relying on what Lois McNay (1999) calls creative agency, where "the existence of values also presupposes a creative process by which values are fashioned and transmitted" (p. 189).

⁵ Don Latham (2004) describes this power to destroy the body as "the ultimate way for the individual to undermine society's ability to exert control over the body" (p. 143).

⁶ Hintz (2002) highlights proactive characters in the works of Monica Hughes, and Sambell (2004) posits Philip Reeve's work as seeking to "empower young readers to become active agents of future change," as she believes "most children's science fiction authors do" (p. 263). A few examples of popular recent YA dystopian series with similarly proactive protagonists include Veronica Roth's *Divergent* (2012), Ally Condie's *Matched* (2010), and Scott Westerfeld's *Uglies* (2005), to name just a few.

⁷ It is necessary to qualify that Peeta is always a character constructed through Katniss's first person narration. Collins only articulates Katniss's view of him, a perspective that figures him as almost a savior contrasted with her perception of her own flawed existence.

REFERENCES

Anderson, M.T. (2002). *Feed.* Cambridge, MA: Candlewick.

Bradford, C., & Baccolini, R. (2011). Journeying subjects: Spatiality and identity in children's texts. In K. Mallan & C. Bradford (Eds.), *Contemporary children's literature and film: Engaging with theory* (pp. 36-53). Houndmills, UK: Palgrave Macmillan.

Bradford, C., Mallan, K., Stephens, J., & McCallum, R. (2008). *New world orders in contemporary children's literature: Utopian transformations.* New York: Palgrave.

Butler, J. (1993). *Bodies that matter: On the discursive limits of "sex."* New York: Routledge.

Butler, J. (1997). *The psychic life of power: Theories in subjection.* Stanford, CA: Stanford University Press.

Collins, S. (2008). *The hunger games.* New York: Scholastic.

Collins, S. (2009). *Catching fire.* New York: Scholastic.

Collins, S. (2010). *Mockingjay.* New York: Scholastic.

Condie, A. (2010). *Matched.* New York: Dutton Book.

Easterlin, N. (1999). Making knowledge: Bioepistemology and the foundations of literary theory. *Mosaic, 32,* 131-147.

Gergen, K. (1991). *The saturated self: Dilemmas of identity in contemporary life.* New York: Basic Books.

Gibbs, R. (2006). *Embodiment and cognitive science.* Cambridge, MA: Cambridge University Press.

Gross, P., & Levitt, N. (1994). *Higher superstition: The academic left and its quarrels with science.* Baltimore, MA: Johns Hopkins University Press.

Grosz, E. (1994). *Volatile bodies: Toward a corporeal feminism.* Bloomington, IN: Indiana University Press.

Hart, F. E. (2001). The epistemology of cognitive literary studies. *Philosophy and Literature, 25*(2), 314-334.

Hayles, N. K. (1993). Constrained constructivism: Locating scientific inquiry in the theater of representation. In G. Levine (Ed.), *Realism and representation: Essays on the problem of realism in relation to science, literature, and culture* (pp. 27-43). Madison, WI: University of Wisconsin Press.

Hintz, C. (2002). Monica Hughes, Lois Lowry, and young adult dystopias. *The Lion and the Unicorn, 26*(2), 254-264.

Latham, D. (2004). Discipline and its discontents: A Foucauldian reading of The Giver. *Children's Literature, 32,* 134-151.

McCallum, R. (1999). *Ideologies of identity in adolescent fiction: The dialogic construction of subjectivity.* New York: Garland.

McNay, L. (1999). Subject, psyche and agency: The work of Judith Butler. *Theory, Culture and Society, 16*(2), 175-193.

Ness, P. (2009). *The knife of never letting go.* Cambridge, MA: Candlewick.

Roth, V. (2012). *Divergent.* New York: Katherine Tegen Books.

Sambell, K. (2004). Carnivalizing the future: A new approach to theorizing childhood and adulthood in science fiction for young readers. *The Lion and the Unicorn, 28*(2), 247-267.

Trites, R.S. (2000). *Disturbing the universe: Power and repression in adolescent literature.* Iowa City, IA: University of Iowa Press.

Ventura, A. (2011). Predicting a better situation? Three young adult speculative fiction texts and the possibilities for social change. *Children's Literature Association Quarterly, 36*(1), 89-103.

Vitz, P.C. (2006). The embodied self: Evidence from cognitive psychology and neuropsycholgoy. In P. C. Vitz & S. M. Felch (Eds.), *The self: Beyond the postmodern crisis* (pp. 113-128). Wilmington, DE: ISI Books.

Westerfeld, S. (2005). *Uglies.* New York: Simon Pulse.

PART TWO

"I Have a Kind of Power I Never Knew I Possessed": What Philosophy Tells Us about Life in Panem

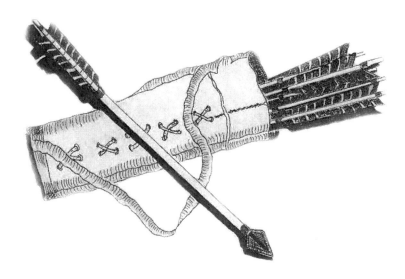

BRIAN MCDONALD

4. THE THREE FACES OF EVIL

A Philosophic Reading of The Hunger Games

By the end of Suzanne Collins's (2010) novel *Mockingjay,* Katniss has discovered that the evils of Panem cannot be cured with only a warrior's courage or an archer's skills. Instead, any hope of a new order to emerge from the dark debris of the old depends on Katniss's becoming a philosopher. On the face of it, this claim may seem absurd. What do the abstractions of the philosophical mind have to do with Katniss Everdeen, the most intensely concrete and practical of survivalists? Throughout the series, staying alive in her world has depended upon lightning reflexes and decisive action, not a philosopher's plodding and seemingly idle reflections on such matters as the nature of Goodness, Beauty, and Truth. Such philosophic preoccupations would seem like troublesome baggage for Katniss to carry into the battles she has to wage, as she makes clear to Peeta when, on the eve of their first Hunger Games, she cuts off his earnestly expressed reflections on maintaining identity and "purity of self" with the impatient snort, "who cares?" (Collins, 2008, p. 142).

Nevertheless, Katniss *comes* to care about such matters, following Peeta down the unfamiliar path of probing reflection at key points in the trilogy. The mounting horrors she must combat make the most philosophical of questions—the problem of evil—the most urgent of issues, and the tragic resolution of *Mockingjay* (Collins, 2010) makes clear that battling systematic evil in Panem is not the same thing as *overcoming* it. Though Katniss helps the rebels topple the Capitol, Gale's bomb destroys Prim and Alma Coin schemes to restart the Hunger Games. Only as Katniss comes to *understand* the nature, motives, and mechanisms of the evil in which she herself is caught does she learn how effectively to stand against it and make her last minute decision to aim her arrow at Coin instead of Snow. That decision, as well as the longer process by which she comes to refuse suicide, marry Peeta, have children, and embrace whatever good there is in life, is the culmination of an extended and painfully winding journey in which she has learned to look past the immediate pressures of her horrific experiences and discover that, under certain circumstances, thinking can turn out to be the most moral of activities.

In this chapter, I argue that the Hunger Games trilogy can be read as a dark parable dramatizing the truth behind Socrates' famous declaration that the unexamined life is not worth living. If we peer beneath the stormy surface of their violent, video-gamelike action into the depths of Collins's novels we will discover a summons to heed the still small voice of reflection. We may thus decide the most courageous quality of its two major characters is their dedication to a relentless questioning that in turn awakens a capacity for independent moral judgments. This

S. P. Connors (ed.), The Politics of Panem, 65–84.

reflective capacity to resist conformity to already formulated directives turns out to be the surest prophylactic against evil. To make this argument, I first examine differing but complementary reflections on the nature and motivations of moral evil as conceptualized by three philosophers: Ignorance as understood by the Greek philosopher Socrates (469-399 BCE); the perverse will as understood by the Church Father Augustine of Hippo (354-430 BCE); and "banality" as understood by the modern political philosopher Hannah Arendt (1906-1975). Drawing on their work, I argue that Katniss, under Peeta's mentoring, comes to understand that, left unchecked, the violent skills and vengeful spirit she shares with Gale can only perpetuate in a new guise the evils of the old Panem. It is only as her hunter's heart embraces a philosopher's courage that she learns to judge soundly and aim her final arrow at the right target. It is this same courage that allows her to battle an enemy more deadly than Snow—suicidal despair—and resume life with Peeta in a genuinely new order that she has helped to bring about through her willingness to hunt down truth, the most elusive quarry of all.

"SO UNLIKE PEOPLE": EVIL AS IGNORANCE

The view that equates evil with ignorance is most closely associated with the name of the great Athenian philosopher Socrates, to whom is attributed the aphorism that to know the good is to do the good. For Socrates, evil is not an actively willed and deliberate choice but rather a failure of cognition. No one chooses evil *as* evil; we only choose what we judge to be good since it is the nature of the good to benefit the one who practices it just as evil harms its practitioner. Who then would knowingly choose the bad since as Socrates says in the Dialogue with Meno, "For what is the depth of misery other than to desire bad things and to get them?" (Plato, 1956, p. 38). It is precisely because knowledge is wedded to the good and the good to human happiness that Socrates famously declares, "[T]he unexamined life is not worth living" (Plato, 2006, p. 776). He means that examination is the only path to wisdom, and wisdom is the means of acquiring that beneficent virtue, absent which no human life can be worthwhile.

In Collins's trilogy, Octavia, Flavius, and Venia—the Capitol style team that, with a mindless and chatty gaiety, preps Katniss for whatever horrors lie ahead—demonstrate why Socrates equated evil with the ignorantly unexamined and thus less than fully human life. When she first meets her prep team in the Remake Center, Katniss is struck at how their non-involved cluelessness makes them curiously inhuman. Recounting their efforts to transform her physical appearance, she states:

> I stand there, completely naked, as the three circle me, wielding tweezers to remove my last bits of hair. I know I should be embarrassed, but *they're so unlike people* that I'm no more self-conscious than if a trio of oddly-colored birds were pecking at my feet. (Collins, 2008, p. 62, emphasis added)

In these characters, Collins is clearly taking satirical aim at the "the wilder-the-better" tattoo/makeup culture of our current era, but her satire also effectively makes Socrates' point about the equation of evil with ignorance. This threesome's chirpily enthusiastic "makeover" of tributes' bodies preparatory to their transformation into corpses is devoid of active malice. Quite the contrary, their practiced violations of Katniss and other victims are conducted in a spirit of an appallingly ignorant quasi-innocence made possible by a moral myopia so blindingly intense it transforms them from human beings into "oddly-colored birds." Interestingly and ironically, this avian imagery calls to mind the bird similes with which Katniss enhances the attractive humanity and loveable innocence of children such as Prim ("little duck" [p. 15]) and Rue ("like a bird" [p. 99]). The difference is that the latter have acquired a painfully existential knowledge of the reality of evil (victims often do) while the former's cluelessness enables them to carry on the work of harming others with nary a troubling thought disturbing their "incomprehensibly silly lives" (Collins, 2009, p. 37). If Socrates were to have encountered Katniss's prep team in the Agora of Athens— and did not immediately write them off as hopeless cases—he would almost certainly have regarded them as badly in need of the kind of remedial education that he provided for the youth and adults of Athens in the kind of probing dialogues recorded by his disciple Plato.

Plato's (2006) account of one of the most famous trials in history, "The Apology of Socrates," shows the great philosopher, on trial for his life, attempting to give such remedial education to accusers who, literally not knowing what they do, have charged him with "impiety" and "corrupting" the youth of Athens (p. 764). Socrates points out the ironic injustice of these charges since his alleged crimes consisted of teaching his listeners the path to wisdom through subjecting their own and others' hazy and ungrounded opinions to examination (pp. 762-764). This could hardly be impiety since, as Socrates reminds his jury, the oracle at Delphi, as reported by a reliable witness, had shown that the god [Apollo] had virtually commissioned him to do this (pp. 762-764; 768-771). The alleged "corruption" was nothing more than his youthful followers practicing his own method of cross examination on others, irritating the latter by exposing their own lack of wisdom (p. 764). Exasperated Athenians were not only unwilling to examine their own lives; they much preferred to remain ignorant of what Socrates taught and charge him with beliefs he never held (p. 764). In reading his words as recorded by Plato, we get a vivid sense that the real culprit is not the impiety and corruption of Socrates, but that of his judges; instead of buttering them up, he assumes the role of judge rather than victim by conducting his own cross-examination and asking acerbic questions such as: "[A]re you not ashamed that you take care to acquire as much wealth as possible … but about wisdom and truth, about … your soul, you take neither care nor thought?" (Plato, 2006, p. 770).[1]

Socrates' cross-examination of his chief accuser, Meletus, is not only an act of self-defense, but a case study in the reasoning behind his assertion that evil must always be a function of ignorance. First, he forces Meletus to admit that no one "wishes to be harmed rather than benefitted by those around him" (Plato, 2006, p. 766); therefore, when Meletus charges him with *intentionally* corrupting the youth, he is asserting this exact absurdity-that Socrates was deliberately going about trying to make bad neighbors who would be sure to harm and not benefit him (p. 766). Therefore, any alleged corruption could only be unintentional, a matter for "private instruction and admonishment," not a crime to be punished by law (p. 766).

Of course, for Socrates, the flip side of equating ignorance with evil is asserting that thoughtful reflection is a path to wisdom and virtue, thus the following famous passage:

> ... it's the greatest good for a man to discuss virtue every day, and the other things you've heard me discussing and examining myself and others about; on the grounds that the unexamined life isn't worth living for a human being. (Plato, 2006, p. 776)

His fellow-citizens (as he predicted) did not believe him and in their fear-driven ignorance felt his infectious habit of fearless inquiry might threaten rather than uphold a virtuous civic order. Thus they condemned him to death. History has since reversed their verdict and vindicated the warning words he gave to his accusers that a guilty verdict would damage themselves more than him since "to kill a man unjustly ... is far worse" than to die unjustly (Plato, 2006, p. 770). His steadfast devotion to the good of his soul over mere maintenance of life proved that even in his death Socrates was the one whose life had been truly worth living.

Peeta, the most "Socratic" character in Collins's series, expresses a similar dedication to honest examination and the preservation of his humanity even in the face of death as he reflects aloud to Katniss on the eve of their first trip into the arena:

> "I want to die as myself. Does that make any sense?" he asks. I shake my head. How could he die as anyone but himself? "I don't want them to change me in there. Turn me into some kind of monster that I'm not." (Collins, 2008, p. 141)

Peeta, like Socrates recognizes that he is likely to die no matter what he does, but also like Socrates, he can think beyond the immediacy of death and realize that what is at stake is not just his life, but his humanity. He can ask the question of whether the short life that lies ahead of him is worth struggling for if his mere survival is purchased at the expense of making him both a "monster" and a mere prop for the violent entertainment of others, "just a piece in their Games" (p. 142).

Peeta's self-examination allows us to set up a kind of Socratic scale for coordinating degrees of ignorance with degrees of complicity in the Capitol's evil. Peeta's knowledge makes him the most aware and least complicit. It is perhaps worth noting that his main strategy is one of defense rather than attack—the peaceful ruse of camouflage—and he never commits active violence in the arena. Katniss, on the other hand, might represent a step down on what I am calling the Socratic scale. Quickly cutting their rooftop discussion short, she tells Peeta that he can go ahead and plan a noble death, while she will concentrate on getting back to District 12 alive (Collins, 2008, p. 142). In eschewing self-examination, we might argue that Katniss takes a step up on the complicit-with-evil scale. Choosing the protective shield of ignorance over the nakedness of reflection, she is also deciding to be a pawn in the Capitol's game—although we must instantly recognize this does not mean she lacks Peeta's moral seriousness. She has, after all, made a commitment to stay alive for the sake of Prim, and this may well account for her self-protective refusal to face frontally the conflict between an ethic of family loyalty and the issues Peeta raises. None of these considerations apply to Katniss's prep team, discussed above, as their utter ignorance makes them dreadfully efficient worker bees in the Capitol hive, and nearly perfect exemplars of what makes Socrates equate evil with ignorance. In this way, they are least aware and most complicit in perpetuating evil.

But Peeta's dilemma may also represent something missing in the Socratic claim. Completely aware that he will be cooperating with a monstrously unjust system, Peeta informs Katniss that when it comes time to fight, he will still do it (Collins, 2008, p. 142). Though we later learn that his major motive for staying alive is to sacrifice himself for Katniss, the very fact that he will eventually have to work against his own principles for the sake of his love proves that cognition is not a cure. Overcoming ignorance does not provide a way out of evil. Peeta is trapped in the same double-bind as Katniss and there is no escape through knowledge.[2]

Perhaps more importantly, this very fact draws our attention to those who have created that double-bind in the first place. How can an ingeniously designed system of evil entertainment such as the Hunger Games—or its real world equivalent, the Roman Colosseum—be explained by something as pallid as ignorance? Complacent ignorance might account for the complicity of many—but can such ignorance explain away the motives of those who created this politically calculated and sadistically brilliant system in the first place? Anything that tends to make the good a reflex action of cognition and evil simply a form of ignorance seems inadequate to some manifestations of deliberate malevolence. For a penetrating examination of what might make such evil attractive, I turn next to someone who examined it under the searching light of autobiographical analysis, the 4th century Church father and philosophical theologian, Augustine of Hippo.

"DESTROYING THINGS IS EASIER THAN MAKING THEM"

Socrates was not unaware that there was culpability in evil—after all he accused Meletus of lacking moral seriousness in his charges (Plato, 2006, pp. 766-768)— but he tried to account for this by making a distinction between true knowledge and merely correct notions. As Brickhouse and Smith (2000) explain:

> Socrates distinguishes knowledge from [merely] true belief or true opinion, on the ground that the former is stable and the latter alterable. ... If one really knows something, Socrates thinks, nothing can persuade one to change one's mind so that one thinks that one had previously been mistaken and did not know. That is why Socrates thinks that knowledge is a "lordly thing ...."
> (p. 179)

But with the coming of Christianity, knowledge lost its lordly status and seemed to become servant rather than master of the will. As Arendt (2003) writes, the will was "a faculty about which ancient philosophy knew nothing and ... was not discovered in its awesome complexities before Paul and Augustine" (pp. 71-72). The Apostle Paul states bluntly that the Good and the will are in open conflict: "For the good that I will to do I do not do; but the evil I will not to do, that I practice. ... O wretched man that I am!" (Rom. 7:19, 24 New Revised Standard Version). Much of Augustine's work is an elaboration of Paul's "wretched' mystery: that to know the Good is *not* necessarily to do it.

The mystery of the nature of evil and the perverse will that actively embraces it tormented Augustine, and much of his early and most famous work, *The Confessions* (2006), is devoted to solving this mystery. At one point, he attempts to detect the motive of a childhood theft in which he and some friends not only stole some pears, but later threw them away, turning the theft into gratuitous vandalism. What could explain this kind of irrationality? Augustine considers all possible motives for evildoing in order to discover the one that will answer his thrice-repeated question: "What was it ... I loved in you O theft of mine?" (pp. 30-32). Since I argue that his particular solution to that question will illuminate the perverted will to evil evident in Collins' Hunger Games trilogy, it is worth taking time to examine the process by which Augustine works through the mystery of motive.

First, the key word in Augustine's (2006) question is "love." Love—or better, passionate desire—is the theme of book II of *The Confessions*. Desire, not reason, is the engine that drives the will. Furthermore, and this may seem surprising, Augustine argues that our desire is *always* for something good since it is either directed towards God, the highest good for those with a properly ordered "love life" (to use a modern colloquialism), or for one of the lower goods that God created (pp. 30-31). In the most literal sense possible, we can desire nothing but good things because the good God made them, and it is their very goodness that makes them desirable (pp. 30-31).[3]

But while there are nothing but good things to desire, Augustine (2006) argues that we can desire them in the *wrong* way through "immoderate inclination" in which "things higher and better are forgotten, even You, O Lord our God, and Your Law" (p. 30). Since God cannot make evil, the *only* place that evil can exist is in a perverse will that distorts desire. Thus, *concupiscence* ("immoderate inclination" [p. 30]) overturns moral hierarchies and, to use Augustine's example of theft, elevates a desire for a lower good above the higher good of God's law. Augustine proceeds to go through a whole inventory of such wrongful acts to show how they are all motivated "through the desire of gaining or the fear of losing one of those lower goods" (p. 30).

Through an Augustinian lens, the essence of the evil manifest in the Capitol doesn't lie in the love of spectacle, ingenious applications of science and technology, or even in the exercise of power since these are all good and desirable things in their proper place. Instead, it is the grotesquely "immoderate inclination" that leads the Capitol's rulers and citizens to love the lower goods of entertainment, technological ingenuity, and power more than the higher goods of human decency, respect for nature, and justice. It is this total inversion of the moral pyramid, and not the elements of which it is composed, that is responsible for evil.

But what underlying motive would make humans want to invert the pyramid in the first place? This is what baffles Augustine (2006) and makes him turn a teenage theft into a case study on foundational motives for wrongdoing. An ordinary theft would be pretty understandable. It has an obvious (if ignoble) motive. Pears are beautiful and tasty; appetite wants them; we grab and eat. But Augustine explains that *his* theft did not occur because the tastiness of a pear was more alluring than the beauty of God's law, rather:

> ... it was not pears that my empty soul desired .... I threw them away, tasting only my own sin and savouring that with delight; for if I took so much a bite of any one of those pears, it was the sin that sweetened it. (p. 31)

Here he puts his finger on the infuriating nature of vandalism. It is a seemingly senseless act whose perpetrators, benefitting nobody including themselves, apparently find destruction "sweet" for its own sake.

But for Augustine (2006), the "sweetness" of sin is *never* for its own sake—even when it appears to be so—but rather for the sake of a certain "show of beauty in sin" (p. 31). Sin without this deceptive "show" would have no appeal, though it is only a show because unlike the real Beauty, it can't deliver on the goods it promises. Whatever pleasure or beauty seems to adhere to sin is a shadow stolen from the Good, the misguided attempt to possess the beautiful things of God's world or the attributes of God on our own terms through acts of "perverse imitation" (p. 32). Augustine goes through a brief catalogue of these "perverse imitations" in which the sinful mind and heart, like funhouse mirrors, generate distorted reflections of God's own attributes: pride mimics God's greatness; cruelty his power; lust parodies his love; and so on (p. 31). Augustine concludes, "By the mere fact of their imitation they declare that You are the creator of all that is, and that there is no place for them to go where You are not" (p. 32). We may note that Augustine might see as a crowning irony that the very possibility of this perverse mimicry only gives testimony to the greatest of God's good gifts to humans, the freedom of the will.

Augustine's (2006) catalogue of human parodies of Divine goodness has finally prepared him for the answer to his question: "Of what excellence of my Lord was [this vandalism] making perverse imitation?" He writes:

> Perhaps it was the thrill of acting against Your law ... getting *a deceptive sense of omnipotence* from doing something forbidden without immediate punishment. I was that slave, who fled from his Lord and pursued his Lord's shadow .... O monstrousness of life and abyss of death! Could you find pleasure only in what was forbidden, and only because it was forbidden? (p. 32, emphasis added)

"Deceptive sense of omnipotence" explains the thrill of gratuitous law-breaking: it creates a pleasing delusion that one is a godlike being free of moral restraints just as God is above the restraints of the moral law that he created. At the same time, this rush of omnipotence is only a "perverse imitation" of the real thing, since unlike God, one has no power to create the moral law, only to manufacture the delusion of negating it. Augustine may have seen the pear tree episode as his own personal enactment of that original sin, which took place among the first humans in another garden, that of Eden. In an earlier work, *On Free Choice of the Will* (1993), he certainly describes the fall of the first humans as motivated by something very much like his own deceptive sense of omnipotence, calling Adam's wholly free and irrationally motivated turning from God the action of one who "wants to be his own good, as if he were his own God" (p. 120). The result of this "perverse imitation," as with Augustine's pears, was predictably destructive since human beings acting independently against God cannot really add anything to the fullness of created Beauty or Goodness, only subtract from it.

We may deduce from Augustine that there are only two ways of responding to the good things made by God: either embrace them with the kind of attentive and receptive creativity that Peeta shows with his art or vandalize them as the Capitol does through its oppressive tactics and policies. As Katniss concludes, "Destroying things is much easier than making them" (Collins, 2008, p. 211).

"HOW FREAKISH THEY LOOK"

Augustine's (2006) ideas can help explain why the very principle of Capitol art and ethics seems to be that of "vicious and perverse imitation" (p. 32), a vandalizing parody of anything beautiful and anything good. At its most harmless level, Capitol cosmetics and body art seem devoted to the idea of making oneself ugly in order to make oneself "original." On more than one occasion Katniss remarks on this repellant lust to deface in order to "make special," most memorably in *Catching Fire* (Collins, 2009) as her prep team prepares to go to work on her:

> Flavius tilts up my chin and sighs. "It's a shame Cinna said no alterations on you."
>
> "Yes, we could really make you something special," says Octavia ....
>
> Do what? Blow my lips up like President Snow's? Tattoo my breasts? Dye my skin magenta and implant gems in it? Cut decorative patterns in my face? Give me curved talons? Or cat's whiskers? I saw all these things and more on the people in the Capitol. Do they really have no idea how freakish they look to the rest of us? (pp. 48-49)

The answer to Katniss's question is, of course, "No," because the Capitol dwellers, in "seeking to be their own good," have cut themselves loose from any given canons of beauty and the result is the kind of destructive artificiality Katniss describes in her first glimpse of the Capitol: "All the colors seem artificial, the pinks too deep, the greens too bright, the yellows painful to the eyes" (Collins, 2008, p. 59). In the Capitol, nature is something to be set upon and made into ever more unnatural combinations. The role of art is no longer to enhance nature, but to deface it.

And yet, as Augustine suggests, all perverse imitation can do is show how much fuller is the given Good and the Beauty already implanted in the world and beyond the capacity of humans to create (though they can reproduce these qualities in art or honor them in acts of love or heroism). While the moral and theological landscape of Collins's Hunger Games series occupies a different universe than Augustine's writings, the opening chapters of *Catching Fire* might have been deliberately set up to emphasize the stark difference between perverse imitation and the beauty of the natural. For example, they exhibit what appears to be a deliberate pattern of alternating contrasts between the natural and the artificial. The novel begins with Katniss awaiting the beginning of the Victory Tour. She wonders whether Effie Trinket will arrive "wearing that silly pink wig, or if she'll be sporting some other unnatural color" (Collins, 2009, p. 3). Further gloomy thoughts about having to maintain an artificial cheeriness on the Tour and her equally artificial pretense of being Peeta's lover then give way to thoughts of Gale, "who is only really alive in the woods, with its fresh air and sunlight and clean, flowing water" (p. 5), and where he can exercise his "natural gift" for hunting (p. 6).

The unnatural makes a particularly ominous reappearance with the visit of President Snow and his tight, puffy, surgically repaired lips, reeking of blood and the disagreeably sweet odor of a genetically enhanced lapel-rose. Exuding a sense of omnipotence he knows is as "fragile" (Collins, 2009, p. 22) as it is fake, Snow settles himself into "this ... place he has no right, but ultimately every right to occupy" (p. 20). This wholly artificial man has come to order Katniss to do a better job of faking her love affair with Peeta by adhering convincingly to the Capitol's script in her upcoming Victory Tour (pp. 28-29).

Later, splashing in her bathwater, Katniss is relieved by a nostalgic memory of paddling about in the waters of a lake in the woods to which her father took her as a girl; this agreeably natural memory is interrupted, however, by the intrusion of her makeup team into her bathroom, lead by Octavia's displaying her new and unnaturally spiked "aqua hair" (Collins, 2009, pp. 34-35). This in turn is followed by a light but telling interlude with Cinna in which Katniss lingers lovingly over descriptions of the natural and comfortable fashions he has designed for her, but this exchange is interrupted as "Effie Trinket arrives in a pumpkin orange wig to remind everyone, 'We're on schedule!'" (p. 40)—thus gratifying Katniss's earlier curiosity about what kind of outlandishly unnatural wig Effie would be wearing (p. 3).

In *Catching Fire* (Collins, 2009), this almost rhythmic pattern of alternating the Capitol's perverse imitations with natural beauties seems designed to prepare the way for a revelatory moment in which art, as embodied by Peeta, is shown to be a loving enhancement and imitation of nature, not fodder to be seized and wrenched into ever more grotesque configurations. As I have argued in another essay (McDonald, 2012, pp. 10-12), Peeta's understanding of art reflects the classical view of *mimesis,* an attentive and responsive imitation of that which is given in the world. In one of the most unexpected and astonishing passages in the whole series,

Peeta comforts a dying morphling (and fellow artist) in the Quarter Quell by describing the fulfilling beauty of *mimesis*:

> "With my paint box at home, I can make every color imaginable. Pink as pale as a baby's skin. Or as deep as rhubarb. Green like spring grass. Blue that shimmers like ice on water."
>
> The morphling stares into Peeta's eyes, hanging on to his words.
>
> "One time, I spent three days mixing paint until I found the right shade for sunlight on white fur. You see, I kept thinking it was yellow, but it was much more than that. Layers of all sorts of color. One by one," says Peeta. (Collins, 2009, p. 312)

In this scene, Peeta's words express the moral side of *mimesis,* showing that true art is not mere mimicry, but rather an act of love and respect for that being artistically represented. His intense contemplation of a beautiful color, and the subsequent discipline that made him spend three days mixing paint to get it just right, is for him a communion with that beauty, or as Augustine might say, with Beauty itself. And there is also a moral beauty in the way that Peeta discerns the morphling's need in her dying moments.

Peeta's morality as evidenced in this scene is thus of a piece with his aesthetic sense since both are based upon an alert responsiveness to what is present before him. Capitol aesthetics, however, are perfectly matched to perverted Capitol morality: a desire to destroy and remake instead of caring and careful attentiveness that enhances. Peeta's artistic and moral contemplativeness seems to share something in common with Augustine's (1993) description of the soul which contemplates the highest wisdom, "realiz[ing] that it is not the same as God, and yet that it is something that, next to God can be pleasing" (p. 122). On the other hand, those practicing the aesthetic and ethic of the Capitol represent the person who "takes pleasure in himself and wills to enjoy his own power in a perverse imitation of God," and in doing so "becomes more and more insignificant as he desires to become greater" (p. 122).

Although the idea of God is absent from the Hunger Games trilogy, it is important to recognize that the actual existence of God plays no *necessary* part in Augustine's psychology of sin for the simple reason that one doesn't have to believe in a god to want to be one! For example, the philosopher Sartre (1993) as well as the psychoanalytically oriented authors Brown (1959) and Ernest Becker (1973) all argue from different perspectives that the human will is fundamentally motivated by the *causa sui* project, the desire to be the cause of oneself. In other words, to quote Brown, the fundamental desire is that of "becoming God" (Brown, 1959, p. 118). Though the world of Collins' fiction is devoid of deity the thirst for omnipotence is omnipresent—with the same destructive consequences Augustine described.

Ironically, this *faux* show of omnipotence that leads only to destruction means that the Capitol residents, whether watching the bodies pile up in the arena or defacing their own for the sake of "originality," are practicing the most banal kind of conformity. Yet that kind of banality, as will be argued below, may turn out to be the most potent weapon of all in evil's arsenal.

"AT LEAST YOU TWO HAVE DECENT MANNERS": EVIL AS BANALITY

Though Socrates and Augustine at points have conflicting views of evil, on the whole, they might better be understood as complementary "variations on a theme": Socrates understands evil as ignorance, though he doesn't account for the phenomenon of the weak will nor does he ask what makes wrongdoing attractive. Augustine shares the Socratic belief that we only choose what we judge to be good, but his account of wrongdoing's deceptive show of beauty fills in some of the Socratic blanks. Hannah Arendt (2003), to whose work I turn next, fills in more of those blanks by arguing that mere "banality" can lead ordinary people to become complicit in truly horrendous evils.

The final phrase in the subtitle of Arendt's (1963) controversial work *Eichmann in Jerusalem: A Report on the Banality of Evil* went "viral" (to use a computer age metaphor). Based on her observations of the 1961-1962 trial and condemnation of the Nazi war criminal Adolph Eichmann, Arendt concluded that it was possible to be an active collaborator in monstrous evil without being personally a monster. All it required was a "joiner" mentality separated from any capacity for exercising independent judgment. Hence the phrase "banality of evil," and its most characteristic representative in the Hunger Games trilogy is arguably Effie Trinket.

Effie Trinket, unlike Snow and those at the top of the power tree, is not motivated by any apparent perverse lust to play god, or by any extraordinary instinct of cruelty. She is by will and habit wholly insensate to the evil she helps coordinate, but she is always infallibly "nice." She is able to perform her duties so smoothly because she refuses to exercise any independent thought about the rightness or wrongness of those duties. It is the kind of outlook one imagines must be prevalent among middle managers in criminal organizations (or governmental bureaucracies!). She is ambitious, effective, and eager for promotion to a higher status job than that of shepherding the woeful District 12 tributes; she is therefore able to help grease the skids for immense atrocities while fussing all the time over "manners." This combination of bright efficiency with blindfolded conscience makes Effie the very embodiment of evil's banality.

In a volume of posthumously published essays, Arendt (2003) explained Eichmann's "banality" in terms that could well apply to Effie Trinkett:

[I] meant with this no theory or doctrine, but something quite factual, the phenomenon of evil deeds, committed on a gigantic scale, which could not be traced to any particularity of wickedness, pathology, or ideological conviction in the doer. … However monstrous the deeds were, the doer was neither monstrous nor demonic, and the only specific characteristic one could detect…was something entirely negative: it was not stupidity but a curious, quite authentic inability to think. (p. 159)

Certainly Effie displays an Eichmann-like banality in the macabre cheerfulness with which she conducts her charges to almost certain death. She also demonstrates her "curious, quite authentic inability to think" on many occasions, including a moment of completely unselfconscious irony when she proudly tells Peeta and Katniss that in talking them up before Capitol sponsors she emphasized their having "overcome the barbarism of [their] districts" (Collins, 2008, p. 74).

Katniss' observation that "manners matter deeply to [Effie]" (Collins, 2009, p. 51) is particularly relevant to Arendt's (2003) understanding of evil's banality, since Arendt was convinced that the Nazi totalitarianism proved that supposedly deeply rooted moral traditions might turn out for most populations to be an easily replaceable set of manners or "mores" (pp. 43, 50). As a Jewish philosopher who left Germany just ahead of the Holocaust, Arendt said that she and her fellow Jews were stunned at "the behavior not of our enemies but our friends," whose eagerness "not to miss the train of History" led speedily to an "overnight change of opinions" and the easy breaking of "lifelong friendships" in order to swap previously sacrosanct moral standards for Hitler's Aryan racialism (p. 24). She reflected:

> ... it was as though morality suddenly stood revealed in the original meaning of the word, as a set of *mores*, customs and manners, which could be exchanged for another set with hardly more trouble than it would take to change the table manners of an individual people. (p. 50, emphasis in original)

Kohn (2003) explains that for Arendt this easily exchangeable nature of values did not mean that she believed with the 19th century philosopher Nietzsche that the principles of morality are in *fact* "exchangeable," in having no ground except that of power (p. xviii-xix). Rather, she assumed that most people are so intensely thoughtless they are capable of simply sleepwalking into any collaboration with evil. For Arendt (2003):

> ... [I]t seems to be much easier to condition human behavior and to make people conduct themselves in the most unexpected and outrageous manner, than to persuade anybody....to start thinking and judging instead of applying categories and formulas which are deeply ingrained in our mind, but whose basis of experience has long been forgotten and whose plausibility resides in their intellectual consistency rather than in their adequacy to actual events. (p. 37)

In other words, moral categories that have been emptied of any real connection to people's experience are of no use at all in the face of great totalitarian upheavals such as occurred in the first half of the twentieth century. Resistance to such events requires that independent exercise of thought so necessary before any judgment can earn the right to be called "moral." The majority of people will refuse the obligation of such reflective and moral autonomy and accept what some set of authoritative "others" tell them. Exchanging their morals for "mores," they'll quickly swap out their former ethical manners for the new ones that have been introduced: "unable to pit their own judgment against history as they read it" (p. 24).

A chilling corollary of Arendt's (2003) thesis is that it is precisely banality's lack of vicious motives that might paradoxically make it the most potent of all evil forces. The banality of evil means "that no wicked heart, a relatively rare phenomenon, is necessary to cause great evil" (p. 164). Dramatic wickedness may claim our attention, but banality is what makes evil most effective. For Arendt:

> We are here not concerned with wickedness ... but with evil; not with sin and the great villains who become the negative heroes in literature ... but with the nonwicked everybody who has no special motives and *for this reason is capable of infinite evil*; unlike the villain, he never meets his midnight disaster. (p. 188, emphasis added)

No more striking phrase could indicate the power of "nonwicked" banality than the assertion that unlike the more overt "villain" who by the very reactive forces he sets in motion must have a stopping point, the "everybody with no special motives" has, theoretically, no checking point for the evil that unthinking compliance and lack of moral substance permits, Such "everybodies" have signed over the right to independent thinking to the ideology, person, or movement they serve. President Snow will "meet his midnight disaster," but the citizens of the Capitol are willing to follow him as far as he is willing to go just as the rebels are willing to follow Coin unquestioningly later in Collins's series. While individual horrific acts (such as the recent massacre of children at Sandy Hook) may wreak unspeakable devastation on particular communities, they are unconnected to the conveyer belt of a social system manned by the unthinkingly compliant, and thus flame themselves out on the spots they occur. On the contrary, when true believers in certain violence-prone political or religious ideologies meet the opportunities of unstable historical times and seize the levers of a social and political system, they may turn evil into the dominant principle of the whole society and extend it systematically through the mechanism of an army of citizens empty of anything but a banal and unreflective capacity to obey the superior force.

"TO LOOK INTO THE CONFUSING MESS OF LIFE AND SEE THINGS AS THEY REALLY ARE"

Arendt's (2003) reflections on evil's banality led her to consider the factors that motivated some people to rise above banality and resist the encroachments of evil, and her answer is relevant to the assertion with which I began this essay: namely, that Katniss had to become a philosopher not only to ignite a revolution against the Capitol's oppressive evil, but also to avoid becoming an enabler of future evil as intense as the one against which that rebellion was raised. For Arendt (2003), if an avoidance of thinking and its corollary, independent judgment, caused the flourishing of evil, its only possible cure lay in the opposite direction, that of reflection. She was convinced that neither religious convictions nor moral upbringing moved people to silent or overt opposition; rather, for her, the one common denominator shared by such noncollaborators was the most fundamental of all philosophical acts: *thinking* (p. 45). She concluded that reflection, often regarded as the most private and least obviously practical act of all, could, in certain circumstances, turn out to have the most political impact of all (pp.188-189).

Whatever degree this is the case in actual life, it certainly is true in the fictional world of Panem, Indeed, Collins's trilogy might well have been written to dramatize just this thesis as is shown vividly in a previously discussed sequence of events touched off by Peeta's rooftop reflections prior to his and Katniss's entering the arena for their first Hunger Games:

> "I keep wishing I could think of a way to ... to show the Capitol they don't own me. That I'm more than just a piece in their Games," says Peeta.

> "But you're not," I say. "None of us are. That's how the Games work."

> "Okay, but within that framework, there's still you, there's still me," he insists: "Don't you see?"

> "A little. Only ... no offense, but who cares, Peeta?" (Collins, 2008, p. 142)

And yet within less than a hundred pages, Peeta's remembered words trigger Katniss' first overt act of rebellion. When Katniss sings the dying Rue to her eternal sleep and later sprinkles wildflower blossoms over her body, it is the previously scorned thought planted by Peeta that has blossomed into the flowers decorating Rue. Faced with Rue's death, Katniss states:

> Then I remember Peeta's words on the roof. "*Only I keep wishing I could think of a way to ... to show the Capitol they don't own me. That I'm more than just a piece in their Games.*" And for the first time I understand what he means.

> I want to do something, right here, right now, to shame them, to show the Capitol that whatever they do or force us to do there is a part of every tribute they can't own. That Rue was more than a piece in their Games. And so am I. (Collins, 2008, pp. 236-237, emphasis in original)

As if to underline the importance of reflection (as well as foreshadow future developments), Katniss at first recalls Gale's "ravings against the Capitol," but finds that they only make her "feel my impotence" (p. 236). It is Peeta's words that give her an idea for a nonviolent and nonvengeful form of protest in the midst of violence, one that she will repeat under different circumstances and with different aims in a remarkable event in *Mockingjay* (Collins, 2010) to be discussed later in this essay.

I have referred earlier to Peeta's "Socratic" role in the novel. Socrates referred to himself as a "midwife" whose goal was to help birth reflection in others (Plato, 1935, pp. 24-27). Peeta has clearly performed that role. His own reflective massaging of Katniss' mind, initially dismissed by her, has brought to birth the uncomfortably yoked twins of thought and action. The need to think is often the enemy of action and vice versa. They can, however, become rare and powerful collaborators in an action-oriented person like Katniss who can be brought to the point of reflection. Her actions in turn have been given a mockingjay's wings and taken flight (ironically courtesy of the Capitol's airwaves!) to enter the hearts and minds of others.

Just as Peeta's "Socratic" midwifery brought forth fruit with Katniss, Arendt (2003) was also stimulated by the Socratic example to consider whether the act of reflection *itself* served as a natural inoculation against evil. She wondered: "Could this activity be of such a nature that it *'conditions' men against evildoing*?" (p. 160, emphasis added). She concluded that it does by considering and then joining together two separate assertions from *The Gorgias*. The first has become an ethical commonplace since the time of Socrates (and in part because of him): "it is better to be wronged than to do wrong" (as cited in Arendt, 2003, p. 181); the second is: "It would be better for me that my lyre ... should be out of tune ... than that I, *being one,* should be out of harmony with myself and contradict me" (as cited in Arendt, 2003, p. 181, emphasis in original).

Arendt (2003) finds this need to be in harmony with oneself the "prerequisite" and basis for the moral judgment that it is better to endure wrong than to perform it (p. 183). As she explains, when you put the two Socratic claims together, it amounts to this:

> It is better for you to suffer than do wrong because you can remain the friend of the sufferer; who would want to be the friend of and have to live together with a murderer? Not even a murderer. (p. 185)

Peeta's reflections might have been specifically designed to make Arendt's point: he doesn't want to be turned into a monster *precisely because he can't live with a self that has become one.* That this highly moral judgment seems to rise naturally from the very act of reflection not only seems a confirmation of Arendt's views that thinking may "condition a man against evil" but also indicates the connection between the two separate faculties of reflection and moral judgment. To summarize her reasoning: Thinking erodes our confidence in the "mores" of our society, which is the prerequisite for an authentic exercise of judgment. This judgment requires that we not approach particular situations with a prefabricated set of directives given to us by others and swallowed unreflectively by ourselves. Because it deals with particulars that cannot be subsumed under these directives, reflection and the moral judgment that derives from the questions it poses requires a degree of sensitivity, discernment, and risk that rule-following does not call for (Arendt, 2003, pp. 188-189).

An analogy might be made to the genuine artist who is also able to discern the truth in the particular and represent it faithfully. Thus Peeta, philosopher and artist, embodies precisely the substance and implications of what Arendt describes. And his own "conditioning" has a similar effect on Katniss, turning their disturbing conversation on the tributes' dormitory roof into the single most important event in the novel since through it, Peeta has begun to evoke in her the same quality she will later attribute to her sister Prim: "An ability to look into the confusing mess of life and see things as they really are" (Collins, 2010, p. 184). Peeta's willingness to rise above that mess and see through it has two dramatic effects. First, his words, rejected at the time but burned into her memory, come back to Katniss in the arena after she sings the dying Rue to her death. They inspire her to decorate Rue's corpse with flowers, a gesture that makes both of them more than a "piece in the Capitol's Games" and lights a fuse that ultimately explodes into the districts' revolt. Secondly, Peeta's insistence on seeing through the mess and not simply being sucked into it becomes the triggering event for the novel's most crucial subplot. If the plot of *Mockingjay* (Collins, 2010) centers on whether Katniss and those she loves will prevail in the revolution she sets off, the subplot deals with whether that victory will turn them into exactly what Peeta fears—a new breed of monsters. And the only thing that stands between them and monsterhood is the fragile barrier of independent thought and judgment, that "conditioner" against evil that Peeta has helped plant in Katniss's mind.

"I NO LONGER FEEL ANY ALLEGIANCE TO THESE MONSTERS CALLED HUMAN BEINGS"

If the most important victory is that over monsters within and not enemies without, then the Hunger Games series' most important episodes are not those involving suspenseful actions, but the more subtle and quiet scenes in which Peeta and Katniss respond to the compelling call of an aesthetic and moral beauty all but drowned out by the blare of the Capitol's noisy artificiality and cruelty. I use the word "call" advisedly because Collins, resembling Augustine in this way, writes in a manner suggesting that the qualities of Goodness, Beauty and Truth are built into the world, while evil represents a perverse parody of them. She conveys this sensibility by displaying the indecency and ugliness of the Capitol as a form of artificiality imposed on the world by human willfulness, while the qualities of Goodness and Beauty seem to belong naturally to it and express themselves as a kind of summons to those who are reflective and aware. She also shows how this responsive awareness might be effective in the partnership of Peeta and Katniss. Aided by Peeta's "midwifery," Katniss is able to combine her effective warrior's skills with Peeta's sensibilities in a way that makes a new order possible. And her embrace of Peeta's reflection and artistry also represent her increasing estrangement from Gale, who remains only a warrior and whose actions, if uncorrected, might well have signaled a restarting of the old regime's horrors in a new form.

In their partnership, Peeta seems to be Katniss's mentor in discovering Truth just as he seems to serve as a powerful example of Goodness, but they both discover and embody the given Beauty in the world through parallel but independent routes. Katniss invokes beauty through her songs and Peeta through art. That we are meant to see these as elements in a parallel partnership is made especially clear in two scenes from *Catching Fire* (Collins, 2009) and *The Hunger*

Games (Collins, 2008) that seem to me to be deliberately constructed as mirror images. The first, examined earlier in this chapter, is Peeta's comforting the dying morphling with a description of the beauty of artistic mimesis. Peeta's scene beautifully mirrors Katniss's response to the dying Rue in *The Hunger Games:*

"Sing," she says, but I barely catch the word.

Sing, I think. *Sing what?* I do know a few songs. Believe it or not, there was once music in my house too. Music I helped make. My father pulled me in with that remarkable voice—but I haven't sung much since he died ...

Sing. My throat is tight with tears, hoarse from smoke and fatigue. But if this is Prim's, I mean, Rue's last request, I have to at least try. (Collins, 2008, p. 234)

Both scenes involve an intervention by comforters to ease the dying of victims whose deaths serve no other purpose than to satisfy the savage entertainment lusts of Capitol dwellers, or to reinforce the power of the Capitol rulers. In both scenes, this lust is counteracted by the invocation of some form of beauty much less noisy and immediately powerful than the Capitol's blaring artificiality and indecency, but much more "real" and somehow rooted in the "nature of things." In both cases, that "something" seems to call out to each person in the form of an "inspiration." Katniss's lullaby "comes to me," just as Peeta's experience with sunlight on leaves calls him to reproduce it in his own art. In both scenes, the act of comforting makes no utilitarian sense at all, and perhaps this explains the major contrast between the two: Katniss is initially dumbfounded by the request to sing in a way that calls to mind her befuddlement about Peeta's words. On the roof with Peeta and in the woods holding Rue in her arms, it is as though she is called upon to exercise unfamiliar powers. And yet, it is in trying out and then exercising those unfamiliar powers that Katniss is able to venture out of the darkness toward greatest accomplishment. Whatever hope remains for her in the novel comes from her seeing Goodness and Beauty not as something useless and hampering survival, but as a form of quiet power that will eventually reveal the Capitol's as more fragile. For this reason, one of the trilogy's movements is a slow evolution of Katniss's feelings away from Gale towards Peeta.

"I'M TIRED OF BEING A PIECE IN THEIR GAMES"

In *Mockingjay* (Collins, 2010), we see Katniss complete her evolution into a person of reflection. With Peeta essentially decommissioned—or worse, turned into a weapon against Katniss because of the torments and tracker jacker poison administered to him by the Capitol—Katniss comes fully into her own as a thinker, mostly through a series of increasing separations from Gale. That increasing separation and subsequent full flowering of her independent reflection is shown on many occasions in the final volume of the series. In one important episode, Gale, with the technical assistance of Beetee, develops a strategy for destroying the virtually impregnable "Nut," the mountain serving as the center of military weapons production for the Capitol. A combination of nicely placed detonations will set off a series of avalanches designed to totally destroy the operations—and all human life inside. The sheer brutality of Gale's strategy, which will destroy not only equipment and soldiers, but also District 2 civilians and workers, horrifies Katniss. Like Gale, she has been crushed with grief and rage at the firebombing of her own District 12, but unlike him, she is distraught by the thought of deliberately creating cave-ins all too reminiscent of the coal-mining accident that killed her father. Gale, on the other hand, is almost imperturbable in his "War is Hell" mentality, and he is quite willing, in Katniss's disapproving words, to make "a coldhearted decision … for other people and those who love them" (Collins, 2010, p. 205).

Perhaps in some deference to Katniss, the train tunnel to the Nut is left open so that some can escape, and Katniss, in the midst of a speech urging the surrender of any other troops in District 2, is suddenly confronted by a young escapee from the Nut's destruction who turns a gun on her and demands that she give him one reason why he shouldn't kill her. The "Peeta within" triggers Katniss's response as she replies, "I can't" (Collins, 2010, p. 215). In an astonishing gesture that exemplifies the kind of action that Peeta said he would never be able to perform in the arena, she lowers her bow and arrow and kicks them away, exclaiming, "I'm done killing [the Capitol's] slaves for them" (p. 215). Taken aback in much the same way that Katniss was when Peeta first expressed his rooftop reflections, the man does not shoot, but instead denies he is a slave. Katniss responds:

> "I am …. That's why I killed Cato … and he killed Thresh … and he killed Clove … and she tried to kill me …. But I'm tired of being a piece in their Games."
>
> Peeta. On the rooftop the night before our first Hunger Games. He understood it all before we'd even set foot in the arena. (pp. 215-216)

Unfortunately, the advance in reflection this represents does no one good but herself—though of course from a Socratic perspective this is vitally important; nevertheless, what could have been a powerfully reconciling and uniting gesture—much as her burying Rue in flowers was—is destroyed when someone in the confusion (not the young man she has spoken to) shoots and wounds Katniss (p. 217).

Throughout the remainder of *Mockingjay* (Collins, 2010), the increasingly reflective side of Katniss wages war with the archer who becomes obsessed with putting an arrow into President Snow, the cause of all evil, and for a while in the surprising denouement it appears that kind of vindictiveness which is more characteristic of Gale than Peeta will win out. Katniss, who has spent the first two volumes trying to escape being a mere piece in the carnivorous power games of President Snow, comes within a whisker of turning herself into a pawn of a new power game planned by Alma Coin. Coin has used Gale and Beetee's ingenious delayed action bomb to see to it that wounded children and the rescue workers caring for them—including Prim—die horrifically. She arranges this so that this act of senseless savagery will be blamed on the Capitol and President Snow. Wanting to take over herself, Coin plans to institute a new version of the Hunger Games and she counts on Katniss's grief-filled hatred for President Snow to make her an ally in consenting to the new policy. Had Katniss not been willing to think her way out of her excessive fog of hatred for Snow and end this would-be coup by aiming her arrow at Coin instead, the revolution of which she was the chief inspiration, symbol, and lead warrior would have been in vain. Coin would surely have eliminated Katniss after she did Snow, and under her rule the banality of evil would have continued its triumphant march into Arendt's "infinity" with an army of new Effie Trinkets to keep the parade going.[4]

That Katniss thwarts, rather than joins, this parade is a result of her having learned to become a thinker as well as a survivalist over the course of the trilogy. Under the tutelage of Peeta, she has engaged in what Socrates would call the primary vocation of the philosopher—to abandon the unexamined life and reflect on what virtues are required to meet the situation's need. Her courageous and morally-directed assassination of Coin (as well as her subsequent decision to live, to marry, and to have children instead of kill herself) is the culmination of a developing process of philosophical and moral examination that at long last have led her to a life truly worth living.

NOTES

[1] I am indebted to my colleague George Dunn (2012), editor of *The Hunger Games and Philosophy*, for pointing out to me years ago that Socrates actually turns his own trial into an indictment of Athens. I also wish to acknowledge the many helpful suggestions George made on this essay when it was in manuscript form.

[2] For a discussion about the way in which "moral luck" makes difficult any simple application of Socrates' belief that it is better to endure rather than inflict injustice, see Dunn's (2012) "The odds have not been very dependable of late": Morality and luck in the Hunger Games trilogy. In G.A. Dunn & N. Michaud (Eds.), *The Hunger Games and philosophy: A critique of pure treason* (pp. 63-73).

[3] We might compare this to Socrates, who claimed, for a somewhat different reason, that we are capable of choosing only what we judge to be good. What Augustine adds is the claim that the objects of our choices really *are* good. The problem is that we choose them in the ignorant (and idolatrous) belief that they are the sort of goods that can give us ultimate satisfaction.

[4] For a different discussion of the moral basis for Katniss's assassination, see Averill (2012), "Sometimes the world is hungry for people who care": Katniss and the feminist care ethic. In G.A. Dunn & N. Michaud (Eds.), *The Hunger Games and philosophy: A critique of pure treason* (pp. 162-176).

REFERENCES

Arendt, H. (1963). *Eichmann in Jerusalem: A study in the banality of evil*. New York: Viking Press.

Arendt, H. (2003). *Responsibility and judgment* (J. Kohn, Ed.). New York. Schocken.

Augustine, A. (2006). *Confessions* (F. J. Sheed, Trans., 2nd ed.). Indianapolis: Hackett. (Original work issued between 397 and 398)

Augustine, A. (1993). *On free choice of the will* (T. Williams. Trans.). Indianapolis: Hackett. (Originally issued in three books between 387-395)

Becker, E. (1973). *The denial of death.* New York: Free Press.

Brickhouse, T. C., & Smith, N. D. (2000). *The philosophy of Socrates.* Boulder: Westview.

Brown, N. O. (1959). *Life against death: The psychoanalytic meaning of history.* New York: Viking Press.

Collins, S. (2008). *The hunger games.* New York: Scholastic Press.

Collins, S. (2009). *Catching fire.* New York: Scholastic Press.

Collins, S. (2010). *Mockingjay.* New York: Scholastic Press.

Dunn, G. A., Michaud, N., & Irwin, W. (Eds.). (2012). *The Hunger Games and philosophy: A critique of pure treason.* Hoboken, NJ: John Wiley & Sons.

Kohn, J. (2003). Introduction. In J. Kohn (Ed.), *Responsibility and judgment.* New York. Schocken Books.

McDonald, B. C. (2012). "The final word on entertainment": Mimetic and monstrous art in the hunger games. In G. A. Dunn & N. Michaud (Eds.), *The Hunger Games and philosophy: A critique of pure treason* (pp. 1-24). Hoboken, NJ: John Wiley & Sons.

Plato. (1935). The Theaetetus (F. M. Cornford, Trans.). In *Plato's theory of knowledge.* London: Routledge & Kegan Paul. (Originally written circa 399-347 BCE)

Plato. (1956). Meno (W. H. D. Rouse Trans.). In E. H. Warmington & P. G. Rouse (Eds.), *Great dialogues of Plato.* New York: New American Library. (Originally written circa 399-347 BCE)

Plato. (2006). The apology of Socrates (C. D. Reeve Trans.). In S. Lawall (Ed.), *The Norton anthology of Western literature* (8th ed., pp. 758-779). New York: Norton. (Originally written circa 399-347 BCE)

Sartre, J. P. (1993). *Being and nothingness* (H. E. Barnes, Trans.). New York: Washington Square Press. (Originally published in 1943)

SEAN P. CONNORS

5. "I WAS WATCHING YOU, MOCKINGJAY"

Surveillance, Tactics, and the Limits of Panopticism

The individual is often something more than a passive and compliant reed buffeted about by the imposing winds of the more powerful .... (Marx, 2003, p. 372)

Although they are set in the future, dystopias are very much concerned with the present. At their core, they represent an attempt on the part of writers to use literature as a vehicle to examine contemporary social and political issues that could, if left unattended, bring about undesirable consequences for people. Dystopian narratives are not diametrically opposed to utopian literature. Rather, as Booker (1994) argues, the two are part of the same project, with the former illuminating the darker side of utopian ideals. In this way, dystopian fictions paradoxically challenge readers to ask how "the future human hells they depict have been created in the name of a quest for stability, perfection, and a man-made utopia" (Sambell, 2004, p. 248).

In an industry known for capitalizing on commercial trends, the success of Suzanne Collins's Hunger Games trilogy, which in 2012 surpassed sales of the seven-volume Harry Potter series to become the best-selling books of all time on Amazon (Haq, 2012), and which spawned a lucrative film franchise starring the actress Jennifer Lawrence, has inspired a host of imitators, including (to name a few) Veronica Roth's Divergent series, James Dashner's Maze Runner series, and Scott Westerfeld's Uglies series. Although the financial interests of profit driven publishers and film studio executives explain this in part, one might still wonder whether the genre's rise in popularity is partially attributable to its reflecting the psychological concerns and anxieties of contemporary audiences.

At the start of the twenty-first century, environmental issues such as rising oceans, severe storms, and devastating wildfires have prompted members of the science community to caution that the planet will become less hospitable to humans if steps are not taken to address the problem of global warming. Following the attacks of September 11, 2001, concerns about terrorism, both in the United States and abroad, have undermined civil liberties, often with the support of a public willing to exchange privacy for security. In 2013, when Edward Snowden leaked information about the depth and breadth of the National Security Agency's (NSA) clandestine domestic surveillance program, many in the media were quick to draw comparisons to George Orwell's (1949/1987) *Nineteen-Eighty-Four* and the shadowy figure of Big Brother. In this social political milieu, it is perhaps not

S. P. Connors (ed.), The Politics of Panem, 85–102.

surprising that a 2012 report published by Bowker, a market research group, found that Collins's Hunger Games series, which shares Orwell's (1949/1987) concerns about the threat that surveillance technologies pose to individual liberty, is read by a sizeable number of adults as well as adolescents (Bowker, 2012).

Today, the use of databases by governments and corporations to collect, store, and retrieve information about individual citizens is characteristic of what some call a "surveillance society" (Lyon, 1994, p. 3). Ours is a culture in which authorities are able to monitor a person's whereabouts with relative ease, be it by tracking a GPS signal emitted by a cell phone or following the digital trail left by one's use of a money card. Each day, surveillance cameras capture our movements in public and private spaces, and advertisers, through a practice known as retargeting, reconstruct our shopping paths through online spaces to recommend products and goods that they assume will appeal to us. In our culture, voyeurism is a popular form of entertainment, as evidenced by the success of reality television programming. In short, "To participate in modern society is to be under electronic surveillance" (Lyon, 1994, p. 4).

The panopticon, an eighteenth century architectural structure that Jeremy Bentham designed to serve as a prison, and which philosopher Michel Foucault (1977/1995) later theorized to explain how surveillance functions to promote and maintain social order, is often cited as a metaphor to explain how power works in a society whose "institutions employ a range of disciplinary practices which ensure that life continues in a regularized, patterned way" (Lyon, 1994, p. 7). Viewed by some as an alternative to Orwell's (1949/1987) Big Brother, the panoptic metaphor is not without critics. Some note that surveillance is only one of several mechanisms that Foucault (1977/1995) associated with disciplinary power (Norris & Armstrong, 1999). Others argue that Foucault (1977/1995) overlooked the "peculiar and paradoxical outcomes of panoptic power" (Lyon, 2006, p. 9), including its susceptibility to human ingenuity. Yar (2003), for example, argues that in the panoptic schema, "the subject of the gaze is rendered in terms of its *passivity*," making it all but "impossible to give an adequate account of creativity and resistance" (p. 261, emphasis in original). Others accuse Foucault (1977/1995) of discounting human agency (Lyon, 1994). Are people at the mercy of the gaze, as Foucault (1977/1995) often seems to suggest, or are they capable of resisting and subverting it?

In this chapter, I examine Suzanne Collins's Hunger Games trilogy through the lens of philosophical criticism (Gillespie, 2010) with the intention of demonstrating how it functions to circumscribe the limits of panopticism as a metaphor for disciplinary power. To do so, I place Foucault's (1977/1995) work on surveillance —specifically, his thesis about the power of the gaze as a mechanism to promote and maintain social order—in conversation with the work of Michel de Certeau (1984), whose investigation of the seemingly insignificant maneuvers that people execute in their daily lives to navigate power structures acknowledges them as agentive beings. Having outlined these philosophical frameworks, I next apply them to Collins's trilogy. In doing so, I argue that whereas the Capitol relies on surveillance as a strategy to promote and maintain control over Panem, Katniss and other characters in the trilogy, through a series of tactics, consistently manage to subvert its gaze by paradoxically making themselves more visible to its surveillance mechanisms. In this way, Collins reminds adolescent readers that even in a surveillance society (Lyon, 1994) they are not without power.

READING LITERATURE THROUGH THE LENS OF PHILOSOPHICAL CRITICISM

This chapter examine Collins's Hunger Games novels from the perspective of what Gillespie (2010) calls philosophical criticism, a broadly defined approach to reading literature that is concerned with "probing important philosophical issues, those big questions that have been with humankind for most of the time we have been writing" (p. 172). While literature and philosophy are commonly regarded as separate scholarly ventures, the two actually share a long history. In *Love's Knowledge*, Nussbaum (1990) notes that for some ancient Greeks, "dramatic poetry and what we now call philosophical inquiry in ethics were both framed by, seen as ways of pursuing, a single and general question: namely, how human beings should live" (p. 15). In the same way, modern philosophers such as Nietzsche, Sartre, Camus and others have seized on literature as a vehicle to present and explore their ideas.

According to Gillespie (2010), there are different ways to practice philosophical criticism. Readers might, for example, place a literary text it in its proper philosophical context to better understand it. As a former high school English teacher, for example, I found that introducing students to tenets of existential philosophy prior to asking them to read Camus's *The Stranger* deepened their appreciation for the novel. Alternatively, readers can examine how a work of literature asks and explores philosophical questions. In this chapter I take a different approach, applying philosophical frameworks attributed to Foucault (1977/1995) and de Certeau (1984) to Collins's Hunger Games trilogy with the intention of demonstrating how the latter can help readers appreciate the limits of panopticism as a metaphor for explaining how social order is produced and control maintained.

Regardless of the approach one takes, philosophical criticism (Gillespie, 2010) is well suited for use in high school and university literature classes. According to Appleyard (1990), "The adolescent reader looks to stories to discover insights into the meaning of life, values and beliefs worthy of commitment, ideal images, and authentic role models for imitation" (p. 14). My own experiences teaching students in high school and university settings supports his observation. Perhaps because they are at a point in life when they are beginning to ask questions about the universe and their place in it, I find that adolescents are generally eager to wrestle with philosophical questions. This is especially true when those questions pertain to the power they hold in relation to the different social institutions that structure their lives.

Despite the concern that Eric Snowden's revelations about the NSA's domestic surveillance program sparked about Big Brother, surveillance is, for better or worse, a routine part of life in contemporary society. In a culture where school violence is not uncommon, this is particularly true for adolescents, many of whom pass through metal detectors when they enter school, encounter security guards or uniformed police in the hallways, and pass beneath the omnipresent gaze of security cameras that surveil their movements on campus. Yet despite the presence of surveillance mechanisms designed to produce what Foucault (1977/1995) calls "docile bodies" (p. 138), adolescents are remarkably adept at devising creative strategies that allow them to resist and subvert the gaze (Weiss, 2010).

In the sections to follow, I examine Foucault's (1977/1995) analysis of disciplinary mechanisms. Next, I introduce the work of de Certeau (1984), who celebrates people's ability to work subversively within systems of power to accomplish their own ends. In contrast to Foucault (1977/1995), whose arguments about the disciplinary power of the gaze can sometimes feel deterministic, de Certeau (1984) acknowledges people as agentive beings with the ability to manipulate oppressive power systems in the service of accomplishing their own ends. Readers who question the appropriateness of applying these complex philosophical frameworks to a work of young adult dystopian fiction might remember that the dystopian genre, committed as it is to engaging in social critique, shares intellectual concerns similar to those embraced by social and cultural critics such as Foucault, de Certeau, and others (Booker, 1994).

DISCIPLINARY POWER AND THE PANOPTIC PRINCIPLE

In *Discipline and Punish*, Foucault (1979/1995) argues that the seventeenth and eighteenth centuries marked a turning point in how authorities exercised power to produce and maintain social order. In constructing his argument, he distinguishes between two modes of power: sovereign power and disciplinary power. As conceived by Foucault, sovereign power aims to exert its authority over others with the intention of controlling their behavior (Fendler, 2010). Prior to the eighteenth century, sovereign power typically manifest itself in the form of public torture and executions, a practice that Foucault (1977/1995) describes as highly calculated and which he suggests was designed to create a spectacle with the intention of terrorizing those who observed it. In doing so, the goal of sovereign power was "to make an example [of a guilty person], not only by making people aware that the slightest offence was likely to be punished, but by arousing feelings of terror by the spectacle of power letting its anger fall upon the guilty person" (p. 58). By leaving its imprint on the individual, literally and metaphorically, sovereign power established a monarch's dominion over his or her subjects. Adopting a broader view of sovereign power, Fendler (2010) argues that it is evident in modern democratic societies in the form of laws, which are in turn upheld and enforced by institutions such as the police and the judicial system.

According to Foucault (1977/1995), governments grew less comfortable with the prospect of perpetuating the barbarism associated with public torture and executions in the early nineteenth century. Rather than punish the body, they instead sought to discipline the soul (p. 16). To accomplish this they adopted mechanisms designed to promote self-regulation and compliance with prescribed norms of behavior. In contrast to sovereign power, this new mode of power, which Foucault (1977/1995) calls disciplinary power, aims to produce "docile bodies" (p. 138). Rather than impose itself on an individual, it instead holds people accountable for exercising power over themselves. As such it represents a "specific technique of a power that regards individuals both as objects and as instruments of its exercise" (p. 170).

Disciplinary power operates according to a different set of principles than sovereign power. According to Foucault (1977/1995), it fractures space with the goal of dividing people into smaller, more manageable groups. Timetables are enforced to control and regulate the movement of bodies in those spaces, and people are subject to repetitive practices designed to train and harness their natural abilities. Disciplinary power also fixes people in hierarchical relationships, and by making them visible to one another, it renders them subject to constant evaluation. On a final note, Foucault argues that the knowledge that academic disciplines such as the social sciences produce functions to establish behavioral norms against which people are measured, and against which they in turn measure themselves. Underscoring this point, Fendler (2010) states, "We discipline ourselves on the basis of messages we get from society—knowledge, rewards, and images—of how we are supposed to live" (p. 44). In doing so, we assume responsibility for ensuring that we comply with behavioral expectations that others establish for us.

Foucault (1977/1995) regards the panopticon, a building that Jeremy Bentham designed to serve as a prison in the seventeenth century, but which was never built, as a metaphor for how power functions in modern society. A circular structure with a guard tower located at its center, the panopticon housed prisoners in individual cells located along its perimeter. Each cell was partitioned by three walls, with a small window built into the rear wall to backlight the prisoners. As a result, while the prisoners were unable to see (or communicate with) each other, they remained visible to the prison guards at all times. Additionally, because blinds shaded the windows in the guard tower, the prisoners could never be certain whether their captors were watching them, the result of which was intended to induce feelings of paranoia. Faced with the knowledge that they were potentially subject to the gaze of the guards, it was assumed that the prisoners, left with no alternative, would comply with the behavioral expectations their captors imposed on them. For this reason, Foucault (1977/1995) understands visibility to function as a "trap" (p. 200). That is, "It is the fact of being constantly seen, of being able always to be seen, that maintains the disciplined individual in his subjection" (p. 187).

Foucault (1977/1995) views the panopticon as a metaphor that can be used to understand how disciplinary power functions in the many institutions that pervade modern life. Describing the advent of the modern police force, for example, he writes:

> ... in order to be exercised, this power had to be given the instrument of permanent, exhaustive, omnipresent surveillance, capable of making all visible, as long as it could itself remain invisible. It had to be a faceless gaze that transformed the whole social body into a field of perception: thousands

of eyes posted everywhere, mobile attentions ever on the alert, a long, hierarchized network .... (p. 214)

Foucault describes how the gaze functions in other institutions as well, famously pointing out that "prisons resemble factories, schools, barracks, [and] hospitals, which all resemble prisons" (p. 228).

Although the panoptic metaphor is helpful in explaining how surveillance produces compliance, it is not without critics. Norris and Armstrong (1999) argue that surveillance is one of several mechanisms that Foucault (1977/1995) associated with disciplinary power, and its effects must be understood in that larger framework. Others argue that by conceptualizing people as passive, panopticism fails to acknowledge their ability to resist the gaze. Lyon (2006), for example, describes a research study that took place in a maximum security prison and revealed how inmates, through activities such as self-mutilation, "react[ed] against the negative visibility that would produce 'compliant selves' by making themselves even more visible," the result of which allowed them to disrupt "the basic seeing/being seen dissociation that the panopticon is intended to sustain" (p. 6).

Contesting the pathologization of vision that she suggests is implicit in panopticism, Yar (2003) argues that if the gaze were as powerful as Foucault (1977/1995) assumes, then the only recourse people would have to resist it would be to avoid it entirely. As she demonstrates, however, this is not the case. Quite the opposite, there are occasions when people voluntarily make themselves visible to the gaze for the express purpose of capturing and holding it. As evidence of this, Yar (2003) describes loosely organized guerrilla theater groups which perform works such as Orwell's (1949/1987) *Nineteen-Eighty-Four* in front of private (e.g., banks, businesses) and public (e.g., police, public transportation) surveillance cameras with the intention of practicing social commentary. These groups make their performances available to audiences around the globe, either by advertising them in advance or by publishing them on the internet post facto. In doing so, they "*reverse* the unidirectionality of the gaze, such that the 'guardians of the spectacle' are themselves turned into the objects of moral judgment" (Yar, 2003, p. 266). Actions such as these suggest that, in addition to subverting the gaze, people can also turn it against itself. Mann and his colleagues (2003), for example, use the term "sousveillance" to refer to a phenomenon whereby people "resist surveillance through non-compliance and interference 'moves' that block, distort, mask, refuse, and *counter-surveil* the collection of information" (p. 333, emphasis added).

The examples offered by the scholars cited above hint at the limits of panopticism and suggest that surveillance is not always guaranteed to produce the sort of "docile bodies" that Foucault (1977/1995, p. 138) envisioned. In doing so, these scholars raise the possibility that, in his quest to identify a metaphor that accounted for the workings of disciplinary power on a broad scale, Foucault may have overestimated the power of the gaze while underestimating the power of human ingenuity. In the section to follow, I turn to the work of French scholar Michel de Certeau (1984), who examined the "tactics" that people execute in their daily lives to work within power structures to accomplish their own ends. By acknowledging humans as agentive beings, de Certeau offers an alternative to the deterministic certainties of panopticism.

TACTICS AND THE ART OF RESISTANCE

In *The Practice of Everyday Life*, de Certeau (1984) examines how consumers, often constructed as passive users of rules and resources that "systems of production" (e.g., commerce, cities, education, etc.) impose on them, appropriate those same rules and resources and use them in ways that run counter to the intentions of their creators. Criticizing Foucault's (1977/1995) work for privileging disciplinary mechanisms at the expense of those they are imposed on, de Certeau (1984) argues that it is necessary to understand how "society resists being reduced to [disciplinary power], what popular procedures (also 'miniscule' and quotidian) manipulate the mechanisms of discipline and conform to them if only in order to evade them" (p. xiv). In the remainder of his text, he examines the ingenuity that people display in resisting disciplinary power.

Of interest here is the distinction that de Certeau (1984) draws between "strategies," that is, actions taken by entities that wield power (e.g., businesses, cities, schools, governments), and "tactics," a term that he uses to refer to actions taken by those on whom strategies are imposed. According to de Certeau, strategies are exercised by the powerful. They are executed by a subject that inhabits a space that separates it from its environment, the result of which affords it a tactical advantage. Provided with a power base, the subject is able to gather and organize its forces, make plans, and, most importantly, surveil its competitors. As de Certeau (1984) argues, this division of space "makes possible a *panoptic practice* proceeding from a place whence the eye can transform foreign forces into objects that can be observed and measured, and thus control and 'include' them within its scope of vision" (p. 36).

Conversely, de Certeau (1984) argues that those who are surveilled, and who thus occupy a weaker position, respond to strategies using tactics. Tactics are the property of those who lack access to an institutional space (what de Certeau calls a "proper"). In the absence of a place to stockpile resources and hatch plans, the weak must instead operate in view of the powerful, rendering them subject to the principle of panopticism. They are not, however, without power in these situations. Forced to operate on enemy territory, de Certeau (1984) argues that the weak can exhibit cunning and capitalize on opportunities to seize power as they present themselves. In this sense, he regards a tactic as inserting itself into "cracks that particular conjunctions open in the surveillance of the proprietary powers. It poaches in them. It creates surprises in them. It can be where it is least expected. It is a guileful ruse" (p. 37). As such, tactics allow the weak to function within power structures that others impose on them.

The distinction that de Certeau (1984) makes between tactics and strategies is significant because it positions people as agentive beings capable of resisting oppressive power structures. Unlike Foucault (1977/1995), who deterministically renders subjects helpless in the face of the gaze, de Certeau (1984) celebrates human ingenuity and acknowledges otherwise inconsequential activities such as an employee's writing emails on company time or a person's jaywalking as acts of resistance. On a broader scale, the concept of tactics make it possible to appreciate the creativity that colonized people have historically shown in resisting their oppressors. Describing how indigenous Indians responded to the presence of Spanish colonizers, for example, de Certeau (1984) argues that "their use of the dominant social order deflected its power, which they lacked the means to challenge: they escaped it without leaving it" (p. xiii). The dominant culture is not, in other words, necessarily imposed on people in a top-down fashion. Rather, as they go about the routines of everyday life, people make "innumerable and infinitesimal transformations of and within the dominant cultural economy in order to adapt it to their own interests and their own rules" (p. xiv).

Acknowledging the tactics that people use to turn systems of power to their advantage is a step toward understanding how prisoners such as those Lyon (2006) described are paradoxically able to subvert the gaze of their captors by staging spectacles that draw attention to themselves. Likewise, it explains how theatrical groups such as those Yar (2003) studied manage to turn the gaze of surveillance cameras back on those doing the surveilling, thereby practicing sousveillance (Mann et al., 2003). In the sections to follow, I argue that de Certeau's (1984) philosophical framework also helps us to understand how, in the dystopian future that Suzanne Collins envisions, Katniss Everdeen and other characters manage to circumvent the disciplinary mechanisms set in place by the Capitol despite their having to act under its ever-present gaze.

"I STEP OUT OF LINE AND WE'RE ALL DEAD": SOVEREIGN POWER AND THE SPECTACLE OF TERROR

The country of Panem, located in what was once North America, is made up of twelve districts ruled over by a distant city known as the Capitol. According to state propaganda, a thirteenth district was decimated following a failed uprising, but as readers of Collins's series know, this was not the case. The relationship between the Capitol and the districts is based on principles of colonialism: the people of the districts labor to generate goods and resources which are in turn transported to the Capitol to support its citizens' lavish lifestyle. In return, the districts receive a meager supply of food and other necessities, and as a result they struggle to sustain themselves.

Although this chapter is concerned with the Capitol's use of disciplinary power to produce and maintain social order, it is worth noting, as Macaluso and McKenzie do in this volume, that it leverages others modes of power against the districts, including what Foucault (1977/1995) calls sovereign power. As explained above, Foucault characterizes public torture and execution as ritualized practices that are designed to achieve an intended effect. By creating a spectacle, they communicate to those who witness them that even the slightest challenge to a ruler's power is subject to punishment. Moreover, they are designed to evoke feelings of terror in those who witness them in an attempt to curb future transgressions against the state. For these reasons, Foucault concludes that, "from the point of view of the law that imposes it, public torture and execution must be spectacular" (p. 58).

Throughout Collins's series, the Capitol embraces sovereign power as a strategy that enables it to exercise and maintain control over the districts. In District 11, the heart of Panem's agricultural system, residents found to have held back crops and produce are publicly whipped (Collins, 2008, p. 202). As Katniss and Peeta discover when they visit the districts on their Victory Tour, those who defy the Capitol can be summarily executed (Collins, 2009, p. 63), and, in some cases, whole districts are annihilated (Collins, 2010, p. 3). The most spectacular, and highly ritualized, example of the Capitol's exercising sovereign power, however, is evident in its sponsoring the Hunger Games.

A gladiatorial-like competition that pits 24 teenagers, a male and female from each of the twelve districts, against each other in mortal combat, the Hunger Games were instituted following the Dark Days, a period in Panem's history when the districts rose up against the Capitol (Collins, 2008, p. 18). The Games take place in arenas throughout Panem, and, as if the prospect of teenagers spilling each other's blood weren't enough, the Capitol leverages different technologies it has at its disposal to heighten the savagery. For example, the Gamemakers orchestrate natural disasters, introduce genetically engineered animals known as "muttations," and expose tributes to toxins and other agents of death. To reach as wide an audience as possible, and to increase the potency of the spectacle it creates, the state broadcasts the Hunger Games on television. In the Capitol, the Games constitute a popular form of entertainment akin to reality television. In the districts, however, where people are forced to watch them under penalty of law, the Hunger Games are a constant reminder of their helplessness in the face of an enemy powerful enough to take their children. As Katniss states, "Taking the kids from our districts, forcing them to kill one another while we watch—this is the Capitol's way of reminding us how totally we are at their mercy" (Collins, 2008, p. 18).

The Capitol's use of sovereign power is readily identifiable to readers of Collins's novels because of the brutal ways it is enacted. As the series progresses and the Capitol's hold on the districts gradually unravels, it relies more heavily on violence to create spectacles that instill fear in its enemies. When, towards the end of her second appearance in the Hunger Games, Katniss challenges the Capitol's power by shooting an arrow into the electric force field that encloses the arena, the Capitol responds by firebombing District 12, killing all but a fraction of its citizens (Collins, 2009, p. 391). Later, in *Mockingjay*, when Capitol planes bomb a hospital, incinerating all those inside, the events are broadcast live on television under an edict from President Snow (Collins, 2010, p. 99). Equally, if not more, important to its ability to produce and maintain control over those it governs, however, is the Capitol's reliance on disciplinary mechanisms, the most notable of which is its use of surveillance.

"THERE ARE ALWAYS EYES FOR HIRE": DISCIPLINARY POWER AND THE GAZE

Summarizing what are in essence the constituent principles of panopticism, Foucault (1977/1995) states:

> It is a type of location of bodies in space, of distribution of individuals in relation to one another, of hierarchical organization, of disposition of centres and channels of power, of definition of the instruments and modes of intervention of power .... Whenever one is dealing with a multiplicity of individuals on whom a task or a particular form of behaviour must be imposed, the panoptic schema may be used. (p. 205)

This view of panopticism, which emphasizes an arrangement of bodies in space, hierarchical organization, and susceptibility to the gaze, constitutes a framework that can be used to understand how the Capitol organizes Panem in a way that effectively allows it to exercise disciplinary power.

To begin, the thirteen districts that comprise Panem are isolated from one another geographically, making travel between them on foot difficult, as well as hazardous. According to Katniss, the forests are rife with predators, and, as becomes clear when she and Gale witness the capture of two runaways, they are also subject to patrol by Peacekeepers. The Capitol takes additional steps to limit people's mobility. The perimeter of District 12, which Katniss and her family call home, is enclosed by a chain-link fence that ought to be electrified, but which seldom works as it should. While the official narrative states that the fence exists to protect the districts from predators that roam the forests beyond town, it also holds their citizens in a fixed location, lessening the likelihood of their interacting with people from other districts.

The security measures in place in other districts are more extreme. In *Catching Fire*, when Katniss and Peeta visit District 11 on their Victory Tour, they are surprised to observe a thirty-five foot high fence topped with barbed wire and surveilled by armed guards in strategically placed watchtowers (Collins, 2009, p. 55). By securing the districts in this way, the Capitol effectively severs the lines of communication between them, which in turn minimizes the likelihood of their organizing to promote their own interests. As Katniss states, "It's to the Capitol's advantage to have us divided among ourselves" (Collins, 2008, p. 14). In this way, the districts are not unlike the prisoners in Bentham's panopticon, unable to communicate with each other as a result of their seclusion in compartmentalized cells.

The Capitol also arranges Panem in a hierarchy, which allows it to divide the districts against each other and further impede their ability to unite and promote their own interests. At the apex of the hierarchy is the Capitol, whose citizens enjoy a range of comforts and luxuries, and whose access to different technologies helps to ensure its military dominion over its enemies. Beyond that are the districts, some of which are more affluent than others, a result of their courting the Capitol's favor. According to Katniss, the Capitol coddled the inhabitants of District 2, who "swallowed the Capitol's propaganda more easily," and who subsequently regarded the Hunger Games not as a form of subjugation, but as "an opportunity for wealth and a kind of glory not seen elsewhere" (Collins, 2010, p. 193). People in District 2 also serve as Peacekeepers, a position that entails their oppressing residents in the other districts, thereby reinforcing the Capitol's hegemony. District 12, on the other hand, is the weakest of the districts, both in terms of the power it wields and its access to material resources.

Like Panem as a whole, individual districts are stratified socioeconomically. District 12, for example, is divided between a "merchant class that caters to officials" (Collins, 2008, p. 8) and the impoverished residents of the Seam who struggle to earn a living laboring in the Capitol's coalmines. Those in the merchant class who take on leadership roles are granted additional privileges. When Katniss visits the home of the mayor, for example, she discovers that he has access to a television, which keeps him abreast of news in the Capitol and ensures that he is privy to information his neighbors are not (Collins, 2010, p. 88). This class structure, intentionally erected and sustained by the Capitol, works against the interests of the individual districts by perpetuating social inequities and pitting their citizens against one another. This is evident when Peeta's mother, a member of the merchant class, runs a starving Katniss off rather than feed her. Threatening to call the Peacekeepers, Peeta's mother expresses her frustration with "brats from the Seam pawing through her trash" (Collins, 2008, p. 29). From a Marxist perspective, the caste system the Capitol erects through its policies produces and sustains inequalities between (and within) the districts. In doing so, it divides them against one another, decreasing the likelihood of their working together to pursue a common cause, and in turn tightening the Capitol's grip on power.

A third aspect of the disciplinary framework that Foucault (1977/1995) associates with panopticism is the practice of surveillance. In its relationship with the districts, the Capitol occupies a position that is reminiscent of the guard tower in Bentham's panopticon. Although it does not reside at the geographical center of Panem, the Capitol nevertheless engages in a range of surveillance practices that allow it to fix the districts in its gaze and enforce compliance with state authorized modes of conduct. To support the Capitol's ability to spy on its enemies, for example, scientists working for the state genetically engineered a special strain of bird known as the jabberjay, a creature that is capable of replicating the human voice and repeating extended passages of conversation to which it is privy (Collins, 2009, pp. 91-92). Katniss also cites the existence of paid informants who work for the Capitol (p. 152). Most important, the Capitol positions surveillance cameras throughout the districts, the result of which affords the state a constant window onto the lives of those it governs. Cognizant that they are watched, the people of Panem seemingly have no alternative but to self-regulate and comply with the Capitol's expectations to ensure their safety and the safety of their loved ones. Recognizing this, Katniss explains that while Gale is willing to criticize the Capitol when they are alone in the woods, he would never dare do so in District 12, where he is subject to its ever-vigilant gaze (Collins, 2008 p. 14).

It is not necessary for people to know with any degree of certainty that they are being watched for them to practice self-discipline (Foucault, 1977/1995). Rather, Foucault argues that the mere knowledge that one is potentially subject to the gaze is sufficient to induce compliance. Before Katniss and Peeta leave District 12 to begin their Victory Tour, President Snow visits her at home in the Victors' Village and reveals his knowledge about her meeting Gale in the woods, a space that she had previously assumed existed outside the Capitol's surveillance web. Confronted with the possibility that she was watched, Katniss immediately turns introspective. She thinks, "Surely they haven't been tracking us in there. Or have they? Could we have been followed? That seems impossible. At least by a person. Cameras? That never crossed my mind until this moment" (Collins, 2009, p. 24). Prior to leaving, Snow reveals that he also knows about a kiss Katniss shared with Gale, which sends a chill down her spine. From this point forward, the knowledge that "President Snow is watching me" (Collins, 2009, p. 43) results in Katniss's becoming more hyper-vigilant.

Foucault's (1977/1995) thesis about the power of the gaze to promote self-discipline is evident when Katniss participates in her first Hunger Games as well. Just as the Gamemakers alter her physical appearance when they "remake" her prior to the start of the Games, applying make-up, grooming her, and dressing her in fine clothing, they also alter the way she carries herself. From the moment she volunteers to participate in the Games, television cameras document her every move, rendering her subject to the Capitol's gaze. This knowledge in turn prompts Katniss to alter her behavior in order to comply with what she assumes are her audience's expectations of her. Upon saying goodbye and boarding a train for the Capitol en route to her first Hunger Games, for example, she refuses to cry for fear that doing so will lead her audience to construct her as weak (Collins, 2008, p. 40). Once in the arena, she performs the role of star-crossed lover to earn sponsors, a role that she is forced to reprise later in the series to appease President Snow and convince the citizens of Panem that she and Peeta are deeply in love. The result of Katniss's continually performing roles that others establish for her is identity confusion. Indeed, after leaving the arena following her first Hunger Games, she stares at a reflection of herself in a mirror and tries "to remember who I am and who I am not" (Collins, 2008, p. 371).

Lavoie (2011) argues that the end result of knowing that one is continually subject to examination by a camera is "a self-propelling machine of fear, paranoia, and *watchedness*" (p. 60, emphasis in original). In Collins's novels, panopticism represents a disciplinary mechanism that the Capitol uses to retain control over the districts. In addition to surveilling the districts, it positions them in a hierarchy, the result of which allows it to divide them against themselves. As Foucault (1977/1995) predicts, these measures appear to be effective in promoting discipline. When the Capitol, faced with the prospect of losing control over the districts, sends Peacekeepers to District 12, for example, Katniss wonders how she could have been so naive as to think that her neighbors could muster the courage to participate in an uprising (Collins, 2009, p. 130). Though their lives are untenable under the Capitol, the people of the districts are seemingly unable to resist it. But is this the case?

In the section to follow, I argue that when one reads Collins's novels from a de Certeaudian (1984) perspective, it is possible to appreciate the myriad tactics that characters employ to subvert the surveillance technologies the Capitol imposes on them. Far from self-regulating automatons, they are instead found to be agentive beings whose ingenuity makes it possible for them to work within the existing power system to accomplish their own ends. In the end, it is neither the military might of District 13 nor its decision to forge an alliance with the other districts that vanquishes the Capitol. Rather, it is the seemingly paradoxical decision that Katniss and other characters in the novels make to exploit the gaze of Snow and other leaders in the Capitol by making themselves more visible to its surveillance mechanisms.

<h2 style="text-align:center;">"I HAVE A KIND OF POWER I NEVER KNEW I POSSESSED":
VISIBILITY AND THE ART OF RESISTANCE</h2>

In *The Practice of Everyday Lives*, de Certeau (1984) argues that tactics—that is, actions taken by the weak in response to the powerful—have no alternative but to "play on and with a terrain imposed on it and organized by the law of a foreign power" (p. 37). As explained above, tactics are akin to guileful ruses, as "[t]he weak must continually turn to their own ends forces alien to them" (p. xix). In the absence of a space to which they can retreat and scheme, those who use tactics must practice vigilance, constantly searching for fissures in power structures they can exploit to their advantage. In this way, tactics are parasitic. As de Certeau argues, "Everyday life invents itself by *poaching* in countless ways on the property of others" (p. xii, emphasis in original).

The story of the jabberjay offers a compelling metaphor for understanding how characters in Collins's trilogy use tactics to manipulate power imbalances in the service of accomplishing their own ends. As Katniss recounts, the jabberjay was a genetically engineered bird that scientists working for the Capitol created for surveillance purposes (Collins, 2009, pp. 91-92). Given its ability to replicate the human voice and repeat extended passages of dialogue, it can be said to constitute a "strategy" (to use de Certeau's [1984] term) the Capitol used to spy on its enemies. Eventually, however, rebel fighters in the districts figured this out, and they responded with a simple, but effective "tactic" that allowed them to exploit the situation and turn it to their advantage—specifically, they fed the birds lies, which they in turn carried back to the Capitol. Thwarted, the Capitol abandoned the jabberjay project, assuming that the birds would go extinct in the wild. This was not the case, however. Rather, before that could happen, the all-male jabberjays mated with mockingbirds, creating a new breed of bird known as the mockingjay (Collins, 2009, pp. 91-92). Able to sing human melodies as well as bird songs, the mockingjay thrived in the wild, and for the people of Panem, it came to symbolize the Capitol's failure. As Katniss explains, leaders in the Capitol "hadn't counted on the highly controlled jabberjay having the brains to adapt to the wild, to pass on its genetic code, to thrive in a new form. They hadn't anticipated its will to live" (Collins, 2009, p. 92). Importantly, the Capitol repeats these same missteps in its dealing with Katniss.

The parallels between the story of the mockingjay and Katniss's relationship with President Snow and the Capitol are striking. As it had the jabberjay, the Capitol overestimates its ability to control and manipulate Katniss. In her quest to survive the Hunger Games and return home to her mother and sister in District 12, she proves a clever adversary. Throughout the series she uses a variety of tactics to subvert the disciplinary mechanisms the Capitol imposes on her. Her acts of resistance are seldom spectacular. Instead, Katniss works quietly within the power system the Capitol erects to manipulate it and turn it to her advantage. It is no coincidence that she, like the jabberjay, experiences a metamorphosis over the course of the series that results in her transforming into the Mockingjay, a symbol of the Rebellion.

In *Catching Fire*, two minor characters, Wiress and Beetee, teach Katniss how to identify seams, or weak spots, in the force field the Capitol creates to trap tributes in the arenas it constructs for the Hunger Games. The characters refer to these seams as "chinks in the armor" because "they reveal what was meant to be hidden and are therefore a weakness" (Collins, 2009, p. 286). In much the same way, Katniss demonstrates an impressive ability to expose and manipulate weaknesses in the Capitol's disciplinary mechanisms, the most notable of which is its use of surveillance as a mode of control. According to Yar (2003), if the panoptic principal were as powerful as Foucault (1977/1995) assumed then the only option people would have to resist it would be to avoid it entirely. Yet in Collins's novels, the exact opposite is true—rather than entrap Katniss, her decision to make herself visible to the prying eyes of the Capitol instead empowers her. Throughout the series, visibility represents a tactic that she and other characters use to disadvantage the Capitol.

In her first Hunger Games, Katniss strategically exploits the gaze of television cameras in the arena and the Capitol to create pathos in her audience. This tactic proves valuable, as it results in her earning sponsors, which in turn betters the odds of her surviving the Games. When, halfway through the competition, the Gamemakers announce a rule change that will allow two tributes to emerge from the arena, Katniss recognizes that her ability to return to District 12 is contingent on her allying with Peeta. She consequently raises her "face up to the moonlight so the cameras can be sure to catch" her smile (Collins, 2008, p. 248). Later, when Peeta falls ill, she again plays to the cameras, this time adopting the role of star-crossed lover, one that she knows her audience is eager for her to perform. When she kisses Peeta prior to visiting the Cornucopia to get him medicine, she explains, "I imagine the teary sighs emanating from the Capitol and pretend to brush away a tear of my own" (p. 281). Later, when the Capitol rescinds the aforementioned rule change, she and Peeta threaten to commit suicide by consuming poisonous berries in full view of the cameras (pp. 344-345). By doing so, the pair turn the gaze back on the Capitol, which ensures their survival, and weakens the state in the eyes of the districts.

Other characters exploit the Capitol's gaze using similar tactics. In a television interview that takes place prior to their first Hunger Games, Peeta confesses his love for Katniss, establishing the couple as an audience favorite and earning them sponsors (Collins, 2008, p. 130). Later, after President Snow threatens Katniss, the couple, with Haymitch's support, orchestrates a public marriage proposal, much to the delight of the Capitol audience (Collins, 2009, p. 73). Still later, when Peeta gives a television interview prior to their entering the arena for a second time, he stuns the television audience by revealing that Katniss is pregnant with his child, a story that he has only fabricated, but which immediately realizes its intended effect. Attesting to the impact that Peeta's words have on the viewing audience, Katniss characterizes them as exploding like a bomb that "sends accusations of injustice and barbarism and cruelty flying out in every direction" (Collins, 2009, p. 256). In the aftermath, as she attempts to process her feelings about what Peeta did, she is surprised to discover that rather than anger, she instead feels "empowered" (p. 258).

Cinna also exploits the Capitol's gaze as a tactic to weaken it. While there are several examples of his doing so throughout the series, the most noteworthy arguably occurs in the prelude to Katniss's second Hunger Games when he cleverly exploits her wardrobe to earn her the favor of the Capitol audience while simultaneously communicating a political message to the people in the districts. Prior to her appearing on television for an interview with Caesar Flickerman, President Snow instructed Cinna that Katniss was to wear the wedding gown the Capitol designed for her, a grim reminder of all she had sacrificed by choosing to challenge its power. Although Cinna complies with Snow's directive, he modifies the dress. As a result, when Katniss, at the conclusion of the interview, spins for the cameras, the dress spontaneously combusts, revealing an underlying outfit that causes Katniss to resemble a mockingjay (Collins, 2009, p. 252). The effect of her transformation is not lost on Caesar, who immediately recognizes the garment's symbolic import. As Katniss narrates:

> A shadow of recognition flickers across Caesar's face, and I can tell he knows that the mockingjay isn't just my token. That it's come to symbolize so much more. That what will be seen as a flashy costume change in the Capitol is resonating in an entirely different way throughout the districts. (Collins, 2009, p. 253)

While Cinna eventually pays for his act of defiance with his life, his decision to turn the cameras against the Capitol proves effective in helping the rebels build support among the districts for the coming revolution.

Later in the series, District 13 perpetuates Cinna's symbolic positioning of Katniss as the Mockingjay in order to unite the districts against the Capitol. Like Cinna and the other characters mentioned above, it exploits the Capitol's surveillance technologies to do so, using them as weapons against it. In the same way that the Capitol uses state controlled television to broadcast the Hunger Games and disseminate its propaganda, District 13 produces a series of short propaganda films that feature Katniss and other tributes in locations throughout Panem. Lacking the technological infrastructure to broadcast these films, however, District 13 instead turns to Beetee, a computer expert, who manages to hack into the Capitol's computer system (another "chink in its armor"!), disrupt its scheduled

SEAN P. CONNORS

programming, and substitute District 13's propaganda in its place (Collins, 2010, pp. 131-134). During the counterculture movement in the United States, Gil Scott-Heron (1970) wrote a poem/song titled "The Revolution Will Not Be Televised," suggesting that those who control the media, and who hold power, are unlikely to televise images that run contrary to their own interests. In the dystopic world that Collins's constructs, however, the revolution *is* televised precisely because the tactic of hacking allows those outside the power structure to subvert it.

These and other examples of characters executing tactics to turn perceived power imbalances to their advantage problematize Foucault's (1977/1995) characterization of visibility as "a trap" (p. 200). Far from ensnaring them, the decision that Katniss and others make to expose themselves to the Capitol's cameras cleverly allows them to deflect its gaze, turning it back on their surveillors. By doing so, they leverage the disciplinary power the Capitol wields against it, a point that is evident when Gale assures Katniss that, in the wake of her public engagement to Peeta, President Snow is unlikely to harm her. "You saw how the Capitol crowd reacted," he tells her. "I don't think he can afford to kill you. Or Peeta. How's he going to get out of that one?" (Collins, 2009, pp. 98-99). The answer is, he cannot.

CONCLUSION: EMPOWERING READERS TO BECOME AGENTS FOR CHANGE

By reading the Hunger Games series from the perspective of philosophical criticism (Gillespie, 2010), it is possible to appreciate Collins's novels as sophisticated literary texts that explore complex issues. As I have argued, the series circumscribes the limits of panopticism as a metaphor for the power that institutions wield over the individual to enforce compliance with prescribed modes of conduct. That Katniss and other characters are able to counter the disciplinary mechanisms the Capitol imposes on them through their creative use of tactics suggest that people are not as helpless in the presence of the gaze as Foucault's (1977/1995) work suggests. Rather, from the perspective of de Certeau (1984), they are agentive beings capable of working within power systems to turn perceived inequities to their advantage.

In 2012, at the Assembly on Literature for Adolescents (ALAN) Workshop in Las Vegas, Nevada, I had the opportunity to hear a panel of young adult authors discuss their work writing speculative fiction for adolescents. One of them, Scott Westerfeld, half-jokingly suggested that dystopian literature is ideally suited for adolescents because the modern high school is itself a dystopia. Foucault (1977/1995), who regarded schools as an example of an institution that operates according to panoptic principles, would undoubtedly agree. In a high school, a large number of students are divided into smaller, more manageable groups and partitioned into separate classrooms. Throughout the day their movements are dictated by a rigid timetable, with a bell ringing to signal them when it is time to change locations. In the current education reform era, students are subject to countless evaluations and assessments, the results of which are used to sort and rank them, establishing hierarchies within hierarchies. At a time when school violence is commonplace, surveillance practices have infiltrated schools in the name of maintaining safety. In some cases students enter school and pass through metal detectors under the watchful gaze of security guards. Other schools make use of surveillance cameras that are strategically placed around campus to monitor and record students' movements. Visitors to schools are increasingly asked to surrender a driver's license, which is then scanned into a database. Perhaps there is more truth to Westerfeld's observation than we might care to admit.

Still, it is possible to appreciate the host of creative tactics that adolescents use to navigate and subvert the disciplinary and surveillance mechanisms that schools impose on them. Consider, for example, the growing number of students who, with parental permission, are electing to stay home rather than submit to the barrage of standardized assessments that are part of the modern educational landscape. In Providence, Rhode Island, a group of students dressed as zombies and marched in front of the state capitol to protest a requirement that tied their ability to graduate from high school to their earning a minimum score on a state assessment (Zezima, 2013). By making themselves visible in this way, these students directed attention back to the politicians whose policies they opposed. Drawing on findings from a research study she conducted in a public school in New York City, Weiss (2010) describes a series of creative tactics that students used to circumvent the surveillance mechanisms that school officials imposed on them. These tactics included their befriending the security guards entrusted with surveilling them, finding alternative routes through the building to avoid the gaze of the guards, and staging a walkout that functioned to disrupt the school day and call unwanted attention to school leaders. Faced with disciplinary mechanisms, the students in Weiss's study managed to subvert them.

Historically speaking, educators have been ambivalent about the prospect of bringing popular culture texts like those in the Hunger Games series into the classroom. When they are taught, it is often as a bridge to traditional literature. By inviting students to read Collins's Hunger Games series through the lens of philosophical criticism (Gillespie, 2010), however, teachers can encourage them to approach the novels in much the same way they do other school authorized texts—that is, by interrogating the social knowledge they reproduce. Asking students to talk or write about occasions in their own lives when they, like Katniss, used tactics to resist practices that struck them as problematic or unfair invites them to see themselves as agents who are capable of working for change. Likewise, encouraging them to consider the surveillance mechanisms they encounter inside and outside of school can heighten their awareness of them and empower them by helping them to understand that any power the gaze wields over them is contingent on their acknowledging its authority. Deprived of that, panopticism comes undone.

The kind of reading for which I, like the other contributors to this volume, am arguing, steeped in principles of critical pedagogy, disrupts the unidirectional movement that is common in literature classes where teachers invite students to draw on their lived experiences to comprehend the texts they read. Instead, it invites them to use literature, young adult or canonical, as a platform for examining their relationships with the world and critiquing and transforming those that they

SEAN P. CONNORS

find oppressive. In doing so, it encourages adolescents to understand that, like Katniss and other characters in Collins's trilogy, they too have power to affect change, locally as well as globally.

REFERENCES

Appleyard, J. A. (1990). *Becoming a reader: The experience of fiction from childhood to adulthood.* Cambridge University Press: Cambridge.
Booker, M. K. (1994). *The dystopian impulse in modern literature: Fiction as social criticism.* Westport, Conn.: Greenwood.
Bowker. (2012). Young adult books attract growing numbers of adult fans. Bowker. Retrieved February 27, 2014 from http://www.bowker.com/en-US/aboutus/press_room/2012/pr_09132012.shtml
Collins, S. (2008). *The hunger games.* New York: Scholastic.
Collins, S. (2009). *Catching fire.* New York: Scholastic.
Collins, S. (2010). *Mockingjay.* New York: Scholastic.
De Certeau, M. (1984). *The practice of everyday life.* Berkeley: University of California Press.
Fendler, L. (2010). *Michel Foucault.* London: Continuum.
Foucault, M. (1977/1995). *Discipline and punish: The birth of the prison.* (A. Sheridan, Trans.). New York: Vintage Books.
Gillespie, T. (2010). *Doing literary criticism: Helping students engage with challenging texts.* Portland, Maine: Stenhouse Publishers.
Haq, H. (2012). 'Hunger Games' passes 'Harry Potter' as bestselling Amazon series. *The Christian Science Monitor.* Retrieved February 28 from http://www.csmonitor.com/Books/chapter-and-verse/2012/0821/Hunger-Games-passes-Harry-Potter-as-bestselling-Amazon-series
Lavoie, D. (2011). Escaping the panopticon: Utopia, hegemony, and performance in Peter Weir's *The Truman Show. Utopian Studies, 22*(1), 52-73.
Lyon, D. (1994). *The electronic eye: The rise of surveillance society.* Minneapolis: University of Minnesota Press.
Lyon, D. (2006). The search for surveillance theories. In D. Lyon (Ed.), *Theorizing surveillance: The panopticon and beyond* (pp. 3-20). Portland, OR: Willan Publishing.
Orwell, G. (1949/1987). *Nineteen-eighty-four.* New York: Signet Classic.
Mann, S., Nolan, J., & Wellman, B. (2003). Sousveillance: Inventing and using wearable computing devices for data collection in surveillance environments. *Surveillance & Society, 1*(3), 331-355.
Marx, G. T. (2003). A tack in the shoe: Neutralizing and resisting the new surveillance. *Journal of Social Issues, 59*(2), 369-390.
Norris, C., & Armstrong, G. (1999). *The maximum surveillance society: The rise of CCTV.* Oxford: Berg.
Nussbaum, M.C. (1990). *Love's knowledge: Essays on philosophy and literature.* New York: Oxford University Press.
Sambell, K. (2004). Carnivalizing the future: A new approach to theorizing childhood and adulthood in science fiction for young readers. *The Lion and the Unicorn, 28*(2), 247-267.
Scott-Heron, G. (1970). The revolution will not be televised [poem/song]. Retrieved from http://www.gilscottheron.com/lyrevol.html
Weiss, J. (2010). Scan this: Examining student resistance to school surveillance. In T. Monahan & R. Torres (Eds.), *Schools under surveillance: Cultures of control in public education* (pp. 313-229). New Brunswick, NJ: Rutgers University Press.
Yar, M. (2003). Panoptic power and the pathologisation of vision: Critical reflections on the Foucauldian thesis. *Surveillance & Society, 1*(3), 254-271.
Zezima, K (2013). More parents opting kids out of standardized tests. Retrieved March 1 from http://www.marinij.com/lifestyles/ci_24045024/more-parents-opting-kids-out-standardized-tests

MICHAEL MACALUSO AND CORI MCKENZIE

6. EXPLOITING THE GAPS IN THE FENCE

Power, Agency, and Rebellion in The Hunger Games

INTRODUCTION

Suzanne Collins's (2008) *The Hunger Games* opens with the image of Katniss rolling out of bed, slipping on her hunting gear, and heading for the high, electrified chain-link fence that separates District 12 from the woods beyond. The fence encloses all of District 12 and ostensibly exists to keep out the flesh-eaters that roam the woods, but as many scholars have noted, the fence primarily functions as a way to oppress people and hold them in their mental, physical, and economic pre-determined place (Pavlik, 2012; Wezner, 2012). Importantly, as Katniss explains, this fence has not worked for some time—it is no longer electrified, and it contains several gaps and "weak spots." Katniss takes advantage of these weak spots to roll under the fence and traverse into the uncultivated and uncharted woods on the other side. Even though this act is illegal, Katniss does it because it allows her to hunt, with her illegal bow and arrow, for extra food for her family and to barter with others in her district. The penalty for hunting and foraging is death, but even the Peacekeepers, the official policing arm of the Capitol, and its leader President Snow, "turn a blind eye to the few of us who hunt because they're as hungry for fresh meat as anybody is. In fact, they're among our best customers" (Collins, 2008, p. 5).

This image of barriers riddled by gaps serves several purposes and, as we argue, foreshadows the entire conflict and plot of Collins's (2008) *The Hunger Games.* In particular, we argue that Katniss's ability to find weak points in the fence in order to hunt highlights two key details of the text: first, that the Capitol does not have complete control over its citizens, and second, that Panem's citizens are capable of finding the Capitol's "weak spots" and exploiting them for their own ends. Thus, we read this opening scene as a metaphor for all of the times that the Capitol fails to wield absolute power, the result of which allows its citizens to recognize and exploit its weaknesses. Importantly, this reading of the opening scene counters assertions made by a number of literary critics (e.g., Pavlik, 2012; Risko, 2012; Wezner, 2012) who contend that the Capitol is a totalitarian regime that wields ultimate authority over its citizens. Throughout this chapter, then, we will push back against these assumptions about the novel and advance two claims: that the Capitol's power is never absolute, and that the citizens of Panem also have the capacity to exercise power and agency in ways that help them survive—and ultimately resist—the Capitol's rule. To do so, we read the text through the lens of

S. P. Connors (ed.), The Politics of Panem, 103–121.

Michel Foucault, who argued for a nuanced understanding of power, one that resisted dichotomizing the "powerful" and the "powerless" and which accounted for the many "modalities" of power that a person can exercise. As we will argue, reading Collins's (2008) *The Hunger Games* through a Foucauldian lens suggests that Panem is not a totalitarian state and that Katniss and Peeta are able to win the Games (thus fomenting rebellion) precisely because they are able to exploit the multiple modalities of power that exist in Panem. This insight, we argue, not only has implications for how readers understand the book itself, but also for how we understand oppressive governmental regimes and the nature of dystopian literature.

THE HUNGER GAMES AND FAMILIAR NOTIONS OF POWER

Many literary critics of Collins's (2008) *The Hunger Games* build their argument around the assumption that the Capitol is a totalitarian regime with absolute power over the citizens of Panem. For example, in his essay "Absolute Power Games," Pavlik (2012) portrays the Capitol as having "ultimate power" (p. 30) and "supreme governmental control" (p. 30). Additionally, he contends that "Snow's administration displays the hallmarks of authoritarianism" (p. 32), and he remarks that Snow wields "fascist control" (p. 35). Painting the Capitol as a totalitarian regime is central to Pavlik's argument, in which he claims that because District 13 overthrows the Capitol by using violence, the citizens of Panem simply trade the Capitol's version of "absolute power" for District 13's version of absolute power (p. 37). Like Pavlik, Risko (2012) and Wezner (2012) also describe the Capitol as a totalitarian regime in order to make their arguments. For his part, Risko (2012) uses the work of Agamben to argue that tributes who participate in the Games function as *Homo sacers*, human subjects who have "experienced complete loss of legal protection and acknowledgment" (p. 84). Tributes become *Homo sacers*, Risko explains, because the Capitol reduces them to this state through its control of Panem's power structure. Finally, in her essay "'Perhaps I am watching you now': Panem's Panopticons," Wezner (2012) argues that the Capitol's use of surveillance and the threat of punishment "reinforces the absolute power and authority of the Capitol" (p. 150) and keeps the districts "powerless" (p. 149).

The assumptions about power that sit at the heart of these arguments about Collins's (2008) *The Hunger Games* stand in stark contrast to the image of Katniss escaping through the gap in the Capitol's fence in order to illegally hunt. Indeed, the metaphor of the fence suggests that, contrary to what other scholars have noted, in the world of *The Hunger Games*, there are no simple dichotomies between powerful and powerless, oppressor and oppressed. Indeed, the book is filled with moments when Panem's citizens enact agency and exercise power, calling into question assertions that cast either Snow or the government at large as wielding "supreme governmental control" (Pavlik, 2012, p. 30). To highlight the idea that the Capitol's power is never absolute and that the citizens of Panem have agency, we turn next to theorist Michel Foucault whose nuanced conceptions of power help us to see beyond a familiar conception of power that dichotomizes the powerful and powerless. We believe that Foucault's theories of power—what it is, the forms it takes, how it works—are especially generative when considering one's agency in the world, and we argue that applying his theories to Collins's (2008) novel helps us to see weak spots in the Capitol's proverbial fence.

RETHINKING POWER WITH FOUCAULT

Unlike the conceptions of power that often seem to sit at the heart of criticism about *The Hunger Games* trilogy, Foucault's understanding of power strays from a conception of power as a top-down, all encompassing "something" that is held, wielded, or seized by an individual or group (as in the case of a dictator or totalitarian government). Indeed, this is the very interpretation of power that Foucault works against by arguing that power is not a group or institution, does not work in simple binaries of the powerful and powerless, and does not represent a choice between blanket subjugation or subservience. While he would not deny the existence of certain regimes that have exercised extreme forms of what he calls "sovereign power" (Foucault, 1977), he argues that individuals "must not assume that the sovereignty of the state, the form of the law, or the overall unity of a domination are given at the outset" (Foucault, 1978, p. 92). Instead, Foucault argues that power takes many forms and can be exercised by any individual, including those who are typically seen as powerless. While a political leader, a law, and even a ruling party enact power, so too do average citizens.

For Foucault (1978), "Power is everywhere … because it comes from everywhere" (p. 93)—that is, power is infused in any and all relationships, situations, and contexts and can be used by any and all individuals. This is because, according to Foucault, "power must be understood in the first instance as the multiplicity of force relations" (p. 92). The "force" he speaks of is a metaphorical one: power is a tactic or a strategic move, and thus any individual can exercise power at any given time because he or she is imbued with it in his or her localized "networks" of relationships. In this way, "one is always 'inside' power, there is no 'escaping' it" (p. 95); thus, power is "always already" vested in every moment and in every social relation. When we think of power in this more relational way, we can see how familiar, over-arching, and structural interpretations of power lose their footing; as Foucault (1978) states, "Power comes from below; that is, there is no binary and all-encompassing opposition between rulers and ruled at the root of power-relations" (p. 94). While Foucault's understanding of power can complicate and even upend the way we think about power in the world, we believe his approach can be fruitful and enlightening. As Fendler (2010) argues, Foucault's approach to power allows us to see that:

[W]e cannot 'blame the system,' nor can we 'hold individuals accountable.' We cannot wait for a leader to tell us what to do, and we cannot wait for someone else to declare us to be emancipated. Instead, we are challenged to see a wide variety of possible power moves, many options, and a whole array of possible consequences. (p. 197)

The Foucauldian notion of power, then, stands in stark contrast with familiar assumptions we make about the nature of power: as inevitable, as top-down, as something we either have or lack.

In order to see how the "powerless" exercise power, one has to understand that, for Foucault, there are many different kinds of power that are "always-already" enacted during every moment of our lives. While he recognizes that power is sometimes exercised from the top down (he calls this kind of power "sovereign"), he argues that there are at least three other modalities of power at work in our world: disciplinary power, biopower, and pastoral power. We believe that recognizing these modalities can help complicate our assumptions about power in general, and the role it plays in Collins's (2008) *The Hunger Games* in particular. In doing so it can also help us to "imagine alternatives to power that we had not previously imagined" (Fendler, 2010, p. 197).

FOUCAULT'S MULTIPLE MODALITIES OF POWER

Sovereign Power

Sovereign power refers to the absolute power that a ruler has over his subjects. This modality of power is most commonly enacted in monarchies, but it exists in other forms of government and communities as well: in dictatorships, in hierarchical institutions, and even in democracies, where laws dictate how fast we can drive our car, at what times and where we can buy alcohol, and the amount of carbon that factories can emit into the air.

As Foucault conceptualizes it, the exercise of sovereign power rests on the threat and/or enactment of a brutal and public punishment—often in the form of public executions—for criminal activity. In a state ruled by sovereign power, the law of the state represents the "will of the sovereign" (Foucault, 1977, p. 47), which means that disobeying the laws of the state not only harms the immediate victim, but also the sovereign him or herself (p. 47). Because crimes momentarily "place the sovereign in contempt" (p. 48), punishments must not only enact justice, they must also restore the sovereign's power and remind subjects that one cannot attack the will of the sovereign and escape retribution. This function of punishment—what Foucault calls the *political* function—thus requires that punishments make the sovereign's power manifest "at its most spectacular" (p. 48) so that subjects will see and understand the sovereign's "intrinsic superiority" (p. 49). As Foucault explains, in a state where a sovereign has ultimate power, punishment highlights "the dissymmetry between the subject who has dared to violate the law and the all-powerful sovereign who displays his strength;" it must therefore be "carried out in such a way as to give a spectacle not of measure, but of imbalance and excess; in this liturgy of punishment, there must be an emphatic affirmation of power and of its intrinsic superiority" (p. 49).

In addition to being brutal, in a system of sovereign power, punishment must also be public. The display of the sovereign's power would have little effect if it were manifest only to the criminal; instead, the sovereign's power must be on display for *all* of the subjects because they, too, "must be made to be afraid" (Foucault, 1977, p. 58). As Foucault explains, the public execution reminds all subjects that "the slightest offense [is] likely to be punished" (p. 58). The public and brutal nature of punishment in sovereign power thus helps to perpetuate the ruler's power and reinforces the subjects' belief in the sovereign's inherent superiority and authority.

Part of Foucault's project is to show that power is more nuanced than the way it is conceptualized and exercised in a sovereign state. He accomplishes this by making a distinction between power and domination. While "[t]he sovereign mode of power is easy to recognize and understand because it most closely resembles forces of domination and control with which we are familiar" (Fendler, 2010, p. 44), power is not the same as domination. In the case of the latter, individuals have no choices, alternatives, or opportunities to exercise their own power. Slavery is the closest appropriation of domination: individuals in chains, forced to do things against their own will, with no "out" of their situation. While one could argue that forcing children to participate in the Hunger Games is an example of domination, those children have many options available to them once inside the arena, as evidenced by the way in which Katniss and Peeta participate. Further, because power works in relations, there is a degree of freedom and agency vested in those relations of power, and individuals can use and exercise power at any given moment. Foucault theorized that because all people have freedom, there must be other forms of power besides sovereign power. Indeed, throughout his career, he conceptualized and defined three other modalities of power: disciplinary power, pastoral power and biopower. We briefly explore these modalities in the sections to follow.

Disciplinary Power

Disciplinary power relates to the ways in which we "discipline" our behaviors, language, and thinking in a certain context or community. In this way, disciplinary power provides a set of social expectations for people: it tells us how we are supposed to act or fit in based upon "messages we get from society – knowledge, rewards, and images" (Fendler, 2010, p. 44). These messages, for the most part, convey an idea of what we think is "normal" for a given person in a given context. So, someone who subjects himself to disciplinary power will act differently in church, for example, than at a baseball game because each context calls for its own procedures and expectations. Disciplinary power requires that we, as individuals, exercise self-discipline, but it also requires that others—in the form of people, organizations, or even the media—exercise it by sending us messages that influence how we behave, talk, and think. A persuasive element of disciplinary power is "the gaze," the notion that members of our community are always watching us. The ubiquitous presence of the gaze compels us to engage in socially accepted, normative behaviors. We see disciplinary power at play when some teenagers go shopping. Their social world has sent them messages about how they should dress, and because they feel that their peers are always watching them and are ready to tease them or harass them if they fail to follow these messages, they are willing to comply with them. In this way, the gaze subjects individuals to control without having to be forceful or explicit.

Biopower

Biopower is a type of power related to population control and demographics, appropriately termed because of its connection to human biological issues like reproductive, disease, and racial categorizations. People and institutions that exercise biopower influence how people conceptualize "births, deaths, health, sickness, and demographic (e.g. race, class, and gender) descriptions" (Fendler, 2010, p. 47). Those who write the definitions of mental illnesses also exercise biopower. And lawmakers who argue over definitions of when life begins are wrestling over biopower. Like all modalities of power, biopower can be both destructive and productive. Certain immunizations in the United States, for example, have prevented millions of children from contracting deadly diseases like the measles, mumps, or polio. In this case, this power helps to regulate the health and well being of the nation. On the other hand, using advances in psychology in order to categorize people according to their psychological strengths and weaknesses has the potential to have a profound and destructive impact on a person's life. For example, diagnosing a student with ADHD can push a child into low-level academic tracks in school, which may mean that she will receive inferior, often mind-numbing education, have fewer chances to interact with students in other tracks, and will come to understand herself as a person who is just not capable of sustaining attention while working on cognitively difficult tasks.

Pastoral Power

Pastoral power refers to power that one enacts through service to others. Indeed, the term "pastoral power" comes from the power priests and pastors gain because they help usher their "flock" of parishioners to salvation (Fendler, 2010, p. 45). Foucault (1982) notes, however, that pastoral power is "no longer a question of leading people to their salvation in the next world, but rather ensuring it in this world" (p. 784). Thus, pastoral power refers to the power exercised by those who help to ensure that people have "health, well-being (that is, sufficient wealth, standard of living), security, protection against accidents," etc. (p. 784). In contemporary society, religious leaders certainly exercise pastoral power, but so do people outside of religious institutions. One example of a figure that wields pastoral power is the lifeguard. A lifeguard's power comes from the fact that her job is to ensure that swimmers at the local pool stay safe. Because the lifeguard provides such an important service, swimmers and other pool patrons follow her rules.

Importantly, Foucault's (1982) conception of pastoral power requires that those who exercise it possess a deep knowledge of the people whom they serve. He explains that this modality of power "cannot be exercised without knowing the inside of people's minds, without exploring their souls, without making them reveal their innermost secrets. It implies a knowledge of the conscience and an ability to direct it" (p. 783). Relatedly, as Fendler (2010) explains, those with pastoral power earn their power by making others dependent on them. These two elements of pastoral power also manifest themselves in the case of lifeguards. Certainly a lifeguard could not become a lifeguard unless she proved that she had the requisite skills needed to protect and support the patrons of a pool. And while a lifeguard differs from a religious leader in that she will not need to understand a patron's "innermost secrets" in order to serve them, she most likely will know enough about pool patrons' behaviors—when and where children are likely to run, what it looks like when a child is drowning, etc.—to help prevent injury and accidents.

Having established four modalities of power that Foucault offers as an alternative to familiar notions of power, we next consider how they function in Suzanne Collins's (2008) novel *The Hunger Games*. We begin by outlining how these four modalities of power manifest themselves in the novel. Then, we argue that the existence of these modalities of power makes it possible for Katniss and Peeta to win the Games, thus rebelling against the Capitol.

BEYOND ABSOLUTE CONTROL: MODALITIES OF POWER IN *THE HUNGER GAMES*

The Promise of Punishment: Sovereign Power in the Hunger Games

Critics' tendency to interpret the Capitol as a totalitarian regime with "ultimate power and supreme governmental control" (i.e., Pavlik, 2012, p. 30) suggests that what Foucault described as sovereign power manifests itself throughout the book, particularly through President Snow and his Capitol regime. Indeed, President Snow seems to have a great deal of authority over the citizens of Panem, and what's more, his power hinges on the ever-present threat of brutal retaliation for criminal behavior. Likewise, the Games themselves can be likened to the practice of public execution that Foucault (1977) details in *Discipline and Punish*.

As readers know, the threat of punishment is ever-present in the lives of Panem's citizens. Katniss explains, for example, that she could be shot for hunting (Collins, 2008, p. 17), and later she reminisces about the first time she met Gale, who cautioned her, "stealing is punishable by death" (p. 110). Notably, although Katniss explicitly reflects on the ever-present threat of punishment in Panem, she does so in an offhanded, casual way, which suggests that this threat is so ubiquitous that it warrants no explication or reflection. Of course, the threat of punishment also manifests itself in implicit ways in the text. Collins (2008) underscores the constant threat of punishment when she introduces the Avox servants that Katniss encounters in the Capitol. As Katniss learns during her stay in the Capitol, it is common practice to cut traitors' tongues and force them to live a life of mute servitude (p. 77). Importantly, the Capitol does not only punish its traitors, it does so in a way that will remind its subjects just how much power it has. Indeed, by maiming these traitors and forcing them to interact with other citizens of Panem, the Capitol turns the Avoxes into visual evidence of their ultimate authority. Like the kings who publicly executed criminals in the classical age, the Capitol uses the punishment of traitors as an opportunity to enact and display its "intrinsic superiority" (Foucault, 1978, p. 49).

Because the threat of punishment is ever-present in Panem, the Capitol is able to control its citizens. Hunting and stealing, for example, are punishable by death, and generally speaking, this punishment prevents most citizens from engaging in these activities. Citizens' movements are also controlled. During the day of the reaping, citizens must be present in the town square; if they do not show up, they are arrested and imprisoned (Collins, 2008, p. 6). Furthermore, in addition to controlling people's behaviors, the threat of punishment also controls citizens' words. As Katniss reflects, criticizing the government or complaining about life in District 12 "would only lead us to more trouble. So I learned to hold my tongue and to turn my features into an indifferent mask so that no one could ever read my thoughts" (p. 6). This fear surfaces over and over again throughout Collins's novel. When Peeta and Katniss want to have a private conversation about a risky topic, they go to the roof of their dormitory where the loud wind will drown out their whispers in case anyone from the Capitol is listening to them. And when Peeta suddenly makes an utterance that could be interpreted as a critique of the Capitol, he quickly adds a few sentences so that any eavesdroppers would think he was a "nervous tribute" instead of a rebel (p. 80).

Most importantly, however, the Capitol's sovereign power manifests itself in the Games. As Katniss explains, the Hunger Games are "punishment" for a time long ago when the districts attempted to rebel against the Capitol: "taking the kids from our districts, forcing them to kill one another while we watch—this is the Capitol's way of reminding us how totally we are at their mercy" (Collins, 2008, p. 18). Like the public executions that Foucault analyzes, the Hunger Games are intended to both punish the districts for their treason *and* remind citizens of the Capitol's strength. To use Foucault's (1977) language, the Games serve both a judicial function and a political one—they enact justice and at the same time highlight "the dissymmetry between the subject who has dared to violate the law and the all-powerful sovereign who displays his strength" (p. 49). Thus, when one reads Collins's (2008) novel through the lens of Foucault (1977), killing the innocent children of parents who are themselves innocent of a treason committed generations ago can be understood as a governmental action designed to produce a "spectacle" of "imbalance and excess" (p. 49).

In addition to illuminating the presence of sovereign power in *The Hunger Games* (Collins, 2008), a Foucauldian lens can also highlight the presence of disciplinary power, biopower, and pastoral power. Indeed, the presence of these other modalities of power in the novel suggests that although the Capitol exercises sovereign power—which may seem like the power of a totalitarian state—this modality of power is far from absolute. Like the fence that surrounds District 12, the power the Capitol exercises has gaps and weak spots that allow the citizens of Panem to enact one or more of these other modalities of power. Thus, reading the text through the lens of Foucault highlights two important aspects of the novel: first, the Capitol is not a completely authoritarian state, and second, the citizens of Panem have much more agency than some literary critics assume.

Under the Watchful Eye of the Capitol: Disciplinary Power in Panem

Readers of *The Hunger Games* will note that the Capitol carefully monitors its citizens. This feature helps to illuminate the power of "the gaze" as a mechanism of disciplinary power. For example, after making a sarcastic remark about her own district while talking privately with Gale, Katniss states:

> I glance quickly over my shoulder. Even here, in the middle of nowhere, you worry someone might overhear you. When I was younger, I scared my mother to death, the things I would blurt out about District 12, about the people who rule our country …. Eventually I understood this would only lead us to more trouble. So I learned to hold my tongue and to turn my features into an indifferent mask so that no one could ever read my thoughts. Do my work quietly in school. Make only polite small talk …. Even at home, where I am less pleasant, I avoid discussing tricky topics. (Collins, 2008, p. 6)

This interior monologue reveals the great power "the gaze" has over Katniss. Because she fears who or what is watching or listening, she acts in a way that is expected of her and every other citizen of Panem—in this case, she does not talk disparagingly about the Capitol so that she and her family are not punished.

While the above example of disciplinary power mainly works to sustain the Capitol's authority, the novel is replete with moments when citizens mobilize disciplinary power in ways that help them meet their own ends. For example, once Katniss volunteers for her sister, we see several instances where she submits herself to the behavioral expectations that accompany her role as tribute. For example, even as Prim cries hysterically and pleads with Katniss not to volunteer, Katniss thinks, "… this is upsetting me and I don't want to cry. When they televise the replay of the reapings tonight, everyone will make note of my tears, and I'll be marked as an easy target. A weakling" (Collins, 2008, p. 23). She shares this same sentiment a bit later as she prepares to say goodbye to her family: "Crying is not an option. There will be more cameras at the train station" (p. 34). Katniss does not want to show emotion or weakness in these moments because she knows that her survival could very well depend on whether or not she can appear formidable— after all, the more she can portray herself as a serious contender, the more likely it is that sponsors will support her and provide the kinds of resources that she will need in order to survive the Games. Additionally, it is worth noting that the reason Katniss disciplines herself in this way is because, from the moment she volunteers in place of Prim, she is nearly constantly subjected to the watchful eye of the gaze. It is because she is being watched—and because people will judge her strength and competitive spirit each time the cameras are on her—that she disciplines her behaviors so thoroughly.

The fact that Katniss disciplines her behavior under the watchful eye of the Capitol and Panem's citizens highlights the agency that she has. In this case, Katniss mobilizes the Capitol's exercise of disciplinary power in order to position herself in ways that will promote her survival. Thus, even though in this scene Katniss conforms to the social rules and norms that the Capitol promotes, she nevertheless does so because she believes it will help her *gain* agency and power in the future. Thus, the scene illuminates a key weak spot in the Capitol's metaphorical fence: its disciplinary power can be used by citizens to foster their own agency.

Importantly, the type of power exercised by "the gaze" does not fall solely under the auspices of the Capitol and President Snow. Indeed throughout the novel, there is evidence that citizens unaffiliated with the Capitol's power regime enact disciplinary power upon each other. This is evident in the days before the Games when Peeta tells Katniss, "I want to die as myself... I don't want them to change me in there. Turn me into some kind of monster that I'm not." He concludes by asserting that he feels like he is "more than just a piece in their Games" (Collins, 2008, p. 142). This key moment suggests that the Capitol is not the only agent exercising disciplinary power over Peeta. While the people of Panem and the Capitol are attempting to discipline him and the other tributes to behave in ruthless and cruel ways, Peeta's desire to resist becoming a monster suggests that other people or groups—perhaps his father, community, or school—have disciplined him to resist cruelty and to define himself and his choices in ways that run counter to how the Capitol would define him. His struggle suggests that power can be exercised through agents other than the Capitol, and it points to yet another weakness in the Capitol's fence; after all, because the Capitol is not the only agent that can exercise disciplinary power, it cannot have absolute power over its citizens.

Just a Piece in Their Games: The Role of Biopower

Much of the Capitol's control derives from its exercise of biopower after the collapse of the North American governments and the subsequent Dark Days, events that resulted in its constructing Panem, a country of 13 districts. Indeed, the entire imposed makeup of Panem, including its divisions and allocations of certain resources and privileges, is evidence of biopower. Citizens of each district essentially make their living by participating in their district's principal industry. Because there are few options for other work, the citizens have become accustomed to this way of life and must live with any side-effects that come with it. For example, the citizens of District 12 are born into a coal-mining region and thus live a lifestyle that is different from the lifestyles of other districts. Thus, how Katniss looks is shaped by the biopower the Capitol has exercised in Panem's design. In comparison to citizens from other districts, or to Capitol standards, she is too hairy, dirty, and unkempt. As she explains, "We don't have much cause to look nice in District Twelve" (Collins, 2008, p. 62), and as a result she has to undergo an intense makeover at the Capitol's Remake Center once she has been selected as a tribute. Conversely, residents of the Capitol have a wealth of resources, and their bodies reflect this: they have aqua hair, gold tattoos, high-pitched voices, and green skin. In all of these cases, the districts, and by extension their citizens, are reduced to stable, pre-determined identities; the citizens becomes commodities of the Capitol.

Perhaps the most salient example of the Capitol exercising biopower is evident in its ability to effectively reduce the Hunger Games tributes to mere objects. As Risko (2012) points out, the Capitol has constructed the Hunger Games in a way that denies the competitors their personhood. The Capitol categorizes the tributes as objects in a number of ways throughout the book. For example, the Capitol uses the phrase "the reaping," which suggests that children taken from the districts are objects that can be "harvested." Additionally, tributes are typically referred to by their district number instead of their name, they are judged based upon scores and skills connected to combat, and, perhaps most importantly, they are subjected to the inhumanity of the Games. It is clear that the Capitol usually succeeds in dehumanizing and objectifying the tributes when Katniss, having listened to Peeta remark that he wants to be more than "just a piece in their games," responds, "[B]ut you're not .... None of us are. That's how the Games work" (Collins, 2008, p. 142). The fact that even Katniss accepts her role as a "piece" in the Games suggests that the Capitol's exercise of biopower successfully reduces tributes to mere objects.

Importantly, in order for biopower to effectively shape people's lives, a critical mass of citizens must buy into and enact the categories and definitions the state imposes on them. As a result, the exercise of biopower leaves room for citizens to reject the state's construction of their lives. This kind of rejection occurs throughout *The Hunger Games* and emphasizes the weakness of the Capitol's control. For example, Collins (2008) presents Cinna as someone who acts and thinks differently than his fellow Capitol citizens; because he actually cares about Katniss and Peeta, he attempts to restore and highlight their humanity through dress and makeup. One way he does so is by refusing to dress them in a way that reflects their district's principal industry, as is typically done with tributes. In refusing to emphasize the labor that District 12 does, he encourages the audience to see Katniss and Peeta as more than just workers who produce resources for the Capitol. He would rather make them "unforgettable" (p. 66), and so he chooses to literally light them on fire (with fake flames) when they are first presented to the citizens of Panem as tributes. When she sees the overwhelming response that Cinna's decision elicits, Katniss remarks that, for the first time since the reaping, she feels hope. Because their costume has allowed others to focus on them as people rather than laborers for the Capitol, Katniss's comment affirms Cinna's purpose in asserting an identity different from the one the Capitol has tried to impose on them.

In a much more explicit example of their recognition of (and resistance to) the Capitol's biopower, Katniss and Gale, early in the novel, discuss the brutal nature of the Games and the reaping. They understand that through these rituals they are nothing more than instruments of the state; that is, they serve only to advance the cause and message of the Capitol and those in charge. But because of this, and because of the inhumane treatment of children across Panem, Katniss states, "I never want to have kids." Gale responds by saying, "I might if I didn't live here" (Collins, 2008, p. 9). The fact that Katniss and Gale are able to have children but don't want to suggests that they wish to resist the Capitol's biopower and exercise their own. They hope to regulate their adult bodies for their own purposes, not the Capitol's. By creating this vision for their future, they gain the satisfaction of imagining that they will not produce more human beings who will become mere instruments of the state or endure the pain of watching their own children suffer what they have.

In a similar way, Katniss's "funeral" for Rue is another example of a rejection of the state's biopower. Despite the fact that the Capitol attempts to define the tributes as inhuman objects, Katniss refuses this definition and instead treats Rue like a person. Typically in the Games, the bodies of fallen tributes are left to be collected by the Capitol's hovercraft, much like a piece of trash might be picked up by a machine. For Katniss, however, seeing Rue's corpse reminds her of the wish that Peeta articulated to her a few nights before they entered the arena: "I keep wishing I could think of a way to… show the Capitol that they don't own me. That I'm more than just a piece in their Games" (Collins, 2008, p. 236). With this in mind, she decides to adorn Rue's body, face, and hair with flowers and cover her wounds. When she is finished, Katniss thinks, "She could really be asleep in that meadow after all" (p. 237). In this moment Katniss has returned a personhood status to Rue; unlike the Capitol, which has always treated citizens of the districts as objects, Katniss treats Rue like a human. That this action represents a rejection of the Capitol's power is underscored later in the text when Katniss notices that the Gamemakers did not show her funeral for Rue in the highlight reel, leading her to reflect, "Right. Because even that smacks of rebellion" (p. 363). Thus, by taking care to treat Rue as a person, Katniss has proven that the Capitol does not completely own her, or anyone else for that matter.

These described scenes essentially capture gaps in the Capitol's fence when it comes to biopower. Whereas the Capitol has tried to regulate its citizens and tributes in certain ways—namely, through attempting to control their bodies and regulate how they think about each other—these scenes depict moments when citizens push back and exercise biopower in thought or in deed, proving that the Capitol does not have complete control over them.

The Capitol as Protector: Pastoral Power

The Hunger Games is rife with examples of Capitol leaders attempting to enact pastoral power, the power that one gains through service to others. One way they do this is by painting themselves as benevolent stewards of Panem. This is exemplified in the story the Capitol tells about the development of Panem. In the Capitol's narrative, the country "rose up out of the ashes" of a dystopian North America that was plagued by both natural disasters and warfare over dwindling resources (Collins, 2008, p. 13). The narrative goes on to explain that the Capitol, the authority that emerged out of the chaos, "brought peace and prosperity to its citizens" (p. 13). This narrative paints the picture of the Capitol as a benevolent entity that provides safety, food, and wealth to its citizens. By telling this particular narrative, the Capitol attempts to engender the citizens' respect and their obedience. The pastoral power displayed by the Capitol is emphasized when Katniss sardonically reflects that in District 12, one can "starve to death in safety" (p. 6). This comment underscores the citizens' deep dependency on the Capitol.

While pastoral power can certainly serve the needs of the Capitol and perpetuate its rule, it can also be mobilized by citizens in ways that expose weaknesses in the Capitol's authority and allow them to enact agency and push back against the Capitol's influence. One example of how the enactment of pastoral power exposes weaknesses in the Capitol's control is evident in Katniss's relationship with the Peacekeepers in District 12. Despite the fact that the Peacekeepers are charged with enforcing the laws of the Capitol, they do not always enforce them in uniform or consistent ways. One of the laws that the Peacekeepers do not enforce with regularity is the law against leaving the district and hunting. As we mentioned earlier, hunting is illegal in the district, and Katniss could be killed for it. Despite the Capitol's laws and their consequences, Katniss continues to hunt. She explains her risky behavior by highlighting the fact that the Peacekeepers benefit from her hunting: "the Peacekeepers turn a blind eye to the few of us who hunt because they're as hungry for fresh meat as anybody is. In fact, they're among our best customers" (Collins, 2008, pp. 5-6). Later, she underscores this point by explaining that the "appetites of those in charge" protect her from being shot for hunting. Reading the relationship between Katniss and the Peacekeepers through a Foucauldian lens, then, suggests that Katniss not only exercises some power over the Peacekeepers, but does so by providing a service that supports their health and standard of living. Thus, Katniss's interactions with the Peacekeepers—a group of people who are supposed to enact the will of the Capitol—not only underscores weaknesses in the Capitol's control over its citizens, it also serves as an example of how the citizens of Panem have exploited the Capitol's weaknesses for their own benefit.

In addition to enacting one's own pastoral power, the characters in the novel also find ways to mobilize others' pastoral power for their own benefit. This is especially evident in Katniss and Peeta's ability to marshal the supportive service that Haymitch provides. In Haymitch's case, the support he offers comes in the form of advice, material goods and occasional emotional support. As Effie reminds Katniss and Peeta early in the novel, "[Y]our mentor is your lifeline to the world in these Games. The one who advises you, lines up your sponsors, and dictates the presentation of any gifts. Haymitch can well be the difference between your life and your death" (Collins, 2008, pp. 46-47). Indeed, one reason that Katniss and Peeta survive the Games is because they attend to Haymitch's demands and thus subject themselves to his pastoral power.

Haymitch's pastoral power is particularly evident during the scenes when Katniss nurses Peeta back to health late in the novel. Throughout this time, Katniss comes to realize that Haymitch will support her and send her life-sustaining gifts if she does a good job of pretending to be in love with Peeta. This occurs to her the first night that she is nursing Peeta. After she gives him a kiss during one of the highest points of his fever, Haymitch delivers a pot of broth. Katniss reflects, "Haymitch couldn't be sending me a clearer message. One kiss equals one pot of broth. I can almost hear his snarl. 'You're supposed to be in love, sweetheart. The boy's dying. Giving me something I can work with!'" (Collins, 2008, p. 261). In this moment, it is clear that Katniss understands that Haymitch has the capacity to support the tributes' health and wellness and that he will only do so if Katniss subjects herself to his pastoral power. As a result, Katniss begins to consciously act as if she is in love with Peeta. Throughout their time in the cave, whenever she remembers "the importance of sustaining the star-crossed lover routine" she kisses or caresses Peeta (p. 281). These actions, however, do not initially result in the food that Katniss and Peeta desperately need to fend off starvation while they are hiding out in the cave. As Katniss remarks, "just a kiss" won't be enough to satisfy Haymitch, and she hypothesizes that "he wants something more personal. The sort of stuff he was trying to get me to tell about myself when we were practicing for the interview" (p. 380). After she has this epiphany, she initiates a kiss with Peeta. Perhaps even more importantly, she initiates the kiss after telling him that she has feelings for him. Immediately after they kiss, the two tributes receive a great feast and Katniss reflects that she can almost hear Haymitch exclaim, "Yes, *that's* what I'm looking for, sweetheart" (p. 382). The feast that Haymitch sends not only prevents Katniss and Peeta from starving to death, it also helps them to gain the strength needed to fight the remaining tributes and the mutations that appear at the Cornucopia. The time that she spends nursing Peeta back to life, then, not only exemplifies the fact that agents besides the Capitol can enact pastoral power, but also that Katniss is able to mobilize Haymitch's pastoral power in ways that benefit both her and Peeta.

EXPLOITING THE GAPS: HOW MULTIPLE MODALITIES OF POWER HELP
KATNISS AND PEETA REBEL

Thus far we have argued that throughout Suzanne Collins's (2008) *The Hunger Games* there is evidence of multiple modalities of power. We have highlighted the ways in which these modalities of power weaken the Capitol's power, which in turn prevents it from exercising the kind of "absolute power" that some critics (e.g., Pavlik, 2012; Risko, 2012; Wezner, 2012) attribute to it. Additionally, we have suggested that a variety of characters in Collins's (2008) novel are able to enact agency throughout the book by exploiting weaknesses in the Capitol's power for their own gain. In this section, we extend the latter argument and contend that characters in *The Hunger Games* not only benefit from the multiple modalities of power at play, but that Katniss and Peeta win the 74th Hunger Games *because* of their ability to manipulate them. Specifically, we argue that Katniss and Peeta survive the Games because they act like "star-crossed lovers," a strategy they were able to employ because multiple modalities of power exist.

Playing Star-Crossed Lovers: A Performance for Survival

As we mentioned in our discussion about the role biopower plays in the text, when Peeta declares his love for Katniss, he encourages the audience to see both of them as human beings with an emotional life and the capacity to love, which is a central reason the two earn the sponsorship they need to survive the Games. Haymitch highlights the life-saving effect of Peeta's confession of love when he explains to Katniss that it made her "look desirable," which will earn her more sponsors than she would have gotten on her own (Collins, 2008, p. 135). And indeed, his declaration does ensure that sponsors "line up around the block" to support Katniss (p. 137), providing her with life-sustaining and expensive gifts, including healing balm for her burns, broth for Peeta, and a large pot of stew. The balm for her burns keeps her alive, as does the broth that she gives to Peeta, and the stew prevents them both from starving at a time when Katniss's need to watch over Peeta, coupled with a never-ending downpour, prevents her from hunting. Thus, because Peeta's declaration endears them to the audience and sponsors, it ultimately keeps them alive during the most difficult moments of the Games.

In addition to earning sponsors that helped them survive during the Games, Peeta's declaration of love for Katniss most likely also compelled the Gamemakers to change the rules of the Games, allowing two tributes from the same district to win. As Katniss reflects, "[F]or two tributes to have a shot at winning, our 'romance' must be so popular with the audience that condemning it would jeopardize the success of the Games" (Collins, 2008, p. 247). Because the Games usually require all but one tribute to be killed in the arena, the fact that the audience's support encouraged the Gamemakers to change the rules suggests that the star-crossed lover performance made it possible for both Peeta and Katniss to survive the arena.

Finally, the only reason that Katniss and Peeta get away with threatening to kill themselves with poisonous berries at the end of their first Hunger Games is because the audience sees them as lovers and not as rebels who have found a way to publicly undermine the Capitol. This is underscored throughout the end of the novel and serves, in part, as the impetus for the second novel of the series. Cinna, for example, dresses Katniss as girlishly as possible in order to suggest that she is too innocent and too in love to have come up with the berry trick in order to rebel. Haymitch also emphasizes the life-saving role of the star-crossed lover performance when he tells Katniss that the Capitol is very angry about the trick and that her only defense is that she was "so madly in love that [she] wasn't responsible for [her] actions" (Collins, 2008, p. 357). Even the Gamemakers highlight the couple's love by encouraging Peeta and Katniss to kiss and cuddle during their interviews and by constructing the highlight reel as a "love story" (p. 362) that ends with Katniss pounding on the glass doors of Peeta's room on the hovercraft. These moves on the part of the Gamemakers suggest that they, too, need to sustain the love story. Perhaps like Katniss and Peeta, the Gamemakers know that the Capitol will punish them if the people of Panem come to believe that instead of acting out of love, the two tributes won because they outsmarted the Capitol.

Multiple Modalities of Power: Making the "Lover" Performance Possible

Importantly, the star-crossed lover routine that allows Katniss and Peeta to win could only have occurred in a context where multiple modalities of power not only exist, but also act on one another. Perhaps the mode of power most essential to Katniss and Peeta's survival is pastoral power. Because the Capitol allows wealthy citizens to support the tribute's health and well-being by providing them with food, medicine and other life-sustaining resources, they essentially invite these sponsors to exercise pastoral power. In addition to the sponsors, the tributes' coaches also exercise pastoral power by controlling the flow of sponsored gifts to the tributes. The fact that their coaches and the sponsors exercise pastoral power over them means that when Katniss and Peeta behave in ways that satisfy their supporters—that is, when they act like star-crossed lovers—they gain the support they need to survive.

In addition to the presence of pastoral power, Katniss and Peeta also win the Games because the Capitol attempts to use biopower to define the children who fight in the Games as tributes or mere "pieces in their games" (Collins, 2008, p 142). As we mentioned above, in order for biopower to effectively shape people's lives, people must buy into and act on the categories and definitions created through this form of power. Because biopower requires "buy-in" from subjects, this modality of power leaves space for autonomy because a critical mass of people can always reject the categories a government imposes on them. And indeed, in the case of *The Hunger Games*, the audience's interest in the blossoming love between Katniss and Peeta suggests that a critical mass of Panem's citizens have rejected the way the Capitol categorizes them as non-human tributes or "pieces in the game;" instead, they choose to view them as human beings who have an emotional life and are capable of love. The fact that the audience is able to resist the categories imposed by the Capitol through its exercise of biopower make the star-crossed lover performance possible and thus allows Katniss and Peeta to survive the Games.

Finally, the presence of disciplinary power makes it possible for Peeta and Katniss to survive the Hunger Games. Indeed, the presence of disciplinary power may be the reason that both Katniss and Peeta are able to perform the "star-crossed lover" routine in a way that endears them to the audience. Since disciplinary power relates to the set of social expectations that tell people how to act "normally" in particular situations, and because both Katniss and Peeta seem to follow the behavioral expectations of "lovers," it is clear that Katniss and Peeta have been "disciplined" in ways that help them know how people in love should act. Indeed, we see Katniss consciously think through how she should behave towards Peeta when she thinks about how her parents behaved when they were in love and then attempts to talk to Peeta with the "special tone that my mother used only with my father" (Collins, 2008, p. 261). She continues to perform what she knows about lovers' behavior throughout the rest of the Games, kissing Peeta before she leaves for the Cornucopia, holding him in the night, and having intimate conversations with him as they hide in the cave. Notably, the fact that Katniss has been disciplined in this way was most likely not the result of the Capitol. Indeed, the fact that District 12 is "largely ignored by the Capitol as long as we produce our coal quotas" (p. 283) suggests that the Capitol cares little for the personal lives of the districts' citizens and had little to no concern for how Katniss was disciplined into the norms of lovers. Thus, because Katniss and Peeta were disciplined by their communities and families into an understanding of what it means to be a lover, they were able to win the Games by acting like they were in love.

Importantly, no single modality of power could have allowed Katniss and Peeta to win the Games; instead, the relationship between these three modalities of power—disciplinary power, pastoral power, and biopower—allowed the two to survive the Games and resist the Capitol's sovereign power. Indeed, if Katniss had not been disciplined into knowing how to perform the role of lover, it would not have mattered that Haymitch refused to give her support until she acted more in love with Peeta. And if the television viewing audience as a whole had not rejected the Capitol's objectification of Katniss and Peeta and had not conceptualized them as human beings with the capacity to love, Haymitch would never have encouraged them to look like lovers and it would not have mattered whether Katniss knew how to behave like a woman in love. Thus, it is not only the presence of these multiple modalities of power, but also the interdependent relationship among them, that made it possible for Katniss and Peeta to exploit the weak points in the Capitol's authority.

IMPLICATIONS FOR UNDERSTANDING TOTALITARIANISM AND DYSTOPIA AS A GENRE

In this chapter we have highlighted two points about Suzanne Collins's (2008) novel *The Hunger Games* that are apparent when one reads it in conjunction with Foucault's analytics of power: first, that the sovereign power of the Capitol is not absolute due to the multiple modalities of power always already at play in any relationship; and, second, that characters in the novel use and exercise their own forms of power, created by gaps in the Capitol's system and vision, to further their own gain or simply to survive. This reading of *The Hunger Games,* then, has several implications for the novel and, we suggest, for our understanding of the dystopian genre as a whole.

First, our work suggests that it is difficult to define the governments of dystopian texts as totalitarian, as some scholars (e.g. Pavlik, 2012; Risko, 2012; Wezner, 2012) have done. A totalitarian regime describes a political system where the governing body (e.g., the state, the Capitol, etc.) enacts complete authority and control over its citizens (Arendt, 1973). But as we have pointed out, the multiple modalities of power at play in Collins's (2008) novel allow the characters to enact a good deal of agency. As shown, they are able to exercise power for their own purposes, and in doing so they often manage to undercut the authority of the Capitol. Indeed, most dystopian fiction positions a "hero" or "rebel" figure to save society or initiate the downfall of a political regime. That these figures exist suggests that the oppressive systems depicted in dystopias are not absolute.

MICHAEL MACALUSO AND CORI MCKENZIE

Along these lines, the hero is sometimes positioned—by critics and scholars or even by the characters of dystopian fiction—as just that, an ultimate hero or savior who was born to lead or to fight the system in place. When we think about these multiple modes of power, however, we see that it is not just the "hero" or the innate qualities of that hero that bring about a revolution or cause the downfall of the regime in place. Instead, the regimes of dystopian fiction may fall because the heroes take advantage of the gaps in the absolute power of their social worlds. Thus, while Katniss certainly has the qualities of a strong protagonist, it is not hard to imagine that another character in her position—Peeta, Gale, Rue, or even Prim—could have exploited the gaps in the Capitol's power just as Katniss did. In this way, it is possible to contend that the heroes of dystopian novels are not endowed with super-human strengths or qualities, but instead are mere mortals capable of recognizing and capitalizing on the weak spots in a regime's control.

Finally, in considering these two points—that dystopian worlds operate under a false totalitarian regime and that protagonists are often mere mortals instead of superhuman heroes—one can appreciate that the governmental system in place in dystopias always had the potential to fail, that a revolution was "always-already" in motion even before the novel began. As long as characters do not exist in systems of complete domination, there is always room for freedom and the exercise of power, and with that, there is always the possibility for rebellion. And while dystopian fiction usually presents some worst-case scenario for the future or some extension or exaggeration of our own societal flaws and fads, Katniss's ability to exploit the multiple modalities of power in *The Hunger Games* teaches us an important lesson—that the possibility and potential for freedom and liberation are always present. Despite the incredible odds *not* in our favor, there is always the potential for brave individuals to exploit the multiple modalities of power that exist and to find a way to beat the system. In this way, hope survives, and Collins's (2008) *The Hunger Games* reminds us that improving our situation is only a matter of finding a gap in the fence.

REFERENCES

Arendt, H. (1973). *The origins of totalitarianism*. Houghton Mifflin Harcourt.
Collins, S. (2008). *The hunger games*. New York: Scholastic.
Fendler, L. (2010). *Michel Foucault* (Vol. 22). New York: Continuum.
Foucault, M. (1977). *Discipline and punish: The birth of the prison*. Random House.
Foucault, M. (1978). *The history of sexuality, Vol. 1: An introduction* (Robert Hurley, Trans.). New York: Pantheon.
Foucault, M. (1982). The subject and power. *Critical Inquiry, 8*(4), 777-795.
Pavlik, A. (2012). Absolute power games. In M. F. Pharr & L. A. Clark (Eds.), *Of bread, blood and The Hunger Games: Critical essays on the Suzanne Collins trilogy* (pp. 30-38). North Carolina: McFarland & Company, Inc.
Risko, G. A. (2012). Katniss Everdeen's liminal choices and the foundations of revolutionary ethics. In M. F. Pharr & L. A. Clark (Eds.), *Of bread, blood and The Hunger Games: Critical essays on the Suzanne Collins trilogy* (pp. 80-88). North Carolina: McFarland & Company, Inc.

Wezner, K. (2012). 'Perhaps I am watching you now': Panem's panopticons. In M. F. Pharr & L. A. Clark (Eds.), *Of bread, blood and The Hunger Games: Critical essays on the Suzanne Collins trilogy* (pp. 148-157). North Carolina: McFarland & Company, Inc.

PART THREE

"Look at the State They Left Us In": The Hunger Games as Social Criticism

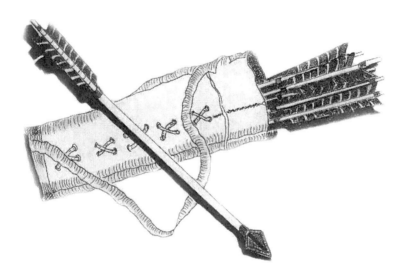

ANNA O. SOTER

7. "IT'S GREAT TO HAVE ALLIES AS LONG AS YOU CAN IGNORE THE THOUGHT THAT YOU'LL HAVE TO KILL THEM"

A Cultural Critical Response to Blurred Ethics in
The Hunger Games *Trilogy*

"My failure," says Snow, "was being so slow to grasp Coin's plan. To let the Capitol and districts destroy one another, and then step in to take power with Thirteen barely scratched. Make no mistake, she was intending to take my place right from the beginning. I shouldn't be surprised. After all, it was Thirteen that started the rebellion that led to the Dark Days, and then abandoned the rest of the districts when the tide turned against it. But I wasn't watching Coin. I was watching you, Mockingjay. And you were watching me. I'm afraid we have both been played for fools." (Collins, 2010, p. 357)

In the Hunger Games trilogy, leaders of the "good side" are essentially no different from leaders of the "bad side." Generally, leaders of oppressed groups have been perceived as more, rather than less, morally and ethically trustworthy. It is not surprising, however, given recent events in our own times, that the three novels in Suzanne Collins's trilogy, published as they were within the last six years, present readers with a view that reflects a less than innocent vision of right/wrong and good/bad leadership. Expediency, ends justifying the means—these are not new issues in contemporary social, economic, and political arenas. While it may be surprising that moral ambivalence is prominent in realistic fiction targeted at adolescents, a cultural critical perspective can provide us with an explanation as to its prevalence. If literature is indeed a mirror of the culture of the time during which it is produced, the moral and ethical ambivalence present in novels such as Cormier's (1974) *The Chocolate War*, the Colliers' (1974) *My Brother Sam is Dead*, or Brown's (2009) *Hate List* are, from a cultural critical perspective, reflections of the culture that produced them. Parallels, whether intended by the authors or not, can be readily drawn between these novels and the blurring of moral and ethical boundaries in the behavior of publicly visible figures in one field or other – observations which are facilitated by the phenomenal growth of a variety of electronically delivered media, primarily cable television and the internet. "Good bad-guys" (and girls) have become glamorized (e.g., the cable television show *Suits*), and even mainstream police shows such as *Law and Order: SVU*, which ostensibly reinforce a binary between right and wrong, imply that

S. P. Connors (ed.), The Politics of Panem, 125–136.

capitulation to the 'system' often requires that one act not according to one's conscience, but to what one's job demands. Capitulation, and what I see as ethical numbness based on the premise that one's job demands it, undermines ethics in the interests of the established (and accepted) order. Ethical numbness is similar to lower psychological responsiveness to violence, a phenomenon that Swing and Anderson (2007) found in subjects that experienced prolonged exposure to violent video games. Again, this is not new: "Nicht schuldig"—"Not guilty"—was a common defense by German soldiers during the Nuremberg Trials. In dystopian societies such as those depicted in Collins' trilogy, Orwell's (1949/1987) *Nineteen-Eighty-Four*, and Bradbury's (1953) *Fahrenheit 451*, extreme institutionalization oppresses the citizenry, but the insidious effects of institutionalization in *seemingly non-oppressive times and cultures* belies its effects.

An account of cultural criticism and how cultural critics see all texts, whether fiction or nonfiction, provides the focus of the next section. This account includes a brief discussion of how such a perspective influences the way in which we read texts, and frames the remainder of the chapter in which I focus on two questions: first, how are larger social and cultural structures embedded in institutionalized behaviors in both Panem and our world (i.e., the culture that produced the novels); and second, what and how are some of the major ethical orientations in both Panem, and thus, our world, as implicitly and explicitly revealed through the novels in the Hunger Games trilogy? I conclude the chapter by drawing on Jauss's (1982) reception theory as a possible explanation for the significant popularity of the series.

CULTURAL CRITICISM (OR CULTURAL POETICS): ALL TEXTS, INCLUDING FICTION, ARE "REAL"

What is "Cultural Criticism," and why does it offer itself as a potential lens for deeper inquiry into Collins's Hunger Games trilogy? Cultural Criticism provides a frame, or lens, through which we can view a literary text, and offers readers an opportunity to read and analyze such text as "fictionalized representations of human experience at a given time and place" (Tyson, 2006, p. 295). From a cultural critical perspective, therefore, the literary text is not simply fiction: it is a reflection of the society and culture that produced it, and of the author within that society and culture; it is, in essence, a mirror of what already exists, whether or not the citizenry is aware of that, and whether or not it exists in such a way that its oppressiveness is experienced.

Cultural Criticism is an offspring of New Historical Criticism. Depending on the literary theorist, a particular theory may be also called by another name. Bressler (2007) notes that New Historicism "is the name given to the American branch of Cultural Poetics," one of its "originating voices being Greenblatt" (cited in Bressler, 2007, p. 218). According to Tyson (2006), "the literary text [is] shaped by discourses circulating in the culture in which it was produced. Likewise, our interpretations of literature shape (and are shaped) by the culture in which we live" (p. 295). For cultural critics, too, all cultural productions can be "analyzed to reveal the cultural work they perform…ways in which they shape our experience by transmitting or performing ideologies" (Tyson, 2006, p. 296). A cultural critical perspective, then, becomes a frame that calls for a particular way of perceiving not only the culture and times in which novels are set, but also the culture and times in which they were produced and published.

According to Tyson (2006), cultural critics of all persuasions share the view that human history and culture "constitute a complex arena of dynamic forces of which we can construct only a partial, subjective picture" (p. 295). As evident in Collins's trilogy, we may be "constrained within the limits set for us by our culture," and yet those same limits may provide us opportunities to either "struggle" against or "transform them" (Tyson, 2006, p. 295). Unlike New Historicism and Marxism, Cultural Criticism tends to be more "overtly political in its support of oppressed groups," and according to Tyson (2006), it is "especially interested in popular culture" (p. 297). In these senses, it seems a natural lens through which to read and consider the events depicted in the Hunger Games trilogy, perhaps more so than New Historicism, Marxism or other postmodern perspectives. Cultural critics "ask us to make connections between the literary text, the culture in which it emerged, and the cultures in which it is interpreted" (Tyson, 2006, p. 297). Drawing on Greenblatt, Tyson (2006) synthesizes the kinds of questions that cultural critics typically ask of a literary text given this perspective. Primary among them are the following:

– What kinds of behavior, models of practice does the text appear to enforce?
– Why might readers at a particular time and place find this work compelling?
– Are there differences between readers' values and the values implicit in the work readers are reading?
– Upon what social understandings does the work depend?
– Whose freedom of thought or movement might be constrained implicitly or explicitly by this work?
– What are the larger social structures with which … particular acts of praise or blame—that is, the text's apparent ethical orientation—might be connected? (p. 297)

Using Tyson's (2006) identification of typical questions, I've chosen to address two of the above questions in particular in my analysis of Collins's trilogy: (a) what are the larger social structures within which … particular acts of praise or blame—that is, the text's "apparent ethical orientation"—might be connected, and (b), upon what "social understandings does the work depend" (p. 297)? That said, in the process of identifying the larger social and cultural structures both in the trilogy and in our own times and culture, aspects of each of the other questions will inevitably be addressed as well. Throughout this chapter, parallels will be drawn between the world created in the novels and the world as seen through the eyes of the author of the trilogy and the consciousness which generated the text in the first place.

ANNA O. SOTER

LARGER SOCIAL (AND CULTURAL) STRUCTURES: INSTITUTIONALIZED BEHAVIOR AND THE COLLECTIVE UNCONSCIOUS

A particularly striking feature of the society depicted in the Hunger Games trilogy is the overt and pervasive institutionalization of human behavior. This is, of course, common in futuristically set dystopian fiction. However, in this instance, I believe the series, perhaps unwittingly, mirrors similarly overt and pervasive institutionalization of human behavior in the culture and period which produced it, namely, the USA and by extension, what we politically identify as a Western Power. Although published over sixty years ago, observations made about the institutionalization of human behavior by Berger and Luckman (1966) bear repeating as they are remarkably pertinent in the context of reading Collins's trilogy from a cultural critical perspective:

> Institutions ... by the very fact of their existence, control human conduct by setting up predefined patterns of conduct, which channel it in one direction as against the many other directions that would theoretically be possible. (p. 55)

In dystopias, institutionalization typically runs roughshod over individual activity, subsuming individual morality and inhibiting human conduct from moving in the "other directions" that Berger and Luckman envision as "theoretically... possible" (p. 55). Institutionalization per se is not perceived negatively by Berger and Luckman (1966), who regard it as an outgrowth of "habitualization" (p. 53). Danger, however, lurks when we are unaware that what we accept, what we tolerate, is not necessarily the only way to exist in the world, either as individuals or collectively. An outcome of this lack of awareness is unconscious "habitualization" which leads us to discover one day that certain behaviors are now accepted as "normal." Even if individuals resist, are horrified, or object, they are no longer in harmony with what is generally accepted as a given, even if that "given" is not perceived positively.

In our own world, since the decades following the end of the Second World War, we have had increasing exposure to ethically questionable behavior by leaders and institutions once thought to be above suspicion, to be morally upright. Investigative reporting today routinely unveils reports of scandals involving religious leaders, military officials, politicians, teachers, doctors, lawyers, and so on. This constant exposure of highly visible representatives of our world suggests either that (a) such behavior is not new, but was more easily hidden before the era of the internet sleuth, or/and (b) that we have embraced the principle of fame and fortune at whatever the cost and be damned with the consequences. A recurring question implicit in Collins's series challenges us to ask as readers who we can trust, and not trust, particularly among the privileged few. Disguise is both literal and figurative. Again, questions of who and what to trust arise almost daily in media news in the current era. As evident in questions that have arisen about what actually happened with the 2013 bombing of the American Embassy in Ben Ghazi, we do not necessarily take as truthful even the US former Secretary of State's explanations. Expediency among even highly respected international leaders appears to be a more prevalent foundation for action than we had naively believed thirty or forty years ago. Similarly, Katniss's early distrust of Coin suggests that no side is above suspicion of ulterior motives.

Collins was reportedly inspired to write at least the first volume in the series, *The Hunger Games* (2008), as a result of a channel surfing session during which she watched a reality television show followed by footage from the invasion by the US of Iraq. According to a report by John Sellers (2008) in *Publisher's Weekly*, Collins was disturbed by this self-inflicted juxtapositioning of content, which she felt blurred different boundaries "in a very unsettling way" (para. 7). Various sources, including Collins, have noted that the Greek myth of Theseus as well as the Roman gladiatorial games provide the frame for the novels, but I argue that the trilogy as a whole is far more revealing as an unconscious representation of Collins' perception that the world she has created as fiction is indeed the world in which we are living.

The Hunger Games series has been described as dystopian fiction, but unlike other typical fictional dystopias, I would argue that it is not set in a future as distant as we might first assume, and therefore, the trilogy is not a warning of things that might happen, but a mirror of what has happened (and is happening) without our being aware of it. It is perhaps not coincidental, then, that, at the series' conclusion in *Mockingjay* (Collins, 2010), Katniss helps Peeta to regain a sense of the physical and psychological present through querying what he is able to recall as "real" or "not real." The confusion Peeta experiences between "real" and "not real" is a result of his having been injected with tracker jacker venom while a captive of the Capitol prior to his rescue by the rebels. The venom causes a form of mental hijacking that targets the "part of the brain that houses fear" and thus generates "fear conditioning" (p. 180), manifested as sheer terror, hallucinations, and nightmarish visions. Our own post-World War II, post-Cold War, post-Vietnam, post-chemical-warfare Iraq, post-Afghanistan military involvements have generated similar manifestations (termed collectively as PTSD or Post-Traumatic Stress Disorder) in those who served in those events. While not injected with material comparable to tracker jacker venom, we now recognize that the mind is not immune to what occurs on battlefields. Nevertheless, the general impression one has of those who suffer PTSD is that the defect lies in them and not in the nature of the activities in which they are required to be engaged and psychologically detached from.

In Collins's trilogy, the oppressive system has been in place long enough—at least 75 years, three generations if we consider the average generation span as 25 years—to have, as Littauer (2006) argues, resulted in "institutionalized behavior," to the extent that over generations, "legitimizations are learned by the new generation during the same process that socializes them into the institutional order" (p. 62). According to Littauer, the "more conduct is institutionalized, the more predictable and thus the more controlled it becomes" (p. 62). As a consequence, if the process of socialization has been effective, "outright coercive measures" [such as the annual Games in Collins's trilogy] "can be applied economically and selectively" (Littauer, 2006, p. 62). Similarly, as implied in the preceding paragraph, the dysfunctions that emerge with PTSD can be dismissed as the affected soldier's problem and not an outcome of dysfunctional institutionalized expectations on the part of those who have the power to launch wars. Littauer (2006) also argues that "the more on the level of the mean that conduct is taken for granted, the more possible alternatives to the institutional program will recede and the more predictable and controlled the product will be" (p. 62). This insight can serve as an explanation for why the population in Panem does not revolt for at least 75 years against a highly indictable charge of pitting children to kill children in the context of a "game." Within the context of a cultural critical analysis, we can see this action as symptomatic of Littauer's (2006) argument that the apparent "objectivity of the institutional world, however massive it may appear to the individual, is a humanly produced, constructed objectivity" (p. 60). In this sense the seeming (objective) reality of the institutionalized world of Panem has the power to shape the individual and produce a "specific kind of person" (p. 60) who does not, in the end, question the perceived reality in which he or she lives. Only those who have for some reason or other retained their agency, who have not been successfully absorbed into the consciousness of the institutionalized culture created in Panem, and who, as a result, retain a sense of another reality, remain able to resist and challenge this process.

Some other instances of the larger social and cultural structures depicted in the fictional world of Panem that have parallels in our contemporary world include the bifurcation between rural and the urbane world of the Capitol. While not necessarily referencing an actual city, it is tempting to see the Capitol as emblematic of the glamorous, upscale side of Washington, DC. It is also possible to link the two in terms of a divided culture of the very rich and the working poor, a divide that is increasingly familiar to us as more sophisticated technologies thrive in large urban areas and not in remote rural areas, whether they are manufacturing and mining industry-oriented or agriculturally oriented.

When she first visits the Capitol, Katniss observes a further divide evident in what is considered fashionable and not. A leisure class appears to have little to do with its time other than focus on self-glamorization and amusement. Katniss comments on the bizarre body painting and weird and wonderful hairstyles she observes upon first arriving at the Capitol, where definitions of beauty are entirely focused on the superficial. Thus she endures skin peels, exfoliation, and extreme make-up in order to make her presentable to the masses that will view telecasts of the Games. In this way, her accounts of her encounters with the "fashionable" in the Capitol are reminiscent of updates that *Vanity Fair* and other contemporary magazines like it issue regarding what is in style in any given year, or who wore what at the annual Golden Globe or Academy Awards. Further parallels can be found in our own time in the thriving cosmetic industry, increasingly extended to include body piercing, liposuction and other forms of body reshaping. This, along with Muller's (2012) extensive discussion of other parallels, raises the most pervasive question the trilogy poses for me and possibly for other readers: what is real, and what is virtual (or unreal)?

The significance of such a question is underscored by how technology is used to control the population in Panem, much as it is in our own time and place. As citizens of a self-declared democracy, we nevertheless know little about what our own government is capable of were its citizens to revolt. We do know that, under the justification of national security, it has used surveillance (e.g., through the internet, electronic imaging and scanning for access) for longer than we have suspected, and in a more widespread way than we imagined. The centralized bureaucracy in Collins's trilogy is uncannily, and disturbingly, familiar, and even seemingly benign within our own experience. At the time of this writing, I passed through customs at a Dallas airport following my return from an international flight and found that because of electronic passports, if a citizen, one can now pass through immigration in certain parts of the US without having to encounter the physical presence of a passport officer—all is conducted electronically. Luggage scanning and, more recently, full body scanning are similarly common in larger airports: twenty years ago, both would have seemed "futuristic." Whether we pay attention to such institutionalized incursions as evidence of more sinister intentions is beside the point. The point is that we have collectively come to accept them as the norm in an embattled culture, and by extension, that we have embraced what Littauer (2006) cautions is one of the long-term effects of institutionalized behavior—namely, that alternatives to imposed rules and regulations which become normal over time will "recede" (p. 62).

THE HUNGER GAMES APPARENT ETHICAL ORIENTATION AND REFLECTIONS OF OUR OWN MORAL AND ETHICAL DILEMMAS

Ethical utilitarianism accepted by a population, whatever the cause entailed, enables institutionalized authority (whether entrenched or through a resistance movement) to ensure that individuals follow orders. Such utilitarianism can also justify the use of individuals as tools for a greater cause without revealing to those individuals that they are indeed relegated to the status of tools in this way.

Both the Capitol and the rebels exploit and utilize Katniss in her first Hunger Games, and again later in the Quarter Quell Games. A compelling rationale can be made for this: the ends justify the means. In *Catching Fire* (Collins, 2009), as in the first novel of the trilogy, ethical utilitarianism is apparent in the release of audiovisuals to the masses who, although watching from the safety of their homes, are as much in the arena as the tributes. A second example is Beetee's plan to blow out the force field surrounding the arena without Katniss's knowledge that District 13 is heavily involved in these Games. Katniss remains unaware that the figure behind her ultimate rescue, Plutarch Heavensbee, has, for several years, been part of an undercover group intending to overthrow the Capitol. Katniss discovers that she is a tool for the rebels who "used [her] without consent, without knowledge …. At least in the Hunger Games, I knew I was being played with" (Collins, 2009, p. 385). She also learns why the other tributes, including Johanna and Finnick, had to save her even at the cost of their own lives when Plutarch informs her, "[Y]ou're the mockingjay, Katniss …. While you live, the revolution lives" (p. 386). She realizes that all was orchestrated once she stepped into the first Games to save her sister, Prim—"[t]he bird, the pin, the song, the berries, the watch, the cracker, the dress that burst into flames"—and she accepts that she is "the mockingjay .... The one that survived despite the Capitol's plans. The symbol of the rebellion" (pp. 385-386). If there is any ambiguity remaining about Coin's perception of Katniss as a potential threat, or her using Katniss only as far as needed, Boggs, a lieutenant for whom Katniss develops high regard, makes it explicit that if she will not support Coin she will be perceived as a threat since she is "the face of the rebellion" (Collins, 2010, p. 267). Such examples pervade the trilogy as they do in our own world. Moral ambiguity is an outcome of ethical utilitarianism. It is not surprising that serious young adult literature often depicts moral ambiguity in decisions protagonists have to make in the face of institutionalized ethical utilitarianism. This kind of literature marks the passage from innocent childhood to morally complex adulthood. Perhaps this also explains why novels such as *The Hunger Games* (Collins, 2008) are so immensely popular. Adolescent and adult readers alike hunger, literally, to find solutions to our own moral and ethical dilemmas.

What other kinds of ethical "messages" can we discern through Katniss's narration of the Capitol's values? A brief perusal of a small internet sample of teen reactions to the books and promo snapshots of the film adaptations indicates that even youthful readers sense that the novels in the trilogy mirror their own world. While minor emphasis is occasionally placed on the "futuristic" qualities of the world that Collins constructs, the commentary captured in these short 'takes' often suggests that some parallels with contemporary events and values are perceived, among them the callous and seemingly detached school shootings that have become the norm following the Columbine High School massacre in 1999. Video clips on *YouTube* (TheFineBros, 2012, 2013) of what teens and adults think of *The Hunger Games* (Collins, 2008), along with Mead's (2013) blog post, provide clips of readers' perceptions about the novels in the trilogy, and include comments about parallels in our world, including the reality of military service at age 19 in various wars in which the US has been involved. One could point also to rhetoric which characterizes the killing of children, women, and the elderly in Vietnam and Afghanistan as "collateral damage" with the rationale being that US soldiers often found it impossible in those settings to determine who was the enemy and who was not.

The lack of reaction (reflected in a lack of commentary) on Katniss's execution of Coin rather than Snow may suggest that Katniss's action is perceived as justified because it is based on her pervading distrust of Coin from their first encounter and her realization that the rebel victory over the Capitol and Coin's ascendancy to power represent the potential establishment of just another form of tyranny. Perhaps it is discomforting to discover that neither side is pure; neither side has total merit; and, neither side is excluded from potential manipulation of facts, people, or agendas. As we move through the second and third novels of the trilogy, *Catching Fire* (Collins, 2009) and *Mockingjay* (Collins, 2010), moral ambiguity and ethical expediency become increasingly apparent. Haymitch, Plutarch, Coin, and others like them who carry out their bidding are no innocents in the struggle for power—rather, they participate in a parallel game that appears as brutal in its exploitation of humans as that engaged in by the deposed regime.

Even Katniss is not averse to operating in ethically ambiguous regions. At the climax of the first novel, she and Peeta succeed in forcing the Capitol to allow both of them to exit the arena alive, a result of Katniss's gambling that the Gamemakers would accept two winners when she and Peeta threatened to consume poisonous berries in full view of the television cameras. Just as the pair is about to swallow the berries, the Head Gamemaker announces that he accepts the two victors concept. Later, Katniss lies to Caesar Flickerman about her motivation for threatening to consume the berries, stating, "I don't know, I just ... couldn't bear the thought of...being without him" (Collins, 2008, p. 369). Katniss discovers that moral and ethical values are often weighed against the threat of punishment or extinction. She lies about her romance with Peeta to continue the charade since cameras are still everywhere. By maintaining the "star-crossed lovers" story, she and Peeta become the darlings of the Capitol's citizens. Is this any different from the moral and ethical relativity that Katniss witnesses in the Capitol and, later, among the revolutionaries?

By casting Katniss both as primary protagonist and first person narrator, Collins provides us with the filter through which we critique the system that the Capitol represents and through which it is able to control all of Panem until the rebel take-over. Katniss is a reliable enough narrator to enable Collins to reflect, through her protagonist's eyes, issues not only within Panem, but also the culture that spawned the novels—ours. In being provided with a protagonist with whom we can identify (as ultimately do many of the citizens of Panem), we are able to empathetically notice what Katniss notices, including the following: her awareness of the material contrasts between the Capitol and the districts; her awareness of the extent of oppression; and, her awareness of duplicity behind seemingly neutral official behavior and language (e.g., smiling at the cameras when introduced to the citizens of the Capitol).

Katniss's awareness of these dualities invites us to see parallels between the US and the Capitol; between seats of power and sites of oppression; between leaders in Panem (Snow and later Coin) and leaders in our time; between the superficiality of the Hunger Games and the illusory world of so-called "reality" television; between the plasticity and over-adornment of people who live in the Capitol and those who live in our own world.

Within the cultural critical frame, then, the Hunger Games trilogy offers us an opportunity to explore parallel instances of how institutionalized our own behaviors have become. It also invites us to question the extent to which citizens in the culture of the present are aware of how we have been constructed through institutionalized behavior patterns. Ethical and moral ambiguity can be heard in phrases that one hears in the work context, in the street, or in various social settings, such as "It comes with the job," or "It comes with the territory," or "You do what you have to do," all of which can be perceived as symptomatic of institutionalized behavior. To reach and remain at the political pinnacle requires making deals of all kinds, even after one is in power. The American public might well be uneasy about how the US came to be involved in Afghanistan or Iraq as two examples. Ambiguity also remains around the issues of whether or not Saddam Hussein used chemical warfare in Iraq, or whether the Iranians are stockpiling nuclear and biochemical weaponry. Similarly, consider seemingly harmless television series such as "Suits," a series that focuses on the machinations of high roller "good bad-guy and girl" lawyers, and which epitomizes high levels of material success evident in their glass and steel corporate towers, their expensive suites, high-rise condos, expense accounts, and a generally luxurious lifestyle. Characters in this series play by ethically ambiguous codes that are every bit as ruthless as what we see in the Hunger Games trilogy. "Real or not real?" (Collins, 2010, p. 321) as Peeta asks Katniss following his rescue from the Capitol forces in *Mockingjay*. Perhaps what we can imagine (fiction) can only be imagined because it already exists in one form or other.

CONCLUSION: CULTURAL CRITICISM AND THE POPULARITY OF THE HUNGER GAMES TRILOGY

Why might readers find the novels in Collins's trilogy compelling? Why do they find the series a "good read"? Various readers I have talked with about the trilogy confirm the popularity of the novels, particularly the first. Comments such as "I devoured the book," "I couldn't put it down," and "I read it in one sitting" are pervasive. Yet it strikes me that a book which depicts the legalized murder of children could also be seen as revolting. Why is this not pervasive?

In my earlier writing on the appropriateness and benefits of utilizing literary theory with young adult literature (Soter, 1999; Soter et al., 2008), I have drawn on Jauss's (1982) work on the aesthetics of reception. Jauss (1982) lays bare what may explain the popular reception of the Hunger Games trilogy, despite Walter Benjamin's assertion that "Nowhere does a concern for the reception of a work of art or an artform aver itself fruitful for its understanding" (cited in Jauss, 1982, p. xv). If we accept that art is mimetic, then the popular reception of Collins's Hunger Games novels may be explicable because of this very quality. The art, in this case the novel, is a representation of what is perceived to exist at the time of its production, regardless of its place in history—we see ourselves and our world reflected in some way in what we view and read. As the pervasiveness of what are popularly termed "Selfies" (photographs of oneself which are then posted on internet social media sites) suggest, we appear to be endlessly fascinated by what we believe are desired reflections of ourselves and our situations. Recognition of what is imitated and aesthetically rendered brings reading audiences full circle to themselves, to their contexts, times, and experiences. As Jauss (1982) notes:

> A literary work, even when it appears to be new, does not present itself as something absolutely new in an informational vacuum, but predisposes its audience to a very specific kind of reception by announcements, overt and covert signals, familiar characteristics, or implicit allusions. It awakens memories of that which was already read [or lived – *author interpolation*], brings the reader to a specific emotional attitude, and with its beginning

arouses expectations for the "middle and end" which can then be maintained intact or altered, reoriented, or even fulfilled ironically in the course of the reading according to the specific rules of the genre or type of text. (p. 23)

Is the widespread appeal of Collins's Hunger Games trilogy (even among adult readers) driven by a deeper, perhaps subliminal hunger for cultural self-analysis? Adolescents are not oblivious to the moral and ethical ambiguity of the adult world. They are, in the age of easily accessible mass media, constantly exposed to it even if not seeking it. Among highly popular YA authors who have tackled teen perceptions of the moral and ethical ambiguity in the adult world, Crutcher's (1986, 1995) fiction frequently takes on this issue and may explain why his novels are also widely popular. His teen protagonists in *Stotan* (1986) and *Iron Man* (1995) provide two examples of how teens struggle to make sense of the adult world with its contradictions and its tendency toward ethical expediency.

It is not surprising that some parents have been outraged by the violence in the first volume of the Hunger Games trilogy. But one might ask, who is buying the books? Presumably, they are mostly purchased by parents or at least paid for by parents. If the considerable number of blogs and other forms of internet comment postings are to be believed, there is widespread recognition of the dualities (physical, institutional, moral and ethical) that I have discussed in this chapter. Muller (2012) suggests that Collins' "repeated and extensive use of the games trope and the focus on the virtual mode that these subordinate" (p. 61) reflect Collins' concern about the fusing of boundaries between the "virtual" and the "real" (p. 61). We do not, as yet, know, in any conclusive way, what parents think they are exposing their children to; or whether they talk with their children about the books; or whether they read them from cover to cover or preview them before they purchase them for their children. I would argue that at least one of the reasons for the great appeal of this series to millions of teens globally is that at a subliminal level teens recognize that the text is a mirror of the world they inhabit, and as Muller (2012) implies, that they also sense in themselves the capacity for the same darkness witnessed in the series. Whether they want to emulate Katniss, who chooses to "tell her story" "even if it means implicating herself" (Muller, 2012, p. 63), is not possible to predict. However, the novels, in functioning as a mirror of not only our world but of ourselves within it, do offer the possibility for redemptive choice, the possibility of overcoming institutionalized moral and ethical expediency and inertia. If we do indeed see our culture, our times, and ourselves reflected in the trilogy, a cultural critical reading provides us with an avenue for self-examination that may offer a similarly redemptive response once the initial pain of self-recognition is embraced.

REFERENCES

Berger, P., & Luckman, T. (1966). *The social construction of reality: A treatise in the sociology of knowledge.* New York: Anchor/Doubleday.
Bradbury, R. (1953). *Fahrenheit 451.* New York: Ballantine.

Bressler, C. E. (2007). *Literary criticism: An introduction to theory and practice*. 4th Edition. Upper Saddle River, NJ: Pearson/Prentice-Hall.

Brown, J. (2009). *Hate list*. New York: Little Brown.

Collier, J. L., & Collier, C. (1974). *My brother Sam is dead*. New York: Scholastic Press.

Collins, S. (2008). *The hunger games*. New York: Scholastic Press.

Collins, S. (2009). *Catching fire*. New York: Scholastic Press.

Collins, S. (2010). *Mockingjay*. New York: Scholastic Press.

Cormier, R. (1974). *The chocolate war*. New York: Laurel Leaf.

Crutcher C. (1986). *Stotan*. New York: HarperCollins.

Crutcher, C. (1995). *Ironman*. New York: HarperCollins.

Jauss, H. R. (1982). *Toward an aesthetic of reception* (T. Bahti, Trans.). Minneapolis, MI: University of Minnesota Press.

Littauer, K. (2006). *Theories of reading: Books, bodies and bibliomania*. Malden, MA: Polity Press.

Mead, C. (2013). *Why I hope we devour the Hunger Games* [Blog post]. Retrieved from http://lifeteen.com/why-i-hope-we-devour-the-hunger-games/. Retrieved March 2, 2014.

Muller, V. (2012). Virtually real: Suzanne Collins's The Hunger Games trilogy. *International Research in Children's Literature, 5*(1), 51-63.

Orwell, G. (1949/1987). *Nineteen-eighty-four*. New York: Signet Classic.

Sellers, J. A. (June 9, 2008). *A dark horse breaks out: The buzz is on for Suzanne Collins's YA series debut*. Retrieved from http://www.publishersweekly.com/pw/print/20080609/9915-a-dark-horse-breaks-out.html

Soter, A. O. (1999). *Young adult literature and the new literary theories*. New York: Teachers College Press.

Soter, A. O., Faust, M., & Rogers, T. (2008). *Interpretive play: Using critical perspectives to teach young adult literature*. Norwood, MA: Christopher-Gordon Publishers.

Swing, E. L., & Anderson, C. A. (2007). The unintended negative consequences of exposure to violent videogames. *Journal of Cognitive Technology, 12*(1), 4-14.

TheFineBros. (2012). *Teens react to The Hunger Games* [YouTube video]. Retrieved from https://www.youtube.com/watch?v=Ri6wRz_NjiA&feature=kp

TheFineBros. (2013). *Elders react to the Hunger Games: Catching Fire* [YouTube video]. Retrieved from www.youtube.com/watch?v=i0uuBoDcSC8

Tyson, L. (2006). *Critical theory today* (2nd ed.). New York: Routledge/Taylor Francis.

SEAN P. CONNORS

8. "I TRY TO REMEMBER WHO I AM AND WHO I AM NOT"

The Subjugation of Nature and Women in The Hunger Games

Several assumptions surround popular discourse about Suzanne Collins's commercially successful Hunger Games series, including one that regards Katniss Everdeen, its protagonist, as offering young female readers access to a newly empowered subject position. In "Brave, Determined, and Strong: Books for Girls (and Sometimes Boys)," Ward and Young (2009) state:

> When choosing a book for a girl, merely reaching for any old book with female characters isn't enough. Care should be taken to find books that feature strong female literary role models, allowing girls to explore their own identities, claim their own voices, and gain confidence, particularly during the adolescent years. (p. 257)

The authors identify *The Hunger Games,* the first novel in Collins's (2008) series, as a literary text that educators can utilize to help female readers toward these ends. In these terms, Collins is understood to present readers with a self-actualized female character that breaks down gender inequalities.

Gonick (2006) identifies two competing discourses that offer opposing views on femininity: what she calls "Reviving Ophelia," which portrays "girls as vulnerable, voiceless, and fragile," and "Girl Power," which "represents a 'new girl': assertive, dynamic, and unbound from the constraints of passive femininity" (p. 2). At first glance, Collins's (2008) novel appears firmly ensconced in the latter category. Katniss is athletic, adventurous, skilled with weapons and brave, characteristics that are often drawn as masculine in popular culture texts. Moreover, she performs tasks that are associated with men, and, in doing so, she subverts—sometimes overtly, sometimes implicitly—traditional female gender roles. Following her father's death, Katniss provides for her family by hunting, and throughout much of the first novel she laments her inability to tend to the sick with the same degree of care and aptitude her mother and younger sister exhibit. Seen in this light, Collins (2008) does appear to open a greater number of subject positions to young women by portraying a strong female protagonist. At the same time, however, this reading overlooks the seemingly important fact that, at least in the first novel, Katniss *does* struggle to define herself in the face of patriarchal institutions that *do*, in fact, change her, even if only subtly. To survive in a society that is engineered by men to benefit men, Collins (2008) demonstrates that even a strong female like Katniss is forced to construct an alternative identity that enables her to create the

S. P. Connors (ed.), The Politics of Panem, 137–156.

impression of having conformed to gender expectations that her society imposes on her. In this sense, she assumes a sort of double consciousness.

In *The Dystopian Impulse in Modern Literature*, Booker (1994) argues, "The modern turn to dystopian fiction is largely attributable to perceived inadequacies in existing social and political systems" (p. 20). A critical examination of *The Hunger Games* reveals that, by engaging in the kind of social criticism that Booker (1994) suggests is characteristic of dystopian fiction, Collins (2008) accomplishes something considerably more complex in her novel, and potentially even subversive, than is commonly assumed. Specifically, she demonstrates how the same oppressive patriarchal conceptual framework that motivates governments and corporations to exploit nature and degrade the environment, both symbols of the feminine, leads them to enact policies that subjugate and exploit disenfranchised groups, including women, minorities, and people in poverty. In this way, *The Hunger Games* shares an assumption that is characteristic of ecofeminist philosophy—namely, that "the specifics that both environmentalism and feminism separately oppose stems from the same sources: the patriarchal construction of modern Western civilization" (Murphy, 1995, p. 48).

Critics occasionally deride speculative fiction—an umbrella term used to refer to a range of genres, including science fiction (SF), fantasy, utopian and dystopian fiction— as *genre fiction* with the result being that they dismiss it as a form of superficial entertainment. The cultural expectations that have historically accompanied young adult literature—namely, that it must perform a didactic function—coupled with its status as a commodity, subject it to additional stigmas and mischaracterizations. Indeed, as Daniels (2006) argues, there remain critics in both secondary and higher education who insist that young adult literature does not warrant serious "attention because it doesn't offer enough substance to be included within the traditional literary canon" (p. 78). One might assume, then, that young adult dystopian fiction represents the low-person on the literary totem pole.

In this chapter, I advocate reading speculative fiction for adolescents—specifically, young adult dystopian fiction—from the standpoint of critical theory to make visible the genre's potential complexity and to foreground the important political work it is capable of performing. To do so, I examine *The Hunger Games*, the first novel in Collins's (2008) series, from the perspective of ecofeminist literary theory to demonstrate how, in the fictional world that Collins constructs, the patriarchal mindset of the Capitol leads it to treat marginalized groups of people, specifically females, as fodder to be remade and consumed by the powerful.

This reading is evident in Collins's (2008) portrayal of Katniss, a teenage girl who, from the moment she volunteers to participate in the Hunger Games, a state-sponsored spectacle akin to reality television in which children of the poor murder one another for the entertainment of the elite, embarks on a journey that leads her to travel through a world dominated by powerful males. Ensnared in that world's ideology, Katniss struggles to demonstrate to those in power, and also to herself, that they don't control her in the same way that they do the material resources they extract from her community in District 12. At the same time, she discovers that her ability to survive in the Capitol, and later in the Hunger Games, is contingent on her performing gender in ways that parallel her society's expectations of her. As a result of her experiences, Katniss undergoes a metamorphosis that transforms a strong, independent female figure into a young woman who, at least at the conclusion of the first novel, is less sure of herself. Recognizing this, I advocate reading her character as a metaphor for the damage that patriarchal institutions inflict on young females by inundating them with a steady stream of messages that function to actively limit the subject positions they recognize as available to them.

SOCIAL CRITICISM AND YOUNG ADULT DYSTOPIAN FICTION

Arguments for the value of young adult literature abound, though it is perhaps most often celebrated for its ability to motivate reluctant readers, support struggling readers, and explore issues that adults, who, not coincidentally, author the majority of young adult novels, assume are of concern to adolescent readers. These ends are important, but, as others point out, young adult literature is also capable of complexity and literary sophistication, and it can challenge stronger readers as well (Connors, 2013; Miller & Slifkin, 2010; Soter & Connors, 2009). Reading young adult literature has the additional positive affect of preparing adolescents to participate in a democratic society by challenging them to reflect on a range of issues and problems that are endemic to the communities they inhabit (Wolk, 2009). This is especially true in the case of young adult dystopian fiction, a subgenre of young adult literature that, like dystopian fiction for adults, actively participates in social criticism.

In the past decade, a host of young adult dystopian novels have been written for (and marketed to) adolescents, including James Dashner's *The Maze Runner*, M. T. Anderson's *Feed*, Veronica Roth's Divergent series, Cory Doctorow's *Little Brother*, Jeff Hirsch's *The Eleventh Plague*, and Marie Lu's *Legend*, to name a few. Although these books are set in futuristic worlds, they invite readers to grapple with contemporary problems and social ills in much the same way that canonical literature does.

According to McDonald (2012), dystopian novels seize on "a negative cultural trend and imagine a future or an alternative world in which that trend dominates every aspect of life" (p. 9). In doing so, authors of dystopias aim to construct a deeper understanding of the human condition by exaggerating its flaws and imagining the consequences of their being taken to an extreme. In this way, though the genre ostensibly presents stories that are set in the future, young adult dystopian fiction is best understood as inviting readers to wrestle with, and interrogate, contemporary problems and issues. In doing so, it challenges them to ask whether it is advisable for society to adhere to certain beliefs or persist in following a particular course of action. As Sambell (2004) argues:

> The dystopia foregrounds future suffering, then, to force readers to think carefully about where supposed 'ideals' may really lead, underlining the point that these hugely undesirable societies can and will come about, unless we learn to question the authority of those in power, however benign they

may appear to be. In this way dystopian texts emphasize predominantly social concerns. (p. 248)

This concern with questioning authority motivates dystopian fiction to target social, religious, and political institutions for criticism with the intention of making visible impediments they erect in the path of human happiness. This penchant for questioning authority and exploring darker aspects of humanity can make some adults, especially those in positions of authority, uncomfortable. Nevertheless, reading dystopian fiction is a valuable exercise for readers of all ages if for no other reason than that it invites them to read the word and the world (Friere & Macedo, 1987). In this sense, like the larger umbrella category of young adult fiction, young adult dystopian fiction offers "a context for students to become conscious of their operative world view and to examine critically alternative ways of understanding the world and social relations" (Glasgow, 2001, p. 54). The potential for this to happen is heightened when one reads young adult dystopian fiction from the perspective of critical theory.

ECOFEMINIST LITERARY CRITICISM

Before offering an ecofeminist reading of *The Hunger Games,* I should first say a few words about this particular critical lens. Ecofeminist philosophy, which emerged in the 1970s, represents a fusion of concerns shared by ecologists and feminists. Like feminism, ecofeminism does not constitute a stable, unified theory. Rather, as Murphy (1995) argues, it is better understood as a conceptual home for theorists who define themselves in multiple ways—for example, as spiritual ecofeminists, traditional Marxist ecofeminists, cultural ecofeminists, and so on. Despite their philosophical differences, ecofeminists are united by a common concern—namely, a "masculinist linkage of women and nature that denigrates and threatens both" (Murphy, 1995, p. 49).

According to Bennett (2005), ecofeminism is concerned with a host of issues, including—but not limited to—women's rights, animal rights, water and air cleanliness, and the oppression of people in Third World Countries by industrialized nations. Nevertheless, she argues that, at its core, ecofeminism is defined by its commitment to two concepts: its belief in the interrelatedness of all things and its commitment to supplanting hierarchically organized societies with egalitarian communities. In regard to the latter, she states:

> [Ecofeminists] assert that valuing one kind of life over another (white over black, male over female, human animals over other animals, industrialized living over agricultural life) will keep the hierarchy firmly entrenched, leaving traditionally defined "male" qualities—physical power, mechanistic ability, analytical and linear thinking—to be affirmed over "female" qualities—empathy, sensuality, emotion. (Bennett, p. 64)

Reading literature through the lens of ecofeminist theory, then, helps readers to disrupt these binaries and "become more aware of the interconnectedness in life, of cause and effect, and of the importance of taking personal responsibility for the consequences of our actions" (Bennett, p. 65).

In *The Hunger Games*, Collins (2008) presents readers with a futuristic society where the misapplication of science and technology blurs the boundary between public and private. Like Orwell's *Nineteen Eighty-Four*, she also depicts a world in which individual freedom is sacrificed to a surveillance society (Lyon, 1994) that demands compliance through the unceasing and omnipresent gaze of the state. Most importantly, Collins criticizes an oppressive patriarchal conceptual framework that treats marginalized groups of humans, including females, as raw materials it can remake for its own benefit. In the novel, those who occupy a position on the lower rungs of society, and who are subsequently regarded as disposable, struggle to define themselves in the face of definitions that other, more powerful figures impose on them. This includes hegemonic definitions of gender. As will be seen, Katniss struggles to maintain her identity as a strong female figure in a patriarchal system that demands compliance through a logic of domination (Warren, 2000). Read through the lens of ecofeminist literary theory, her involvement in the Hunger Games can be construed as a metaphor for the violence that society inflicts on young women by limiting the range of subject positions they recognize as available to them for performing gender.

"IF I CAN FORGET THEY'RE PEOPLE KILLING THEM WILL BE NO DIFFERENT AT ALL"

In *Ecofeminist Philosophy*, Warren (2000) identifies several features of a conceptual framework that patriarchal societies use to rationalize the oppression of humans by gender. This includes, but is not limited to, "conceptions of power and privilege that systematically advantage Ups over Downs, and a logic of domination" (p. 62). Significantly, Warren argues that this same conceptual framework "is used to justify the domination of humans by race/ethnicity, class, age, affectional orientation, ability, religion, marital status, geographic location, or nationality" (p. 62). She also regards it as offering a rationale for "the domination of nonhuman nature (and/or animals) by humans" (p. 62). Aspects of this conceptual framework are evident throughout Collins's (2008) novel, most notably in the relationship between the Capitol (Ups) and the citizens of Panem (Downs).

The economic structure of Panem, the setting of Collins's (2008) novel, is designed to privilege some groups (e.g., the wealthy, residents of the Capitol) at the expense of others (e.g., the poor, residents of the districts). Early in *The Hunger Games*, readers learn that a series of disasters—some man-made, others environmental—destabilized North America and brought about the collapse of society. From this devastation arose Panem, a country comprising twelve districts, all of which exist under the rule of a despotic government known as the Capitol. The relationship between the Capitol and those it governs resembles that of colonizer-to-colonized in so far as the state controls access to raw materials and industry that, by right, belong to the individual districts. Indeed, the association the Capitol forges between the districts and the goods and resources they produce for

SEAN P. CONNORS

its benefit defines them. District 4, for example, is known for providing seafood; District 11 for generating grains and produce; District 12, which Katniss calls home, for mining coal used to power the Capitol, and so on.

In *The Death of Nature,* Merchant (1983/1980) argues that, in contrast to ancient civilizations that conceptualized the feminine earth as a nurturing mother figure humans were obliged to revere and protect, the modern world, organized as it is by a patriarchal mindset, is driven by a commitment to mechanization and a desire to control nature. The presence of this binary—nature/modernity—is felt throughout *The Hunger Games.* A large city replete with skyscrapers, the Capitol appears to exist apart from the natural world. Indeed, when Katniss encounters it for the first time she describes its colors as "artificial, the pinks too deep, the greens too bright, the yellows painful to the eyes" (Collins, 2008, p. 59). She is also struck by the Capitol's reliance on technology, including its sleek machines, its awe-inspiring aircraft, and its seemingly endless lines of cars parading down city streets.

McAndrew (1996) argues that ecofeminists oppose "science and technology as presently practiced, because science and technology view the natural world as something to be mastered or even conquered, the dominance theme of patriarchy" (p. 371). Significantly, the Capitol uses technology as a tool to control the natural world. This is evident in several ways, most notably in its decision to locate the Hunger Games in ecological environments it constructs. This includes forests, arctic landscapes, and deserts, all of which pose different challenges and obstacles for contestants to overcome. At the same time, the Capitol, through its various machinations, exerts complete control over these environments. Streams and riverbeds are drained overnight; conflagrations are ignited at the push of a button, sending panicked animals stampeding for their lives; temperatures rise during the day and unexpectedly plummet in the evening; the sun rises during what is ostensibly the middle of night, and more. The Gamemakers also blanket these environments with hidden cameras and microphones, literally imposing technology on the land to ensure that they have an omniscient view of the contestants. Despite their seeming authenticity, these landscapes are characterized by a sense of artificiality, as evidenced by Katniss's struggling to determine whether the moon she observes in the arena sky is "real or merely a projection of the Gamemakers" (Collins, 2008, p. 310). Unable to reach a definitive conclusion, she expresses her desire for it to be real, as it would give her "something to cling to in the surreal world of the arena where the authenticity of everything is to be doubted" (p. 310).

The Capitol uses science and technology to control nature in other ways, including engineering "muttations"—genetically altered animals—as weapons against its enemies. Jabberjays, a special kind of bird capable of repeating extended passages of human conversation, enable the Capitol to monitor the schemes of dissidents, while tracker jackers, a form of killer wasp "spawned in a lab and strategically placed, like land mines, around the districts during the war" (Collins, 2008, p. 185), provide a constant reminder to the districts of the power the Capitol wields over them. As Katniss explains, the synthetically altered venom of tracker jackers is sufficiently powerful to inspire hallucinations and, in some cases, death. By using science and technology to bastardize and remake nature in this way, the

142

Capitol is able to preserve—and extend—its grip on power. In doing so, it signifies its commitment to a conceptual framework similar to the one that Warren (2000) associates with patriarchal cultures. Indeed, as McDonald (2012) persuasively argues, the Capitol, through its policies, effectively treats "the natural world as fodder to be set upon and remade into ever more grotesque and unnatural combinations" (p. 13).

In contrast to the Capitol, where people live in comfort, the residents of Panem's twelve districts exist under harsh conditions. Although people in District 12 are responsible for mining coal used to power the Capitol, an undertaking that is fraught with danger, they are poorly compensated for their labor and given minimal access to food and medicine. As a result, illness, starvation and death are rampant, a point that Katniss clarifies when she states:

> Who hasn't seen the victims? Older people who can't work. Children from a family with too many to feed. Those injured in the mines. Straggling through the streets. And one day you come upon them sitting motionless against a wall or lying in the Meadow .... Starvation is never the cause of death officially. It's always the flu, or exposure, or pneumonia. But that fools no one. (Collins, 2008, p. 28)

District 12 is not the only district to suffer in this way. The African American residents of District 11 are responsible for generating crops and produce, yet they are not allowed to partake of the goods they harvest. Those who do are whipped mercilessly while others are made to watch, a punishment that calls to mind the institution of slavery as it was practiced in the American South, and which underscores the Capitol's commitment to governing through what Warren (2000) calls a logic of domination. By treating the residents of the districts harshly, and by conceptualizing power as "power over power" (p. 46), the Capitol enacts another feature of an oppressive conceptual framework. As Warren explains, "When power-over power serves to reinforce the power of Ups as Ups in ways that keep Downs unjustifiably subordinated ... such conceptions and practices of power are unjustified" (p. 47).

Under these harsh conditions, Katniss and her family turn to the natural world for sustenance. When, in the weeks following her father's death in a mining accident, she and her family face starvation, she gathers dandelion greens as a way to survive. In the months that follow, she recalls that, "The woods became our savior" (Collins, 2008, p. 51). In addition to fishing, stealing eggs from nests, and hunting squirrel, rabbit and other wild game, Katniss gathers plants for food, including one her parents named her for. Her mother, an apothecary, earns a living collecting herbs and plants she in turn uses to cure the sick and heal the injured in District 12. She later passes this knowledge on to Katniss's younger sister, Prim. In contrast to the Capitol, then, the Everdeen family values and appreciates nature for its restorative powers, as opposed to remaking and exploiting it for material gain.

According to Warren (2000), philosophers have long "argued that the language one uses mirrors and reflects one's concept of oneself and one's world. As such, language plays a crucial role in concept formation" (p. 27). In *The Hunger Games*, references to nature are interlaced throughout Katniss's speech, and they construct a binary between the world of District 12 (nature) and the Capitol (modernity). Her younger sister, Prim, is said to have "a face as fresh as a raindrop, as lovely as the primrose for which she was named" (Collins, 2008, p. 3). When the back of Prim's white shirt inadvertently comes undone, creating a tail of sorts, Katniss takes to calling her "little duck" (p. 15). In contrast, when she references nature to make sense of her experiences in the Capitol, her language often foregrounds the artificiality of the latter. City lights are said to "twinkle like a vast field of fireflies" (p. 80) while metallic cameras wielded by paparazzi are reminiscent of insects (p. 40). Even the residents of the Capitol, motivated by an aesthetic that leads them to dye their hair and paint their bodies, strike Katniss as alien, so much so that she regards the stylists assigned her as "unlike people" and more like "a trio of oddly colored birds...pecking around my feet" (p. 62). Significantly, when she undergoes a beautification process to remove excess hair from her body, she imagines herself as "a plucked bird, ready for roasting" (p. 61), an apt metaphor given what awaits her in the Hunger Games.

Derrida and other deconstructionists note that binary oppositions exist in a value-laden hierarchy in which one element is granted priority over another (Leggo, 1998). The dystopian world that Collins (2008) constructs in *The Hunger Games* is founded on binaries that privilege the wealthy over the poor, the strong over the weak, and modernity over nature. As will be seen in the section to follow, the same conceptual framework that sustains these binaries also gives the Capitol a rationale for controlling and remaking marginalized groups of people in the same way it does the natural world. In the end, it is the state's ability to dehumanize others that enables it to find entertainment in watching disadvantaged teenagers slaughter one another in an arena. Intuitively, Katniss seems to understand this, because when Gale, her hunting partner in District 12, compares killing tributes in the Hunger Games to hunting animals for food, she tells herself, "The awful thing is that if I can forget they're people, it will be no different at all" (p. 40).

"SOMEHOW IT ALWAYS COMES BACK TO COAL AT SCHOOL": A PROGRAM OF DEHUMANIZING OTHERS

Having foregrounded a series of binaries that structure the relationship between the Capitol and the residents of Panem, Collins (2008) examines the role an oppressive patriarchal conceptual framework plays in leading those in positions of power to enact policies that dehumanize marginalized groups of people. As explained, in Panem the twelve districts exist in a metonymic relationship with the goods they produce for the Capitol, so that District 4 is known for producing fish, District 11 for agricultural products, District 12 for coal, and so on. This conflation of people with goods is accomplished in several ways in the novel, both at a local and a global level.

In District 12, nearly every aspect of a person's existence is tied to the business of extracting coal from the earth. This includes one's experiences in school, where the bulk of "instruction is coal-related" (Collins, 2008, pp. 41-42). Additionally,

Katniss and her family, along with their neighbors, inhabit a section of the district known as the Seam, a not so subtle allusion to a layer of coal sufficiently thick to be mined for profit. Perhaps because it permeates virtually every aspect of their daily lives, the residents of the Seam even begin to resemble coal, a fact that Katniss references when she observes that her neighbors "have long since stopped trying to scrub the coal dust off their broken nails, the lines of their sunken faces" (p. 4).

At a global level, the Capitol reinforces this association between people and resources by insisting that contestants who participate in the opening ceremony of the Hunger Games dress in a fashion that is indicative of their district's principal industry. As a consequence, contestants from District 12 traditionally wear miner's outfits, though Katniss is able to recall a year when the pair, a male and a female, "were stark naked and covered in black powder to represent coal dust" (Collins, 2008, p. 66). By forging this metaphorical association between coal and the people who mine it, the Capitol effectively dehumanizes the residents of District 12, relegating them to the realm of *things*. In doing so, it "mines" and exploits them for its own profit. This is most clearly evident in its sponsoring the Hunger Games, a bloody spectacle that pits 24 teenagers—two from each of Panem's twelve districts—against each other in mortal combat until one emerges victorious.

Having quashed a violent uprising, the Capitol created the Hunger Games to serve as a persistent reminder to the districts of their powerlessness. In addition to requiring parents to sacrifice their children in the Hunger Games, the Capitol forces them to watch the slaughter unfold on television in what is an extreme example of reality programming, thereby reinforcing its position of power over the districts by holding them complicit for participating in their own oppression. As Katniss explains:

Taking the kids from our districts, forcing them to kill one another while we watch—this is the Capitol's way of reminding us how totally we are at their mercy. How little chance we would stand of surviving another rebellion. Whatever words they use, the real message is clear: "Look how we take your children and sacrifice them and there's nothing you can do. If you lift a finger, we will destroy every last one of you." (Collins, 2008, pp. 18-19)

The process wherein contestants are selected to participate in the Hunger Games, along with the discourse that surrounds the competition, can be read as additional evidence of the Capitol's dehumanizing the people of Panem. The names of two "tributes" from each district—one male, the other female—are selected from a glass container in what the Capitol calls a "reaping," an apt metaphor given that children of the poor are effectively harvested and consumed for entertainment by the powerful. Even if they manage to survive, their involvement in the Hunger Games functions to change them into something other than what they are. This is evident in the case of Katniss, who discovers early on that her ability to survive in the arena is contingent on her complying with expectations that males impose on her.

SEAN P. CONNORS

"IF YOU PUT ENOUGH PRESSURE ON COAL IT TURNS TO PEARLS":
REGENDERING KATNISS

To this point I have argued that several popular assumptions surround *The Hunger Games*, one of which regards Katniss as offering young female readers access to a newly empowered subject position. This reading is not easily dismissed, as Katniss does exhibit qualities that are typically drawn as masculine in popular culture texts. She is a skilled hunter who is adept at using a bow and arrow, and after her father is killed in a mining accident she assumes his role by providing for her family. Likewise, Katniss is neither averse to killing nor prone to sentimentality, a fact that is evident when she recalls killing a lynx that took to following her in the woods. Though she regretted losing the animal's companionship, she nevertheless saw its death as an opportunity for her to profit by selling its pelt.

Miller (2012) argues that gender divisions are not as prevalent in the futuristic world that Collins (2008) envisions as they are in contemporary society. She rightly notes, for example, that men and women work alongside each other in the mines of District 12, and that males and females are selected to represent the districts in the Hunger Games where they compete against each other in a single competition as opposed to participating in separate contests according to gender. Furthermore, in the Capitol, men and women dye their hair, wear make-up, and sport tattoos, all of which seems to suggest that they are held to equivalent standards of beauty.

In much the same way that Katniss is thought to open up newly empowered subject positions to young female readers, Miller (2012) regards Peeta, a talented artist who is adept at decorating cakes, and who, with the exception of his physical strength, lacks either the ferocity or the athletic prowess other male contestants exhibit in the arena, as subverting hegemonic masculinity (Madill, 2008). Unlike Gale, Katniss's hunting companion in District 12, Peeta is not especially good with weapons. Indeed, with the exception of cutting short a mortally wounded girl's suffering, an act that could be interpreted as compassionate, and picking poisonous berries that inadvertently result in a death toward the end of the novel, he does not kill in the arena. He is actually wounded for most of the competition, and as a result is unable to care for himself. It consequently falls to Katniss to care for (and protect) him. For these reasons, Miller (2012) concludes that:

> Of the major characters in the Hunger Games trilogy, Peeta is the closest to being an androgynous blend of the most desirable masculine and feminine traits. He's confident and self-reliant like Katniss, but unlike his fellow District 12 tribute, he's also trusting and open. He's physically strong, but he avoids violence and aggression except in self-defense. His occupation of baking matches his warm and nurturing personality. He cleans up a drunk and disheveled Haymitch, offers a chilly Katniss his coat, and is generally kind and thoughtful. (p. 154)

At first glance, as Miller (2012) suggests, gender inequities do not appear to be as prevalent in Panem as they are in contemporary society, and, to a certain extent, Katniss and Peeta *do* disrupt hegemonic femininity and masculinity. Nevertheless,

146

a closer reading of the novel reveals that Collins (2008) accomplishes something considerably more complex than simply engaging in a discourse of "Girl Power" which, as Gonick (2006) argues, detracts attention away from the very real inequalities that females face at the hands of patriarchal institutions. The novel is set in (and produced by) a patriarchal culture, after all, and as such Katniss's agency is circumscribed to some extent in both the world of the text and the world of readers. Peeta might be able to circumvent traditional gender norms without fear of retribution, but Katniss cannot, and this is precisely Collins's point—no matter how strong Katniss is, her ability to survive in the Capitol is ultimately contingent on her performing hegemonic femininity (Krane, 2001).

Shortly before the scheduled start of the Hunger Games, Katniss converses with Peeta atop the roof of the building in which they are staying. As they gaze out at the twinkling lights of the Capitol, Peeta confesses his desire to retain his identity in the Hunger Games. Specifically, he states, "I don't want them to change me in there. Turn me into some kind of monster that I'm not" (Collins, 2008, p. 141). Instead, he expresses his desire "to show the Capitol they don't own me. That I'm more than just a piece in their Games" (p. 142). Katniss, of course, is unable to grasp his meaning, which is symbolically important. Though he incurs a physical injury, Peeta *does* exit the arena with his identity largely in tact. As a male, his society neither demands nor expects him to reinvent himself. Katniss, on the other hand, has no choice but to do so. Ultimately, the odds of her surviving in the arena are contingent on her becoming something other than what she is at the start of the novel, suggesting that females are, in fact, held accountable to a different standard than males in Panem. An ecofeminist reading of the novel invites readers not only to contemplate that double standard, but also to consider the role that male characters play in regendering Katniss.

Though it presents readers with a strong female protagonist, the world of *The Hunger Games* is decidedly male. At home in District 12, Katniss enjoys the companionship of her sister, Prim, whom she loves deeply, and her mother, with whom she is less close, a result of the fact that she holds her accountable for abandoning her family emotionally following her husband's death. She is close to Gale, her male hunting companion, but her relationship with him is by her own account plutonic. In the world of the Capitol, on the other hand, Katniss is surrounded by males, the sole exception being Effie Trinket, a figure so hyper-feminine as to appear cartoonish. It is perhaps not surprising, then, that males play a central role in regendering Katniss. As a contestant in the Hunger Games, she is expected to perform gender in ways that Cinna (her stylist), Haymitch (her mentor), and Peeta (her fellow tribute from District 12) establish for her. This, coupled with the knowledge that she exists under the omnipresent gaze of television cameras, influences the way that she carries herself in both the Capitol and later in the Hunger Games.

Soon after arriving in the Capitol, Katniss is sent to a "Remake Center"—an obvious metaphor for the transformational nature of her journey—where she undergoes a series of cosmetic alternations designed to enhance her appearance. To begin, her prep team scrubs and waxes her, practices that are torturous for Katniss, who complains, "My legs, arms, torso, underarms, and parts of my eyebrows have been stripped of [hair], leaving me like a plucked bird, ready for roasting" (Collins, 2008, p. 61). At the conclusion of this process, however, she is taken by her transformation, suggesting that, at least on some level, she approves of it. Confronted with an image of herself on a television screen, she states, "I am not pretty. I am not beautiful. I am as radiant as the sun" (p. 121).

As explained, the Capitol dehumanizes residents of the districts in a variety of ways, one of which involves its conflating them with raw materials and goods they produce for its benefit. Tributes are made to wear costumes that represent their district's principal source of industry in the opening ceremony of the Hunger Games. In Katniss's case, however, Cinna, her male stylist, elects to forego the coal miner outfit that contestants from District 12 traditionally wear. Although his motivation for doing so—to garner attention for Katniss and ensure that she comes across as memorable—is altruistic, he nevertheless replaces the costume with one that signifies the product her district produces—namely, coal. He and Peeta's stylist dress the couple in stylish black outfits that, when lit, emit real flames, the result of which earns them the approval of the viewing audience, and gains Katniss the moniker, "The girl who was on fire" (Collins, 2008, p. 70). In this way, Cinna's choice of wardrobe symbolically functions to reinforce the same dehumanizing association the Capitol constructed through its legislative policies. Whether he intended it or not, the metaphor can be read as suggesting that, much like flames consume coal, tributes are consumed by the hungry gaze of viewers in the Capitol.

When she goes on a television show following her sensational debut in the opening ceremony, Katniss is forced to submit to Cinna's aesthetic once again. Using a metaphor that reveals volumes about her feelings toward her style team's efforts to remake her, she states, "They erase my face with a layer of pale makeup and draw my features back out" (Collins, 2008, p. 120). The result is so impressive that Katniss again struggles to recognize herself, and, upon seeing her reflection, she is left with the impression that "[t]he creature standing before me in the full-length mirror has come from another world" (p. 120). Foregrounding a similar scene in *Catching Fire,* the second novel in the series, McDonald (2012) interprets the discomfort that Katniss feels when her prep team expresses their desire to transform her into "something special" as evidence of her understanding that "to 'make you something special' really means to unmake what you already are" (p. 14).

Like Cinna, Haymitch also plays a role in regendering Katniss. Though he is himself a resident of District 12, he treats her and Peeta as if they are something other than human when he meets them for the first time. Katniss recalls his circling them, "prodding us like animals at times, checking our muscles, examining our faces" (Collins, 2008, p. 58). Dissatisfied with her cold demeanor, Haymitch insists that Katniss experiment with alternative identities, one of which is that of a naïve girl who talks animatedly about the beautiful wardrobe her prep team assembled for her in the Capitol. This, of course, is completely out of character for Katniss, and at the conclusion of an exhausting afternoon spent playing vulnerable, arrogant, witty, mysterious, sexy and so on, she exasperatedly concedes that none of these identities suit her. She subsequently laments that, at the conclusion of her meeting with Haymitch, "I am no one at all" (p. 118).

Despite her concerns, Katniss does manage to endear herself to the television audience through a combination of humor and beauty. Prior to taking the stage, she reaches an agreement with Cinna to find him in the studio audience and respond to questions the show's host poses as if she were talking to him. Asked to model her dress at one point, Katniss observes Cinna making a subtle circular motion with his finger, as if to say "*Twirl for me*" (Collins, 2008, p. 128), which she does, much to the delight of the audience. Following her performance, however, she is disappointed by the image she cast, which she concedes amounted to little more than "[a] silly girl spinning in a sparkling dress" (p. 136).

Like Cinna and Haymitch, Peeta pressures Katniss to perform hegemonic femininity when, on the same television show, he unexpectedly confesses his unrequited love for her. Furious, she attacks him when they return to their complex. Yet when she expresses her frustration at being used, Haymitch angrily informs her:

> You are a fool .... *That boy gave you something you could never achieve on your own .... He made you look desirable.* [emphasis added] And let's face it, you can use all the help you can get in that department. You were as romantic as dirt until he said he wanted you. Now they all do. You're all they're talking about. (Collins, 2008, p. 135)

Katniss accepts his point, but is troubled by the knowledge that performing a role others prescribe for her means surrendering her autonomy. Angered by this injustice, which she attributes directly to the Hunger Games, she expresses her frustration at being made to "[hop] around like some trained dog trying to please people I hate" (p. 117).

Significantly, Collins (2008) represents Effie Trinket, the lone female character in a position to help Katniss during her stay in the Capitol, as completely ineffectual. With her make-up, stylish clothing, and her constant emphasis on proper manners, the character is a cartoonish equivalent of the "dutiful female" archetype. Throughout the novel, Effie's sole contribution of note includes teaching Katniss to walk in heels while wearing a dress, to maintain proper posture, and to smile when responding to an interviewer's questions, skills that call to mind those one might expect a beauty queen to possess. Despite her dissatisfaction with Katniss's performance in these areas, Effie persists in her mistaken belief that "if you put enough pressure on coal it turns to pearls" (p. 74). Collins likely intended this humorous slip as a sardonic comment on Effie's intellect. Nevertheless, the statement is symbolically important in that it comments directly on her prep team's efforts to transform Katniss, the daughter of a coal miner, into something other than what she is—namely, a desirable female figure.

Collectively, the influence (or *pressure*) that Cinna, Haymitch, Peeta, and, to a lesser extent, Effie, exert on Katniss suggests that she must be desired by males in order to gain the approval of her viewing audience. For this to happen, however, she has to submit to standards of beauty and behavior prescribed for her by males.

In her own words, she is "made beautiful by Cinna's hands, desirable by Peeta's confession, tragic by circumstance, and by all accounts, unforgettable" (Collins, 2008, pp. 137-138). In contrast, the male characters in the novel earn followers as a result of their strength and physical prowess, not their ability to appear physically attractive to an audience. With this in mind, Miller's (2012) assertion that gender is not an issue in Panem is complicated by the knowledge that female competitors in the Hunger Games are, in fact, held to a different standard than males. Indeed, the odds of Katniss's surviving in the arena are contingent on her meeting that standard, a task that is complicated by the knowledge that she is forced to perform under the ever-present gaze of the Capitol.

"I CAN'T SHAKE THE FEELING THAT I'M BEING WATCHED CONSTANTLY": THE PERILS OF SCIENCE AND TECHNOLOGY IN A SURVEILLANCE SOCIETY

Sambell (2004) argues that "children's dystopias seek to violently explode blind confidence in the myth that science and technology will bring about human 'progress'" by illustrating how the two "can be used to bring about oppressive, inhuman and intolerable regimes, rather than 'civilized' ones" (pp. 247-248). As explained above, ecofeminists oppose science and technology when patriarchal societies use them to control and manipulate nature (McAndrew, 1996). Through its commitment to genetic engineering, for example, the Capitol treats "the natural world as fodder to be set upon and remade into ever more grotesque and unnatural combinations" (McDonald, 2012, p. 13). Its misapplication of science and technology leads it to treat people as "fodder to be set upon and remade" in much the same way.

In *The Hunger Games*, Collins (2008) imagines a world in which any sort of ethical code that might hold scientists accountable for their work has been stripped away, leaving them free to enact whatever monstrous visions their minds are capable of producing. Similar to the Capitol wresting nature out of its original form in the act of producing "muttations," it transmutes humans into animals in what is perhaps the most obvious, and extreme, example of its controlling and dehumanizing others. Toward the end of the novel, as Katniss and Peeta prepare to confront Cato, their last remaining opponent in the arena, they are unexpectedly set upon by a pack of wolves. Almost immediately, Katniss become cognizant of the fact that the wolves are unlike any animal she has encountered—they stand on two legs, for example, and gesture to one another with their paws. Upon closer examination, she is horrified to discover that the wolves—which she correctly identifies as a new breed of muttation—resemble her fellow tributes who were killed earlier in the competition, suggesting that the Gamemakers resurrected them for the express purpose of heightening the drama surrounding the climax of the games to further titillate the viewing audience. Likewise, the Gamemakers are able to control these muttations, so that, at the press of a button, they come and go from the battlefield.

This is, of course, an extreme example of how the Capitol uses technology to dehumanize those who come under its power. More insidious are the subtler ways it exploits science and technology to manipulate those it governs. Collins (2008) reserves her sharpest criticism for what Lyon (1994) calls a "surveillance society"—that is, a society that curtails individual freedoms by subjecting people to the omnipresent gaze of the state. She is especially critical of the media, which she holds complicit in blurring the boundary between public and private through its promotion of reality television, symbolized in the novel by the Hunger Games. In Orwell's *Nineteen Eighty-Four*, the Party employs technology, represented in the form of telescreens and microphones, to monitor the public and private lives of its members. In Panem, however, surveillance has taken an even more insidious turn, as it has evolved into a popular form of entertainment. Throughout the novel, the knowledge that others watch her compels Katniss to perform gender in ways that enable her to win the favor of her viewing audience. To do so, however, she must compromise, even if temporarily, her identity as a strong, independent female.

Under the auspices of the Capitol, the citizens of Panem are denied freedom of speech, a result of the fact that the state uses cameras and other forms of surveillance technologies to monitor and control them. Hunting deep in the woods one day Gale tells Katniss, "It's to the Capitol's advantage to have us divided among ourselves" (Collins, 2008, p. 14). This is not a sentiment he would express openly in District 12 due to the ever-present threat of surveillance, suggesting that, though their lives are untenable, the residents of the districts have fallen so completely under the control of the state that they are no longer able to resist its power. Instead, they self-monitor to ensure that they present themselves in a way that is consistent with what they assume the state expects of them. In this way, surveillance technologies promote discipline by conditioning people to behavioral codes established by those in positions of authority.

The same phenomenon is discernable in the Hunger Games, as the Gamemakers exploit many of the same surveillance technologies the Capitol uses to compel discipline. In the latter case, however, surveillance constitutes a form of entertainment as much as it does a form of discipline. From the time they are selected to participate in the Hunger Games, tributes are made subject to the prying eyes of television cameras that compete to capture and document their experiences for a viewing audience. Broadcasting the games is somewhat problematic, however, given that cameras must be able to track the movements of multiple contestants simultaneously in a sizeable space. To account for this, the Gamemakers construct an environment (literally, a forest, arctic plain, desert, etc.) they can manipulate. As explained above, they are able to turn night to day, cut off the flow of streams and rivers, ignite wildfires, and so on. They also blanket the arena with an elaborate web of surveillance cameras and microphones, ensuring that they are able to monitor and capture the movements of individual contestants. As a result, contestants act with the knowledge that they are watched, a situation that calls to mind Bentham's Panopticon, an architectural structure that Foucault (1977) theorized.

Bentham designed the Panopticon, which functioned as a prison, so that authorities could monitor the behavior of inmates without their knowing when (or whether) they were being watched. In this way, the knowledge that they were *potentially* watched was presumed to motivate the inmates to self-monitor and self-discipline. A surveillance society (Lyon, 1994) functions according to a similar precept in so far as it aims to monitor and control behavior through the application of technology. As Lavoie (2011) states, "With an observer or camera virtually everywhere, one cannot presume that one is in a private sphere at any time," the result of which gives rise to "a self-propelling machine of fear, paranoia, and *watchedness*" (p. 60, emphasis in original).

As Wise (2002) explains, "the Panopticon was not reserved for Big Brother only but was to be a public space," which suggests that we not only self-discipline but also "discipline each other" (p. 30). His observation is pertinent to my argument, as reality television programming constitutes a public space, albeit one in which an audience monitors the movements of those positioned on the opposite end of a camera. This complex situation is complicated still further in Panem, however, given that the viewing audience also exists under the gaze of the state. The resultant image is a highly wrought web of watchedness in which virtually everyone, oppressor as well as oppressed, is entangled.

From the time she volunteers to take her sister Prim's place as tribute for District 12, Katniss is acutely aware of the fact that she is surveilled by cameras, the result of which exposes her not only to the prying eyes of the Capitol, but also to viewers who could potentially sponsor her in the Hunger Games. Faced with the knowledge that a sponsor could mean the difference between life and death, she elects to present herself in a way that she assumes will position her as a formidable competitor. When she bids farewell to her mother and sister, for example, she makes a conscious decision not to cry out of concern that doing so will lead her opponents to construe her as weak. Likewise, when she is injured in the arena, she resolves not to show emotion. Faced with the need to help Peeta when he is mortally wounded, however, Katniss has no alternative but to perform a role that is decidedly more foreign to her—that of a love-struck girl. In this way, the knowledge that she is watched compels her to perform hegemonic femininity (Krane, 2001) in order to accommodate her audience's expectations of her.

In District 12, Katniss showed little interest in the opposite sex. Her relationship with Gale, her male hunting partner, was by her own account plutonic, and she characterized herself as lacking the knowledge that enabled other girls to attract attention from males. To gain the support of a sponsor wealthy enough to pay for Peeta's medicine, however, Katniss has no alternative but to adopt the role of star-crossed lover in a narrative that he and Haymitch scripted for her. When she kisses Peeta for the first time, an act that is designed to elicit teary-eyed sighs from her viewing audience, Haymitch rewards her efforts with nothing more than a bowl of soup. Cognizant that he is watching her, Katniss imagines him snarling, "You're supposed to be in love, sweetheart. The boy's dying. Give me something I can work with" (Collins, 2008, p. 261). She subsequently infers that he wants her to share something personal, which she does. Later, when she confesses her feelings for Peeta for the sake of the television cameras, she imagines Haymitch exclaiming, "Yes, *that's* what I'm looking for, sweetheart" (p. 302, emphasis in original). In this way, the knowledge that she is watched by a male compels

Katniss to remake herself—or, more strongly, to regender herself—in a way that allows her to appease her audience.

Later, after Katniss and Peeta double-cross the Gamemakers, an event that I will address momentarily, she catches a reflection of herself in a plate of glass onboard the aircraft returning her to the Capitol. Taken by the image, she exclaims:

> I startle when I catch someone staring at me from only a few inches away and then realize it's my own face reflecting back in the glass. Wild eyes, hollow cheeks, my hair in a tangled mat. Rabid. Feral. Mad. (Collins, 2008, p. 348)

Cleary, Katniss's experiences in the arena dehumanized her, reducing her to the status of an animal. This is not the final imposition that she incurs at the hands of the Capitol, however. In a galling example of hubris, doctors onboard the aircraft take it upon themselves to wipe her body of all signs of physical trauma it endured in the arena. In doing so, they also remove scars and imperfections she acquired while hunting in the woods with her father and Gayle at home in District 12. Were it not for the intervention of Haymitch, the doctors would have augmented her breasts as well. The end result of their labor, coupled with the work of her prep team upon her return to the Capitol, is a distinctly feminine image. Prior to appearing on television for the final interview of the Hunger Games, Katniss describes herself in the following way:

> My hair's loose, held back by a simple hairband. The makeup rounds and fills out the sharp angles of my face. A clear polish coats my nails. The sleeveless dress is gathered at my ribs, not my waist, largely eliminating any help the padding would have given my figure. The hem falls just to my knees. Without heels, you can see my true stature. *I look, very simply, like a girl* [emphasis added]. A young one. Fourteen at the most. *Innocent. Harmless.* (Collins, p. 355)

The above image is made all the more striking by the knowledge that it stands in contrast to the image readers encountered of Katniss at the start of the novel when she appeared dressed in hunting boots, a pair of trousers, a shirt and a cap, a traditionally masculine attire.

By arguing that the presence of surveillance technology functions to regender Katniss, I am not proposing that she is completely under the control of those who watch her. Knowing that the Capitol must have a winner for their game, she and Peeta threaten to eat poisonous berries at the novel's climax, the result of which enables them to turn a surveilling eye back on their surveillors, thus ensuring their survival. Nor do Katniss's experiences in the Hunger Games eradicate all semblance of her former self. As she washes away her makeup and returns her hair to its signature braid prior to returning to District 12, she gradually experiences the sensation of "transforming back into myself" (Collins, 2008, p. 371). Nevertheless, the pressure she faced to reinvent herself in the arena—to become something other than what she was—does appear to alter her, even if only subtly, a fact that is evidenced by her struggling "to remember who I am and who I am not" (p. 371). Likewise, her awareness of being watched is heightened at the novel's conclusion.

Faced with the knowledge that her decision to challenge the Capitol's power has placed her in harm's way, a wary Katniss notes that she is unable to "shake the feeling that *I'm being watched constantly*" (p. 366, emphasis added).

BEYOND "THE BASTARD STEPSON OF REAL LITERATURE"

Gonick (2006) identifies two competing discourses—"Girl Power" and "Reviving Ophelia"—that, upon first glance, appear to offer opposing views on femininity. Upon closer examination, however, Gonick argues that each of them is problematic, a result of the fact that they "direct attention from structural explanations for inequality toward explanations of personal circumstances and personality traits" (p. 2). Read through the critical lens of ecofeminist literary theory, it is possible to appreciate Collins's (2008) *The Hunger Games* as a novel that presents readers with a "new girl" character while at the same time directing attention to the role that patriarchal institutions play in limiting the empowered subject positions that young women recognize as available to them.

Left unquestioned, narratives that celebrate "girl power" can promote a post-feminist ideological assumption that society has successfully ameliorated gender inequities, ensuring that females have access to the same opportunities and privileges as males. This assumption is dangerous, especially at a time when women continue to earn less than men, when they are frequently subjected to male violence, and when they are held to standards of beauty and desirability that potentially place their health at risk. Furthermore, there is reason to believe that while young female readers are capable of identifying characters that challenge hegemonic masculinity and femininity, they may not necessarily approve of their doing so. Having conducted a case study that examined the experiences of four preadolescent girls who read and talked about *The Hunger Games* in the context of a book club, Taber, Woloshyn, and Lane (2013) found "that the girls appeared most comfortable when the characters enacted stereotypical gendered behaviors in the book." Quoting Young (2003), the authors determined that "powerful cultural pressure still exists for young women to uphold an unrealistic standard of beauty" (Taber et al., 2013, p. 13).

In her novel, Collins (2008) captures the complexities of this problem by portraying the tensions that young women face in a culture that invites them to celebrate strong, independent female figures at the same time that it demands that they perform hegemonic femininity. In doing so, she demonstrates how an oppressive conceptual framework that leads governments and corporations to impose themselves on the environment also leads them to enact policies and legislation that actively work to oppress women. Moreover, in the spirit of ecofeminist philosophy, Collins invites readers to be less accepting of technology and, in doing so, to interrogate the role that it plays in reinforcing a patriarchal hierarchy. These are weighty issues for a young adult dystopian novel, indeed. Yet despite the fact that scholars in the field of children's literature acknowledge the literary merit of young adult fiction, it continues its quest to find legitimacy in academic settings where it remains, to quote Chris Crutcher, "the bastard stepson of real literature" (Manes, 2003, para. 2).

For the past several years I have taught an undergraduate course on young adult literature and literary theory. One of the assignments for the course requires students to interview secondary school librarians about young adult authors and titles that are popular with adolescent readers, as well as changing trends the librarians discern in the field of young adult literature. In recent years students have consistently returned to my class and reported that speculative fiction—specifically, young adult dystopian fiction, fantasy, and horror (e.g., werewolves, vampires, and zombies)—constitutes the most popular genre with students. This past year, however, as secondary schools near the university where I work implemented the Common Core State Standards, some librarians lamented that, in spite of speculative fiction's appeal to adolescents, teachers opted not to allow them to read it for independent reading assignments due to the fact that they didn't believe the genre was sufficiently challenging.

Young adult literature's status as popular culture, coupled with the knowledge that it is ostensibly written for adolescents, may lead some critics to dismiss the genre as low culture. Young adult dystopian fiction is at even greater disadvantage, given that it is branded pejoratively as *genre fiction*. As the ecofeminist reading of *The Hunger Games* that I have offered in this chapter demonstrates, however, young adult dystopian fiction participates in social criticism with the intention of foregrounding obstacles that otherwise taken-for-granted institutions place in the path of human happiness. In doing so, it invites readers to imagine other ways of interacting with the world and other possible social relationships. In this way, it participates in the goals of literature with a capital "L." Indeed, as Booker (1994) argues, "If the main value of literature in general is its ability to make us see the world in new ways, to make us capable of entertaining new and different perspectives on reality, then dystopian fiction is not a marginal genre" (p. 176). Read through the lens of critical theory, it is possible to appreciate young adult dystopian fiction as a potentially complex, multilayered form of literature that, to borrow from Aristotle, is capable of instructing at the same time that it delights. In the end, the perceived value and complexity of young adult dystopian literature may depend as much on the questions that we, as readers, ask of individual novels as it does on the novels themselves.

REFERENCES

Bennett, B. (2005). Through ecofeminist eyes: Le Guin's "The Ones Who Walk Away from Omelas." *The English Journal, 94*(6), 63-68.

Booker, M. K. (1994). *The dystopian impulse in modern literature: Fiction as social criticism.* Westport, CT: Greenwood.

Collins, S. (2008). *The hunger games.* New York: Scholastic.

Connors, S. P. (2013). Challenging perspectives on young adult literature. *The English Journal, 102*(5), 69-73.

Daniels, C. L. (2006). Literary theory and young adult literature: The open frontier in critical studies. *The ALAN Review, 33*(2), 78-82.

Foucault, M. (1977). *Discipline and punish: The birth of the prison.* New York: Pantheon Books.

Friere, P., & Macedo, D. (1987). *Literacy: Reading the word & the world.* South Hadley, MA: Bergin & Garvey.

Glasgow, J. N. (2001). Teaching social justice through young adult literature. *The English Journal, 90*(6), 54-61.

Gonick, M. (2006). Between "girl power" and "reviving Ophelia": Constituting the neo-liberal girl subject. *NWSA Journal, 8*(2), 2-23.

Krane, V. (2001). We can be athletic and feminine, but do we want to? Challenging hegemonic femininity in women's sport. *Quest, 53*(1), 115-133.

Lavoie, D. (2011). Escaping the panopticon: Utopia, hegemony, and performance in Peter Weir's *The Truman Show. Utopian Studies, 22*(1), 52-73.

Leggo, C. (1998). Open(ing) texts: Deconstruction and responding to poetry. *Theory Into Practice, 37*(3), 186-192.

Lyon, D. (1994). *The electronic eye: The rise of surveillance society.* Minneapolis: University of Minnesota Press.

Madill, L. (2008). Gendered identities explored: The Lord of the Rings as a text of alternative ways of being. *ALAN Review, 35*(2), 43-49.

Manes, B. (2003). Writing it really real. *Orlando Weekly.* Retrieved from http://www2.orlandoweekly.com/news/story.asp?id=3056

McAndrew, D. A. (1996). Ecofeminism and the teaching of literacy. *College Composition and Communication, 47*(3), 367-382.

McDonald, B. (2012). The final word on entertainment: Mimetic and monstrous art in The Hunger Games. In G. A. Dunn & N. Michaud (Eds.), *The Hunger Games and philosophy: A critique of pure treason* (pp. 8-25). Hoboken, NJ: Wiley.

Merchant, C. (1983/1980). *The death of nature: Women, ecology, and the scientific revolution.* San Francisco: Harper & Row.

Miller, J. (2012). "She has no idea. The effect she can have." Katniss and the politics of gender. In G. A. Dunn & N. Michaud (Eds.), *The Hunger Games and philosophy: A critique of pure treason* (pp. 145-161). Hoboken, NJ: Wiley.

Miller, S. J., & Slifkin, J. M. (2010). "Similar literary quality": Demystifying the AP English literature and composition open question. *The ALAN Review, 37*(2), 6-16.

Murphy, P. D. (1995). *Literature, nature, and other: Ecofeminist critiques.* Albany: State University of New York Press.

Sambell, K. (2004). Carnivalizing the future: A new approach to theorizing childhood and adulthood in science fiction for young readers. *The Lion and the Unicorn, 28*(2), 247-267.

Soter, A. O., & Connors, S. P. (2009). Beyond relevance to literary merit: Young adult literature as 'Literature.' *The ALAN Review, 37*(1), 62-67.

Taber, N., Woloshyn, V., & Lane, L. (2013). 'She's more like a guy' and 'he's more like a teddy bear': Girls' perception of violence and gender in The Hunger Games. *Journal of Youth Studies*, 1-16.

Ward, B. A., & Young, T. A. (2009). Brave, determined, and strong: Books for girls (and sometimes boys). *Reading Horizons, 49*(3), 257-268.

Warren, K. J. (2000). *Ecofeminist philosophy: A western perspective on what it is and why it matters.* Lanham: Rowman & Littlefield.

Wise, J. M. (2002). Mapping the culture of control: Seeing through The Truman Show. *Television New Media, 3*(1), 29-47.

Wolk, S. (2009). Reading for a better world: Teaching for social responsibility with young adult literature. *Journal of Adolescent & Adult Literacy, 52*(8), 664-673.

RODRIGO JOSEPH RODRÍGUEZ

9. "WE END OUR HUNGER FOR JUSTICE!"

Social Responsibility in The Hunger Games *Trilogy*

Everyone laughed at the impossibility of it,
 but also the truth. Because who would believe
 the fantastic and terrible story of all of our survival
 those who were never meant
  to survive? (Harjo, 2008, p. 5)

The telling of stories through literature, especially through adventurous, post-apocalyptic novels with death-defying odds and trials, serves the purpose of informing readers about other worlds and introducing them to societies they may recognize as resembling their own. Young adult dystopias in particular offer readers an opportunity to question the social conditions that adults have created for them, including those that, whether as a result of bigotry, prejudice, or ignorance, condemn people to endure inhumane treatment and wretched conditions. Essentially, young adult dystopias place a mirror before readers, challenging them to examine the world they inhabit and the obstacles it places on the path to social justice. Recognizing this, it is necessary for educators to create opportunities for students to read young adult dystopias critically with the goal of examining not only how they chronicle the human struggle, but also how they advocate liberating people from otherwise disempowering social conditions.

Although it can be read and enjoyed as a fast paced action adventure story, Suzanne Collin's Hunger Games trilogy, like other works in the dystopian genre, depicts real-world problems such as war, violence, and economic disparities with the intention of challenging readers to examine the extent to which they are complicit in helping sustain them. The work of literacy educators who choose to teach Collins' novels is consequently to figure out how they can best guide students in examining their lives with the intention of helping them to explore their identities, identify injustices, and become more socially conscious, responsible stewards of the rapidly changing world they inhabit. This sort of teaching—which I call socially conscious pedagogy—prepares students to resist oppressive power structures and, like mockingjays, triumph with resilience in the face of difficult circumstances.

Dystopian novels explore intersections of control, power, and privilege. These texts can be frightening, offering stern warnings about forthcoming destruction on a global scale unless action is taken to establish a new course for society. Moreover, they leave readers to question the intricacies of power and how it informs the choices available to people. Much has been written about the power of

S. P. Connors (ed.), The Politics of Panem, 157–165.
© *2014 Sense Publishers. All rights reserved.*

young adult literature to foster engagement (see, for example, Nilsen & Donelson, 2009). In the case of young adult dystopias, adolescents may well see themselves represented in characters to the point that they become engrossed in their plight. This is important. So too, however, is encouraging developing readers to read young adult dystopias critically, as doing so creates opportunities for them to heighten their consciousness about social justice issues in both the texts they read and the world in which they live.

In depicting social problems, what do young adult dystopian novels aim to accomplish? According to Basu, Broad, and Hintz (2013):

> YA dystopias are sensitive registers to the explosion of information that characterizes contemporary society, and to the atmosphere of conspiracy that pervades popular political discourse. Many novels feature an awakening, sudden or gradual, to the truth of what has really been going on .... Access to information is often dangerous, but it is repeatedly presented as the only way to become free. (p. 4)

In my own work, I am concerned with how young adult dystopias such as Collins's Hunger Games trilogy work to "awaken" readers to social problems and instill in them a sense of social consciousness. One must be able to name one's reality, after all, and articulate one's position in society to gain a sense of self. This process is facilitated through one's exposure to critical, socially responsible literacies. Coming into consciousness calls for new ways of seeing and understanding the complexity of the world. It also entails searching for ways to work within and, if necessary, to subvert existing power structures to act for change. In sum, a socially just society is one that values and upholds human rights. It is one in which the dignity of every human being is valued. Everyone deserves equal economic, political, and social rights. Literature represents a vehicle that writers have historically used to work toward these ends.

As readers familiar with the Hunger Games trilogy know, the citizens of Panem are deprived of basic rights such as free speech, the ability to move about freely, the freedom to labor where they wish, and the ability to ensure the welfare and safety of their families. The Capitol's use of the Hunger Games, a gladiatorial-like competition akin to contemporary reality television, was introduced to punish those who challenged the Capitol's power. To do so, it pits teenagers against each other in violent situations in which they are made to kill or be killed for the entertainment of an elite class. The futuristic society that Collins envisions is in turmoil as a result of war and violence, and impoverished families are torn apart by the oppressive policies of a totalitarian government. In the Capitol, meanwhile, a privileged class enjoys access to a range of comforts and leisure activities. Moreover, the material resources that they enjoy are produced on the backs of those whom the Capitol has colonized. By choosing to represent Panem in this way, Collins offers a scathing indictment of the economic and social conditions that divide people in the United States at the time of this writing.

In this chapter, I will examine how the Capitol, through its enactment of control, power, and privilege, functions to create a subjugated citizenry that is alienated from itself. To accomplish this, the Capitol relies on a variety of strategies, including a relentless propaganda campaign designed to obfuscate the truth, the use of entertainment to blind people to social and political problems, and mechanisms that function to divide those it governs against themselves. In Katniss Everdeen, however, Panem finds a hero who is socially conscious and who offers readers a model of resistance. In doing so, she provides a vision of a future in which the people's eyes will open and "the sun will rise" (Collins, 2008, p. 234). Often, Katniss's acts of resistance do not entail awe-inspiring acts of bravery and heroism. To the contrary, she more often engages in minor acts of resistance that inspire others to come together as a collective and work for change. Collins's message is clear: only by becoming socially conscious and working together can people liberate themselves from the chains of oppression.

How can educators support students in exploring the Hunger Games trilogy not as an action adventure story, but as a form of social critique? The answer, I suggest, is to create opportunities for them to read Collins's novels critically. According to Selvester and Summers (2012), "Critical literacy gives us a way to read to resist rather than to accept, and to write to reconstruct rather than to regurgitate" (p. 9). Selvester and Summers argue that the main goal of socially responsible pedagogy is to "enable teachers and students to use literacy to support critical self-determination and develop the tools to act in morally, socially, and politically responsible ways" (p. 26). In the remainder of this chapter, I examine how characters in the Hunger Games trilogy, through seemingly minor acts of resistance, exemplify the sort of social consciousness that Selvester and Summers argue is necessary for people to act "in morally, socially, and politically responsible ways."

LOOSENING THE BONDS OF TYRANNY: SOCIAL AWARENESS AND RESPONSIBILITY

A central theme in Collins's trilogy emphasizes the importance of developing a social consciousness and becoming cognizant of inequities that are attributable to oppressive policies. In Panem, the reaping process wherein tributes are selected to participate in the Hunger Games takes the form of a lottery system not unlike the one that was used to draft soldiers during the Vietnam War. Because the poor have the opportunity to enter their names in the lottery multiple times in exchange for a "tesserae"—a small allotment of grain beyond that which they would customarily receive from the government—they are more likely than the rich to be chosen as tributes. Unlike "Career Tributes," who are selected from wealthier districts that have historically curried the Capitol's favor, and who have been trained to accept its ideology unquestioningly, tributes from Panem's poorer districts often lack the training that would enhance their chances of surviving the Hunger Games. As a result, the probability of their dying in the arena is exponentially greater.

For Katniss, however, the challenge of growing up under harsh conditions prepared her for the arena. Indeed, necessity required that she become more resourceful at a young age. Faced with the need to provide for her family, she had to hunt, apply her survival skills, and cope with the challenges her society posed for her. She learned to cope when her life was unexpectedly turned upside down by a series of catastrophes. Katniss adopted the role of surrogate parent and household breadwinner, for example, after her father was "trapped [in a mine], unable to reach sunlight, buried forever in the darkness" (Collins, 2008, p. 59). Having lost her husband, Katniss's mother in turn fell into a deep "immobilizing sadness ... a sickness" (p. 36) that impaired her ability to care for her daughters. Familial circumstances thus instilled in Katniss a level of resilience. More importantly, they imbued her with a burgeoning sense of social consciousness, as she was forced to look past her own interests in order to tend to the needs of her sister and mother.

In the essay "What Good Is Literature in Our Time?", Anaya (1998), reflecting on the relevance of literature to society, states, "We live in a time of transition, a time in which the human spirit can either be crushed or in which it can be transformed into a new level of consciousness" (p. 471). The importance of attaining "a new level of consciousness" in order to avoid falling prey to despair is emphasized time and time again in Collins's trilogy. Forced to compete in the Hunger Games with the knowledge that only one person can be crowned victor and survive the carnage and destruction, tributes certainly have good reason to despair. Katniss experiences feelings of alienation herself as she performs the roles of both hunter and hunted in the arena. Continually faced with the threat of death, Katniss in some ways becomes desensitized to it. As she states, "Gale and I agree that if we have to choose between dying of hunger and a bullet in the head, the bullet would be much quicker" (Collins, 2008, p. 17).

Katniss does not, however, succumb to despair. Rather, she exemplifies the sort of heightened consciousness for which Anaya (1998) advocates. Although she might appear indifferent to politics, she is very much aware of her role as a pawn in the Capitol's system. She is cognizant, for example, that her experiences in school are designed to prepare her for a lifetime spent laboring in the Capitol's coalmines. Likewise, she appreciates how the Capitol manipulates language to mask the truth:

> It's mostly a lot of blather about what we owe the Capitol. I know there must be more than what they're telling us, an actual account of what happened during the rebellion. But I don't spend much time thinking about it. Whatever the truth is, I don't see how it will help me get food on the table. (Collins, 2008, p. 42)

Schooling and education are slanted in the Capitol's favor in Panem, as they are ideologically motivated and function to obfuscate the truth. In Panem, critical literacy is absent from the curriculum given the Capitol's desire to maintain control, order, and power. As a result, most people in the districts are unable to see through the state-sanctioned narratives that are imposed on them. Due to her social consciousness, Katniss stands out as an exception.

Although Katniss demonstrates an ability to see through the official narratives the Capitol disseminates to control people in the districts, she occasionally falls victim to the ploys of those who would manipulate her:

I can never get around the fact that District 13 was instrumental in 12's destruction. This doesn't absolve me of blame—there's plenty of blame to go around. But without them, I would not have been part of the larger plot to overthrow the Capitol or had the wherewithal to do it. (Collins, 2010, p. 6)

In the world of Panem, the ability to see through institutional narratives that work to perpetuate the status quo and make oppression possible is crucial. Indeed, Collins seems to suggest that a challenge for those interested in creating a just society with democratic participation is figuring out how to prepare people to think critically.

As explained above, Collins's trilogy, like other works of dystopian fiction, invites readers to become more socially conscious by encouraging them to consider how the problems that characters in a storyworld face are manifest in the world that readers inhabit. In doing so, it encourages them to interrogate concepts such as power and privilege. In an interview, Collins, highlighting a series of social issues that she understood herself to explore in the Hunger Games series, states:

The sociopolitical overtones of *The Hunger Games* were very intentionally created to characterize current and past world events, including the use of hunger as a weapon to control populations. Tyrannical governments have also used the techniques of geographical containment of certain populations, as well as the nearly complete elimination of the rights of the individual. (Blasingame, 2009, p. 726)

Over the course of the series Katniss discovers that she is not alone in her disdain for the Capitol's oppressive politics. As the series progresses, readers discover, along with Katniss, that people elsewhere hold similar perspectives about the Capitol. Over the course of the trilogy, as Katniss acknowledges the social historical conditions that have worked to subjugate people in Panem, she becomes more willing to challenge them. It should be noted, however, that her ability to do so is attributable to her seeing through state-sanctioned propaganda that works to detract people's attention from serious social problems. This includes the Capitol's reliance on the Hunger Games as a form of entertainment.

As readers know, the Capitol implemented the Hunger Games to incite fear among the districts and to dissuade them from rebelling as they had in the past. The Gamemakers incite terror by subjecting viewers to the horrors of watching teenagers murder other teenagers. These atrocities are captured by a series of surveillance cameras that are carefully positioned in the arenas in which the Games take place, and they are in turn broadcast throughout Panem. Those who inhabit the districts experience agony and anguish as they are forced, under penalty of death, to watch their loved ones meet their demise on television screens. For the citizens of the Capitol, however, who live in comfort, the Hunger Games constitute a form of entertainment. Capitol audiences savor the pleasure of observing a slow, drawn out death such as Cato's at the Cornucopia, as it prolongs the Hunger Games and satiates their barbarism. In this way the savagery of the Games is not unlike the gladiatorial games of the Roman Empire, or the violent videogames that many adolescents interact with today. Once again, Collins invites readers to examine contemporary social issues, in this case challenging them to question the morality of a society that relishes (and actively breeds) violence. At the same time, she invites readers to examine their own complicity in perpetuating this problem. They are, after all, reading a novel about teenagers murdering other teenagers, presumably for entertainment. Like Katniss, who, having spent years "watching tributes starve, freeze, bleed, and dehydrate to death" (Collins, 2008, p. 169), is alienated from the brutalities she must commit, Collins seems to suggest that contemporary audiences are also desensitized to violence.

Throughout the Hunger Games trilogy, the Capitol uses propaganda and entertainment to oppress people. That it does so effectively is evidenced by the fact that the residents of the districts regard themselves as having little to no control over their futures. Collins message is clear: to maintain order one has only to strip people of their social consciousness. To retain the ability to think critically and ask questions is to reserve the power to challenge the status quo and replace it with a new social order.

ENVISIONING A NEW REPUBLIC

Throughout the Hunger Games trilogy, Katniss is instrumental in establishing a new social order that will presumably be more democratic and just for all citizens. It is one in which the right to make choices and secure basic necessities is available to everyone. In the third volume of Collins's trilogy, *Mockingjay*, Katniss reflects on an exchange she had with Plutarch Heavensbee, an architect of the revolution who shared his desire to see the tyranny of the Capitol replaced with a representative democracy not unlike one their ancestors enjoyed. All too familiar with the world her elders have left her, however, Katniss is understandably dubious:

> Frankly, our ancestors don't seem much to brag about. I mean, look at the state they left us in, with the wars and the broken planet. Clearly, they didn't care about what would happen to the people who came after them. But this republic idea sounds like an improvement over our current government. (Collins, 2010, p. 84)

To some extent, Katniss appreciates that the divisions the Capitol manages to forge between districts, as well as within districts, function to disempower people. To escape the tyranny of the Capitol, and to build the sort of republic that Plutarch envisions, Katniss realizes that the districts must be willing to set aside their differences in order to work toward a common good. As the excerpt above suggests, this is not something that adults in Panem have been able to do in the past. Ultimately, Collins seems to believe that the work of building a more equitable world is a project that ultimately falls to the young.

Throughout the trilogy, Collins suggests that the ability to create a more equitable and just world is contingent on people working together as a collective. This is evident, for example, when Panem's previous victors, forced by the Capitol to enter the arena for a second time in the 75th Hunger Games, "join hands .... [A]ll twenty-four of us stand in one unbroken line in what must be the first public show of unity among the districts since the Dark Days" (Collins, 2009, p. 258). Confronted with this unprecedented (and very public) act of resistance, the Gamemakers have no alternative but to terminate the broadcast. Before they are able to do so, however, the viewing audience throughout Panem witnesses the tributes' show of solidarity. Collins's message is clear: only by working together can people hope to effect change.

In a totalitarian government, a single power aims to divide people and control all aspects of public and private life. In *Catching Fire* (Collins, 2009), President Snow unexpectedly visits Katniss at her home in the Victors' Village. His visit reveals the precarious position that she placed herself in by aligning forces with Peeta in the arena and threatening to commit suicide by consuming poisonous berries. It also suggests that the pair's actions afforded them a measure of power. President Snow's questions confirm that he regards Katniss as a threat to the Capitol's power because she did not play by the established protocol. In an attempt to dissuade her from committing similar transgressions in the future, he cautions her:

[U]prisings have been known to lead to revolution. Do you have any idea what that would mean? How many people would die? What conditions those left would have to face? Whatever problems anyone may have with the Capitol, believe me when I say that if it released its grip on the districts for even a short time, the entire system would collapse. (Collins, 2009, p. 21)

Snow's words go unheeded, however, as Katniss eventually emerges as the dystopian hero who, as a result of her continued acts of resistance, manages to inspire a rebellion in the districts.

Throughout the series actions that are ultimately instrumental in bringing down the Capitol begin as quiet acts of collective resistance. At the reaping during which Katniss and Peeta are chosen to participate in their first Hunger Games, for example, the residents of District 12 refuse to applaud their selection. Katniss states, "So instead of acknowledging applause, I stand there unmoving while they take part in the boldest form of dissent they can manage. Silence. Which says we do not agree. We do not condone. All of this is wrong" (Collins, 2008, p. 24). Later, after she arrives in the Capitol, Katniss's ability to survive the Hunger Games and emerge as a symbol of the rebellion is facilitated by her relationship with Cinna, her stylist. After a dress that Cinna designed for her prior to her entering the arena for a second time captures the attention of Panem by making a bold political statement, Katniss acknowledges that "Cinna turned me into a mockingjay" (Collins, 2009, p. 252). The revolution was not, in other words, attributable to a single individual. Instead, it was a result of people working together to support one another.

Quiet forms of resistance and civil disobedience are evident elsewhere in the trilogy. In the opening chapter of *The Hunger Games*, readers witness Katniss break the rules by entering the woods to hunt, a form of trespassing. A "high chain-link fence topped with barbed-wire loops" (Collins, 2008, p. 4) and charged with an electric current isolates District 12 from the outside world in much the same way that fences used during World War II confined prisoners of the Holocaust to concentration camps. While the official narrative advanced by the Capitol suggests that the fence was installed as a way to keep wild animals from entering District 12, the residents of District 12 understand that it was designed to prevent people from running away. Because many of them, including the Peacekeepers, are dependent on the game Katniss provides, however, they choose to turn a blind eye on her forays into the woods, which itself constitutes an act of resistance.

Although Collins advocates working together to combat social injustices, she is not naïve enough to believe that people can ever completely overcome them. Rather, she treats the fight for equity and fairness as one that must continually be waged. When, at the end of the revolution, Plutarch Heavensbee comments on the prospect of Panem's enjoying future peace, he cautions Katniss, "Now we're in that sweet period where everyone agrees that our recent horror should never be repeated. But collective thinking is usually short-lived." He continues, stating, "We're fickle, stupid beings with poor memories and a great gift for self-destruction. Although who knows? Maybe this will be it, Katniss." (Collins, 2010, p. 379). A realist to the end, Plutarch's words serve as a reminder that destruction looms if people are not vigilant in maintaining their sense of history and a sense of social consciousness.

CONCLUSION

Critical literacy aims to equip people with the tools necessary to name the reality they live and challenge the oppressive conditions they face. Critical readers are able to step back from texts such as those that comprise Suzanne Collins's Hunger Games series and examine the intersections of power and control not only in those texts, but also in the world they inhabit. In doing so, readers might reach a conclusion akin to that of Alsup (2014), who states:

> When reading a book like [*The Hunger Games*], which is essentially a novel about a girl's life as a character in a reality TV show, the teen reader vicariously experiences the games on at least three levels: as a citizen of Panem and an audience for a reality show, as Katniss herself who struggles within the games, and as an objective reader of a book by Suzanne Collins about both. Whether we like it or not, such fragmented and layered experiences of reality are perhaps more the norm of today's teens than the exception, despite our culture's prevailing myth of the unitary, stable self. (p. 29)

If, as Alsup suggests, readers do experience the trilogy on three levels, then the need for them to come into consciousness—that is, to "wake up" and maintain a sense of self-awareness—is imperative. With this in mind, educators interested in teaching Collins's novels would do well to ask how they can best support students in questioning the issues she raises while working to heighten their sense of social consciousness.

As teachers, we can connect students with literature that heightens their awareness of their responsibility to work for change, equality, and equity. At the same time, however, we must equip them with the tools they need to read those texts critically. Selvester and Summers (2012) argue that for "teachers and students to participate fully as informed citizens, they must develop literacy knowledge— skills and abilities that make them capable of acting on behalf of themselves and others to nurture a just society (p. 150). Social justice is accessible to all students and teachers when they collaborate as responsible, socially conscious people.

According to Hill (2014), "When adolescent readers can recognize and articulate the constructs of a text, they have become empowered" (p. 17). To equip adolescents with critical reading skills that allow them to act in a world that merits equality, equity, and justice for all is to empower them. In an attempt to make connections and build a conscious and responsible citizenry, many authors of children's, young adult, new adult, and adult narratives use literature to awaken souls and enact change in a world that is rife with injustices and inequities. In that sense, literature is interconnected with our everyday experiences. It holds the promise of greater social responsibility, and it has the potential to transform readers into agents for change, leading them to see the world anew. Recognizing this, educators need to create opportunities for students to enter storyworlds such as the one Collins constructs in the Hunger Games—that is, storyworlds which call on readers to think and act boldly, and which invite them, like Katniss, to become more socially responsible citizens.

REFERENCES

Alsup, J. (2014). More than a 'time of stress and storm': The complex depiction of adolescent identity in contemporary young adult novels. In C. Hill (Ed.), *The critical merits of young adult literature: Coming of age* (pp. 28-37). New York: Routledge.

Anaya, R. A. (1998). What good is literature in our time? *American Literary History*, *10*(3), 471-477.

Basu, B., Broad, K. R., & Hintz, C. (2013). Introduction. In B. Basu, K. R. Broad, & C. Hintz (Eds.), *Contemporary dystopian fiction for young adults: Brave new teenagers* (pp. 1-17). New York: Routledge.

Blasingame, J. (2009). An interview with Suzanne Collins. *Journal of Adolescent & Adult Literacy*, *52*(8), 726-727.

Collins, S. (2008). *The hunger games*. New York: Scholastic.

Collins, S. (2009). *Catching fire*. New York: Scholastic.

Collins, S. (2010). *Mockingjay*. New York: Scholastic.

Harjo, J. (2008). *She had some horses: Poems*. New York: W. W. Norton & Company, Inc.

Hill, C. (Ed.). (2014). *The critical merits of young adult literature: Coming of age*. New York: Routledge.

Nilsen, A. P., & Donelson, K. L. (2009). *Literature for today's young adults* (8th ed.). Boston: Allyn and Bacon.

Selvester, P. M., & Summers, D. G. (2012). *Socially responsible literacy: Teaching adolescents for purpose and power*. New York: Teachers College Press.

PART FOUR

"That's a Wrap": Films, Fandom, and the Politics of Social Media

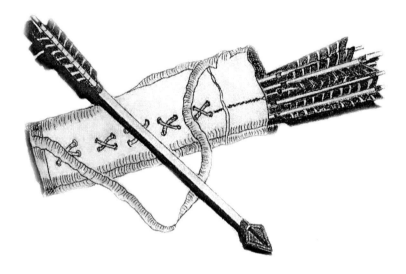

HILARY BREWSTER

10. "SHE HAS NO IDEA. THE EFFECT SHE CAN HAVE"

A Rhetorical Reading of The Hunger Games

First person narration is commonplace in young adult literature. Many award-winning titles—for example, Sherman Alexie's (2007) *The Absolutely True Diary of a Part-Time Indian, Speak* by Laurie Halse Anderson (1999), and *Feed* by M. T. Anderson (2002), among others—are written in this particular narrative mode. Some argue that the prevalence of this narration and the popularity of young adult literature have established first person as the preferred technique (Schuhmann, 1999, p. 314). Yet the first-person narrator—or homodiegetic single focalizer—almost always narrates events retrospectively or in the historical present tense.[1] In the Hunger Games trilogy, however, Suzanne Collins chooses to have her protagonist, Katniss Everdeen, narrate in the simultaneous present tense (often just referred to as present tense), which has an altogether different effect and impact on "readerly dynamics" (Phelan, 2005a).

If we accept for the moment that narrative is "somebody telling somebody else on some occasion and for some purpose(s) that something happened" (Phelan, 2007, p. 3), then the relationship between when the narrator *experienced* the events in relation to when the events *occurred* matters significantly. Retrospective narration is comprised of a narrator who tells about events some time after those events have occurred; it also foregrounds the cognitive and experiential differences between the experiencing-I and the narrating-I (DelConte, 2007, p. 428). In laymen's terms, the narrator already knows the outcome of the events that she is about to relay, which impacts the ethics and motivations of the ways and means of the telling (as constructed by the implied author). This method of narration can highlight how—if at all—the narrator has been impacted by the events that she has experienced, while also tying events together thematically. In young adult literature, this is a technique that authors commonly use in coming-of-age (or *bildungsroman)* masterplots. Historical present tense narration varies only slightly: the narrator tells of past events, but uses the present tense to do so. This technique allows the narrator to tell her story as if she were currently experiencing it, and often enhances the immediacy of her memories of the events (DelConte, 2007, p. 248).

By distinction, simultaneous present tense narration occurs when the narrating-I and the experiencing-I are merged, and the narrator is telling the reader about events as they happen:

S. P. Connors (ed.), The Politics of Panem, 169–188.

This narrative strategy, the homodiegetic simultaneous present, places the reader in a very different relationship to ... the events of his narrative than would any kind of retrospective account. The strategy takes teleology away from the [narrator's] narrative acts: since he does not know how the events will turn out, he cannot be shaping the narrative according to his knowledge of the end. Consequently, we cannot read with our usual tacit assumptions that the narrator, however unself-conscious, has some direction in mind for his tale. Instead, as we read any one moment of the narrative we must assume that the future is always—and radically—wide open: the narrator's guess about what will happen next is really no better than our own. (Phelan, 1994, p. 223)

Working with the tools of rhetorical narrative theory in this chapter, I first explore the myriad ways in which the aforementioned narrative strategy—simultaneous present tense narration—forces the reader to consider how several important elements of narrative inherent in Chatman's (1978) communication model—a key component to this critical approach which acknowledges the implied author, narratee, and authorial audience (implied reader)—are impacted. Next, I examine how Suzanne Collins (2008) uses this particular technique in *The Hunger Games* to complicate issues like reader judgment and engagement, and the doubly-layered rhetorical situation, all of which affect issues of audience and ethics. I conclude the chapter by discussing how the tools of narrative theory, specifically focalization, impact the ethics and audience of the film adaptation of the novel. First, however, I want to outline the rhetorical model of narrative and make the case for why it is a useful critical framework for examining literature, and the Hunger Games series in particular.

THE RHETORICAL MODEL OF NARRATIVE

Chatman's (1978) communication model, referenced above, serves as the skeleton for the rhetorical approach to narrative, or narrative as the art of communication. This model—though it has been criticized recently for some basic insufficiencies— is status quo in narrative theory and especially the rhetorical approach. As shown below, Chatman's model conceptualizes narrative transmission as follows:

Actual author→ implied author→(narrator)→(narratee)→implied reader →actual reader

Though a bit of an oversimplification, the components inside the box are derived from the text, and the two within parentheses are fictional constructs. Booth (1961/1983), believing that the art of literature as communication had been long ignored by critics, pushed this concept further by arguing that narrative is a thoroughly *rhetorical* act of communication in which the narrator and types of narration are selected by an author to engage in a particular type of rhetoric. The degree to which an author is successful at producing a particular emotional and ethical effect is related to her technical and aesthetic choices.

The terms actual author, actual reader, and narrator likely do not need clarification, and in the following section I focus on the narratee, but I want to briefly define the other two components. Citing Booth (1961/1983), Nünning (2005) writes that "the implied author is thus not a technical or formal device, but the source of the beliefs, norms, and purposes of the text, the origin of its meaning ... the implied author imposes his or her ... intention, beliefs, and norms and values ..." (p. 239). More simply, the implied author is the *sense* of the author one gets from reading the text, regardless of the persona of the *actual* author. The implied reader is, therefore, in a way the inverse of the implied author: it is the "most perfect" reader of a given text, based on the text itself. While of course individual flesh-and-blood readers will vary in their response to a text, the implied reader is one who takes on the intentions and beliefs of the implied author. Naturally, this has tricky ethical implications—I imagine most of us do not want to be the implied reader of *The Birth of a Nation* or *Mein Kampf*—but as an element of the communication model, it serves as the textual referent that unites the readership of the text.

Rabinowitz (1977), dissatisfied with the extant binary of implied reader and actual reader, re-examined the role of the audience and developed the idea of the narrative audience, who believes the narrative to be "true"; i.e., when we read Snow White, we have to believe in magic spells and dwarves or the whole story is a sham. Individual readers need to be—and generally are—in the narrative and authorial audiences simultaneously: we need to believe that the world of the text is real and realize that it is constructed all at the same time. Put another way, if we did not immerse ourselves in J. K. Rowling's storyworld, why would we be sad, or maybe even shed real tears, when Dumbledore dies? Yet we also logically understand that our immersion does not make Hogwarts real.

Building on these ideas, Rabinowitz (1987) later developed "the tacit conventions that govern readers' interpretations and evaluations of narrative" (Phelan, 2005b, p. 503). These are the rules of notice, signification, configuration, and coherence. Rabinowitz (1987) argues that we pay attention to certain aspects of narrative (titles, threats, disruptions, etc.), attend to those knowing they are important, put them together as the narrative unfolds, and then, when we are finished, see how all of the parts make up an aesthetic and ethical whole. While these interpretive strategies are specifically for the reader, literary conventions—rules of genre, etc.—are also important for the author.

Both Booth (1961/1983) and Rabinowitz (1977, 1987) place equal importance on the author, reader, and text. Phelan (2007), too, argues that a text's meaning is derived from a constant feedback loop among implied author, textual phenomena, and reader response (p. 18). We judge characters, develop hopes and expectations, construct hypotheses, etc. as we read, and in turn those are confirmed or denied and the process continues. We also make ethical judgments about the narrator in relation to the telling and the told—what happens and how/when we learn about it—and our own personal sets of beliefs and values. This accounts for the differences in individual evaluations, but also for our shared interpretive experiences.

Admittedly, I have not touched on every aspect of the rhetorical approach to narrative. The late Booth, Rabinowitz, and Phelan are not the only theorists contributing to this particular methodology, nor have I outlined every argument made by these three scholars. However, it is the equal importance placed on author, text, and reader, along with the elements of ethics and judgment, that not only drew me to this particular critical approach, but also make it a good fit for analyzing Collins's (2008) novel *The Hunger Games* given her choice in narrative strategy and the disturbing ethics (or lack thereof) inherent in her storyworld.

NARRATING PANEM

As mentioned earlier, many components of Chatman's (1978) communication model have been challenged and debated in scholarship. Chief among these— perhaps only second to the concept of the implied author—is that of the narratee: the fictional entity to whom the narrator is relaying her information. In many first-person texts, the narratee is relegated to the background so quickly that the reader quickly forgets he exists, as in Salinger's (1951) *The Catcher in the Rye*. On the other hand, epistolary fiction, like *The Perks of Being a Wall-Flower* (Chobsky, 1999) foregrounds the narratee with the use of Charlie's "Dear Friend," while others, like *Carbon Diaries: 2015* (Lloyd, 2009) use the reveal of the narratee— Laura's cousin—as a plot device. Many first-person narrators break the fourth wall, referring to the reader as "you" and causing the narratee to blend with the implied reader, much like the narrator and implied author can move closer together or farther apart. However, what becomes of the narratee in instances of present tense narration? Can there be one at all? And how does this impact the "... telling somebody else on some occasion and for some purpose" definition of narrative established above? (Phelan, 2007, p. 3). In this section, I examine this question in relation to *The Hunger Games*.

Collins (2008) opens her novel thusly:

> When I wake up, the other side of the bed is cold. My fingers stretch out, seeking Prim's warmth but finding only the rough canvas cover of the mattress. She must have had bad dreams and climbed in with our mother. Of course she did. This is the day of the reaping. (p. 3)

In this opening paragraph, the reader learns some important pieces of information: the narrator has a sister named Prim; their father is likely not in the picture ("our mother" not "our parents"); and whatever "the reaping" is, it brings on nightmares. That the narrator and her sister are sharing a mattress with a "rough canvas cover" clues us in, perhaps, to their relatively low socioeconomic status. Of course, we do not learn the narrator's name, and won't for four more pages[2] when she reaches the woods to meet Gale, her hunting partner; he greets her by using her nickname, leading the narrator to explain, "[M]y real name is Katniss, but when I first told him, I had barely whispered it. So he thought I'd said Catnip" (Collins, 2008, p. 7).

To whom is the narrator telling her story? Much of Part 1, titled "The Tributes," is narration doubling as exposition. Background information about the uprising and subsequent defeat (or obliteration) of the districts by the Capitol, the Dark Days, Treaty of Treason, and Hunger Games needs to be explained so that when Katniss volunteers as tribute to spare Prim, the urgency and gravity of the situation is understood. Yet as a result of Collins's (2008) decision to have her narrator clarify that "my real name is Katniss," in addition to her relaying a history lesson and details about District 12, the reader can come to one of three conclusions regarding the identity of the narratee.

The first option is that the narrator is telling her story to someone entirely unfamiliar not only with the politics of Panem, but also with Katniss herself—a total stranger outside District 12 and the rest of Panem. The second option is that much of the first section—which takes Katniss from reaping day to the night before the Games officially begin when Peeta tells all of Panem that he is in love with her—is redundant narration: the narrator telling the narratee information that she already has (Phelan, 2005a, p. 11). The third option is either that there is no narratee, or that the narratee is so completely merged with the implied reader that it is not a separate entity in the chain of communication, but without the fourth-wall being broken, as mentioned above. In this particular instance, either of the first two options achieves the same purpose on behalf of the implied author: namely, to inform the implied reader and set the stage for Katniss's trip to the 74th annual Hunger Games. The third option, however, complicates Chatman's (1978) communication model by further questioning the necessity of a key (albeit contested) piece.

This issue regarding to whom Katniss is telling her story continues to be complicated in *The Hunger Games*. At one point in the second section, "The Games," during which Katniss is trying to survive the arena, she settles in for a well-deserved night of rest in a tree. Rue, a tribute from District 11 with whom Katniss formed a short-lived alliance, has been killed, and Katniss honored her sacrifice by singing to her until she passed away. She then covered Rue with flowers before the hovercraft swooped in to remove her body (Collins, 2008, pp. 234-237). After the Gamemakers' nightly ritual of broadcasting pictures of tributes lost during the day, and with the gift of bread sent by the people of Rue's district still in her grasp, Katniss falls "instantly asleep" (p. 247). She narrates:

Sometimes, when things are particularly bad, my brain will give me a happy dream. A visit from my father in the woods. An hour of sunlight and cake with Prim. Tonight it sends me Rue, still decked in her flowers, perched in a high sea of trees, trying to teach me to talk to the mockingjays. I see no sign of her wounds, no blood, just a bright, laughing girl. She sings songs I've never heard in a clear, melodic voice. On and on. Through the night. There's a drowsy in-between period when I can hear the last few strains of her music although she's lost in the leaves. When I full awaken, I'm momentarily comforted. I try to hold onto the peaceful feeling of the dream, but it quickly slips away, leaving me sadder and lonelier than ever. (Collins, 2008, pp. 247-248)

Over a week of time has passed in the storyworld, and this is, obviously, not Katniss's first night's sleep. However, this is only the second time that she has narrated her sleeping and dreaming. Most of the other times she tells us that she fell asleep (whether fitfully or all at once), and perhaps what woke her up—a wall of fire (p. 171), the snap of a tree branch, (p. 158), a cannon (p. 209), or the sun—but not about her dreams. Yet even the first time she tells us about her dreaming, it is narrated in such a way ("my slumbers are filled with disturbing dreams...I bolt up screaming ..." [p. 86]) that it hints at a millisecond moment of historical present tense narration, as opposed to the above paragraph in which she is, literally, narrating her dreams to us as they happen and acknowledging the comfort they give her upon waking. She, then, understands on some narrative level that she has told the narratee about her brain activity *while she was asleep.* How is this possible? If we are heavily invested in the narrative audience (Rabinowitz, 1977), we understand that often upon waking we can recall dreams and perhaps even share them aloud. But, save the occasional moments of talking in one's sleep, we do not tell of our dreaming *while* asleep, and, of course, Katniss is not speaking aloud at this moment. This is interior monologue.

Although seemingly insignificant—it is only a long paragraph in a 300-plus-page novel, after all—it is a scene like the one described above that narrative theory, specifically the rhetorical model, can illuminate and assist in our interpretation of a text. What purpose is served by the implied author including a dream sequence here? Most other nights of Katniss's sleep, even in the arena, are significant only for what she faces upon waking up. Here, though, she has a peaceful dream: something likely unheard of in the midst of her being hunted for entertainment. By taking this moment to give the narratee and implied reader a window into Katniss's unconscious, even in a rather unnatural way, Collins (2008) is highlighting the devastation of Rue's death, the impact of Katniss's first "real" kill, the ongoing unfairness of the games (Rue is the youngest, smallest tribute whom Katniss repeatedly compares to her own sister), and, once again, the atypical nature of this year's competition: Katniss honored Rue's death and was sent a gift from a district other than her own.

Katniss's involvement with the narratee becomes even more complex a few chapters later when she is trying to revive and heal Peeta, who has been badly injured in a fight with Cato, the Career Tribute from District 2. In an effort to relax, Peeta has asked Katniss to tell him a story as he recuperates in their sleeping bag—a "happy story" of which Katniss has very few. Before telling him the edited-for-the-Capitol version (she *is* on camera), she narrates, "here's the real story of how I got the money for Prim's goat, Lady" (Collins, 2008, p. 268), after which she recounts a tale involving her and Gale illegally killing a buck and surreptitiously taking it to the butcher to sell. "This is where I really got the money for the goat, but I tell Peeta I sold an old silver locket of my mother's" (p. 270). By interjecting her storytelling with two interior utterances designed so that the reader knows the truth—both about the money and her reason for omitting this detail in her public sharing of it—the implied author is allowing Katniss to further connect with the narratee and the implied reader. Yet, one might think that once she "pick[s] up the story" to really tell Peeta about the goat, the section would be offset by quotation marks, and it is not. The first time quotation marks are used in this particular scene is when *Peeta* speaks up to say something, after which Katniss narrates, "I had almost forgotten he was there" (p. 272). She is, within the conventions of print, not really talking to Peeta, even though Peeta is her actual narratee at this moment of the double-layered communicative situation. Katniss is communicating with both Peeta and the implied reader at this moment.

Yet at other times when Katniss tells her narratee and the reader that she is thinking to herself about something—sawing the tree branch to release the tracker jackers (Collins, 2008, p. 187), desperately needing water, or a snarky comment she wishes to make to Cato (p. 226)—Collins has offset them with italics. She does this even a few pages after the goat-story scene when Katniss is en route to the Cornucopia and thinking about Gale watching her on television, wishing he could protect her on this potentially deadly hike (p. 281). In this case the implied author clearly wants to highlight Katniss's "almost forget[ting] he was there" for the implied reader's sake. We notice, of course, that thinking about the day she brought Prim the goat is another rare, happy instance for Katniss, much like her oddly pleasant dream earlier. In this way, Collins (2008) is trying to draw as much attention to the cheerful moments as possible *because* they are so rare for an impoverished, fatherless teenager currently vying for her—and her friend's—life in an arena designed to kill her.

To continue the complication of the line of communication between implied author and implied reader we must return to the goat story. As part of Katniss's narration of this story, Collins (2008) writes, "You should have seen Prim's reaction when we walked in with that goat. Remember this is a girl who wept to save that awful old cat, Buttercup" (p. 272). But *Peeta* does not know that story. Katniss has never told him about her family's grouchy orange tabby cat; but she *has* told the narratee and the reader—in fact, it is one of the first things we learn about her (p. 3). If this particular section of text was, as mentioned earlier, offset by quotation marks to indicate that Katniss is talking directly to Peeta—which of course she is because he remarks on how lovely the story is—then we might assume that she shared this information with him earlier, or perhaps even that Collins made a mistake. But within the conventions of print narrative, Katniss is telling this tale as interior monologue that Peeta has access to. Therefore, "remembering" Buttercup is Collins directly communicating with the implied reader vis-à-vis Katniss, which further complicates the question of the existence of the narratee.

READER AS SPECTATOR

The simultaneous present tense narration does more than raise questions about a component of Chatman's (1978) model or Phelan's (2007) definition of narrative. In this section, I argue that Collins's (2008) narration technique is designed to ensure that the authorial audience is also fully immersed in the narrative audience (Rabinowitz, 1977) in order to heighten the mimetic component of the narrative

HILARY BREWSTER

itself. Once Katniss is actually participating in the Games, the present tense narration creates an exceptionally mimetic narrative—*especially if* the reader has stepped fully into the narrative audience and has become so engaged with the text that being in the authorial audience is nearly forgotten, something that the implied Collins is likely hoping for in designing her narrative.

Right before Katniss steps into the cylinder that will bring her from her Launch Room to the Cornucopia, the immediate area of the arena named for its shape and abundance of useful materials, she is sitting nervously with Cinna, her stylist. She narrates her interior monologue, explaining that "nervousness seeps into terror as I anticipate what is to come. I could be dead, flat-out dead, in an hour. Not even" (Collins, 2008, p. 146). As someone in the narrative audience—that is, someone who believes Katniss, Peeta, and the others to be real people—this thought makes utter sense: waiting to enter a gladiator style competition would definitely fill anyone with a sense of terror at the thought of being murdered. Yet this scene takes place not even halfway through the entire novel. A member of the *authorial* audience might think to herself, "Obviously Katniss does not die in less than an hour, probably more, because there is far too much text left for that to happen." It is possible, of course, that Collins might drag out the action of that first hour for the next hundred or so pages, but given how she has treated narrative time thus far, it is unlikely. She spends roughly 50 pages on reaping *day*; there is no reason to think that this implied author will suddenly slow down time and expand an hour into more than twice that many pages.

The realization that Katniss will likely not die is also highlighted by Collins (2008) titling the third and final section of the novel "The Victor." Who else would it be? Naturally, the implied author has also entreated the reader to care just as much about Peeta's survival; although as readers we know that, at least on Katniss's part, the star-crossed lovers schtick is mostly for the sake of the audience in the Capitol, it does not necessarily diminish our rooting for Peeta. If nothing else, the two characters are from the same district, which naturally allies them, and Peeta's (genuine) declarations of love play into a reader's (especially a teenager reader's) desire for love to prevail. The singularly titled third section begins immediately after Claudius interrupts the Games with a heretofore unheard of mid-Game rule change that would allow both Katniss and Peeta to win if they were the final two competitors alive (p. 244). Now we're *really* rooting for them! But would Collins switch focalizers with just a little bit of story left? Though not unheard of in the realm of fiction, this is also probably an unlikely move.

Authorial readers have tacitly accepted the rule of fiction that first person narrators do not die during the narrative.[3] There are, of course, exceptions to this rule (whether these narratives are effective at achieving their ethical or aesthetic purpose is a separate question), but they are few and far between. Of course, in retrospective narration, an authorial reader is aware that the story, no matter how gruesome, violent, or life-threatening, does not result with the narrator dying, because she is telling the story; historical present tense would result in the same conclusion. It is no shock, then, that much of this third section is devoted to *Peeta's* survival. He is deathly ill due to an infection as a result of a deep thigh wound he acquired during a fight with Cato. We, as readers, know—or at least, assume with near perfect certainty—that Katniss will survive. With this new rule change, however, we are even more interested and invested in Peeta's survival, which is exactly what the implied Collins is hoping for.

Yet the present-tense narrative technique employed by Collins (2008) increases the unlikely possibility that Katniss won't survive *just a little*, because it is at least a logical option for both the narrative and the authorial audience that the novel might end with a dramatic death scene.[4] Given the situation in the storyworld— fighting to the death in a closed arena in which not only other tributes, but also the Gamemakers, are trying to kill you—Katniss's life is certainly on the line numerous times. She avoids a rock to the skull because of Thresh's inclination to repay debts (p. 288), and she does not die of dehydration, tracker jacker venom, or massive blood loss thanks only to Haymitch, Rue, and Peeta, respectively. Part of the entire point of this novel is that teenagers, including our beloved narrator, have to kill one another for sport. Whether or not Katniss will survive is built into the narrative progression, even if the outcome is tacitly understood.

To combat the likelihood that readers will straddle the authorial and narrative audiences too well, thus negating part of the suspense and excitement of wondering whether Katniss lives or dies, the implied author must heighten the mimesis of the narration. In what is (both ethically and aesthetically) the climax of the novel, Collins (2008) plays on this possibility. Katniss and Peeta are two of the remaining three victors and they work together to eliminate the outsider in a violent scene on top of the Cornucopia. After Cato's gruesome (near) death-by-muttations—which Katniss mercifully aids with an arrow to his head—the wretched Gamemakers announce that the earlier change to the rules allowing two tributes from the same district to win is revoked. Disgusted, but not surprised, Katniss and Peeta must now decide what to do.

Rather than one of them murdering the other to win, Katniss and Peeta defy the Capitol's manipulative rules and very nearly commit suicide together by swallowing poisonous nightlock berries (Collins, 2008, p. 345). By this point, however, the reader is familiar with Katniss's rebellious tendencies—like covering Rue from District 11 with flowers upon her death (p. 237), for example—and how she intuitively understands how President Snow and the Gamemakers will have to handle these situations. Therefore, even a reader immersed in the narrative audience should pick up on Katniss's real intent with the berries when, on the page before she and Peeta put them in their mouths, she narrates:

> Yes, they have to have a victor. Without a victor, the whole thing would blow up in the Gamemakers' faces. They'd have failed the Capitol. Might possibly even be executed, slowly and painfully, while the cameras broadcast it to every screen in the country. If Peeta and I were both to die, or *they thought we were* … (p. 344, emphasis added)

As action packed as the scenes from the arena are—in an ethically horrifying way, of course—and as nerve-wracking as this particular moment is, even the most engaged reader will recognize that Collins is, in no way, actually letting Katniss die. The stunt with the berries is just that—a stunt, one designed to undermine the Capitol and reveal a flaw in the system, even if, as she and Peeta count down to "three," she thinks "maybe I'm wrong" and "maybe they don't care if we both die" (p. 344). In fact, I might argue that the narration even makes this moment *too* anti-climatic.[5] Katniss narrates, "I lift my hand to my mouth, taking one last look at the world. The berries have just passed my lips when the trumpets begin to blare," and then a frantic Claudius tells the pair to stop and announces that both she and Peeta are the victors (p. 345).

If the implied Collins were trying to heighten the suspense of this suicidal moment, she would have given the reader a chapter ending, cliff-hanging page turn after "world" or possibly "lips" with ellipses, or even ended the novel there on a *true* cliffhanger. Instead, she is concerned with how the Gamemakers and President Snow *react* to Katniss and Peeta's defiant maneuver, which contributes to her continued concern with demonstrating the instability of the oppressive Capitol and the need for—and inevitability of—an uprising, the seeds of which have been planted.

I argue that it is because of this "first-person-narrators-don't-die" convention that Collins (2008) writes Katniss's story in the present tense. If the novel were narrated retrospectively, or even historically, the mimetic suspense of Katniss's time in the arena would be diminished ever so slightly, because the authorial reader would understand on some level—even if she had also mostly immersed herself in the narrative audience—that Katniss survives the Games.[6] By creating a narrative in which the protagonist is no more aware of events than the reader, the stakes are higher not only for Katniss—who is literally fighting for her life—but for the reader's engagement as well. As it is written, the present tense narration makes both ethical and aesthetic sense. Participating in the Hunger Games is not something that Katniss has experienced before—this is not the case by the second installment in the series, though each arena is unique—therefore, for her to be telling of the events as they happen mimics the senses of newness, confusion, and uncertainty for Katniss. Additionally, by using this narrative technique, "Collins provides us with the very kind of entertainment that she is trying to critique: we have become enraptured viewers of a reality show, and are pumped with triumphant, sickened relief when the other guy falls to his death" (Baker, 2011, para. 17). I discuss the implications of this ethical positioning in a later section when I examine the film adaptation.

THE ETHICS OF THE TELLING AND THE TOLD

Given the nature of the rather disturbing content, Collins (2008) also must take special care with the ethics presented in the text. Although other literary theories—feminist, Marxist, post-colonial, critical race, etc.—ask readers and critics to work outside-in, applying a particular, pre-established framework to a text, rhetorical narrative theory works inside-out, using the text itself to determine the set of ethics presented to the reader (Phelan, 2005a). Collins does not shy away from presenting the reader with a very clear set of ethical values by utilizing the single homodiegetic focalizing narrator as her mouthpiece. However, getting the reader "on board" with the larger, macro set of ethics involving Panem, the Capitol, and the Games is not necessarily too difficult to achieve; what becomes trickier is how to continue to be sympathetic for Katniss once she enters the arena and is, like all the other tributes, a murderer.

The narrator's voice is one method by which an implied author can insert herself into the ethics of the story. Certainly, there can be—and often is—distance between the two entities; the greater the distance, the greater the unreliability of the narrator, as is the case with Titus in M.T. Anderson's (2002) *Feed.* However, Katniss seems to act as Collins's (2008) mouthpiece; though not always likeable, necessarily, Katniss's understanding of the politics of Panem and the annual "celebration" of the Hunger Games is precisely the set of ethics a reader should take on without much resistance A government that separates and exploits its people for its own benefit is, for a modern Western audience, surely loathsome. A government that insists on the yearly slaughter of 23 teenagers as punishment for the oppressed and entertainment for its wealthiest members is despicable, atrocious, and unforgiveable. It should, I hope, not take even the least politically aware reader too many steps to recognize that Katniss's disgust and mistrust of the Capitol is the "right" way to feel. This is the ethical position endorsed by the implied author.

To aid in this ethical positioning, Collins (2008) has also created a wholly sympathetic character in her narrator, even when she is in the arena. Unlike the "Careers" from Districts 1 and 2—the districts at least somewhat in the Capitol's favor, and the most financially well-off—Katniss is from District 12, what "used to be" Appalachia (p. 41). To a modern reader—even a teenaged one who might be less aware of America's geopolitical landscape than an adult reader—this should signal inescapable poverty. Katniss happens to live in the poorest part of District 12, nicknamed the Seam. Her father, a coal miner like most of the men in District 12, was killed in a mine accident. Although Katniss breaks the rules of going beyond the district boundaries to hunt, she does it for a good cause—to feed her family. Her willingness to sacrifice for her family is, of course, highlighted when she volunteers to take Prim's place at the Reaping. Katniss is the perfect underdog. And, as Head Gamemaker Seneca Crane tells President Snow in the film version, "everyone likes an underdog."

Yet how can Collins (2008) continue to make Katniss sympathetic once she enters the arena? By definition, being a tribute—even one who volunteered under such noble circumstances—makes her a potential murderer. How can we root for her when she is killing teenagers? This is where the implied Collins uses narrative progression to her advantage.

Technically speaking, Katniss only kills four other tributes in the first volume of the series, and, to the narrative and authorial audiences, each death is justified. Her first two kills, Glimmer and the girl from District 4, die as a result of tracker jacker stings (Collins, 2008, p. 192). Yes, Katniss releases the nest of deadly wasps onto them, but she is trapped in a tree by an alliance of Career Tributes (and Peeta) waiting her out in order to kill her. Sawing off the branch is self-defense, a disengaged method of eliminating her enemies, and, admittedly, quite clever. Katniss does not escape unscathed, either, which aids in our sympathy. Additionally, as a result of this tracker jacker plot-point, her alliance with Rue begins.

Katniss's third kill, her first "real" one, is not self-defense, but also fully understandable. The boy from District 1 ensnares and spears Rue, and Katniss shoots an arrow into his neck, killing him instantly (Collins, 2008, p. 233). Although Cato and the other Careers leave Glimmer to die a tragic, awful death—though they do seek ravenous vengeance on Katniss as a result—Katniss avenges the death of her ally. For a reader rightfully positioned to detest the idea of teenagers killing one another for sport, Katniss's kill is as legitimate as it could be. Rather than viewing her as a maniacal killer, we instead see her as loyal and trustworthy, reactionary rather than aggressive. What is ethically troublesome is that we might even *root* for this kill, given how Collins has spent time fleshing out the almost sisterly bond between Katniss and little Rue from District 11. Yet before possibly celebrating this moment, we bear witness to Katniss's humanity as she sings to and buries her ally.

Mentioned briefly in an earlier section, Katniss's final kill in her first Hunger Games is also understandable and can almost barely be considered a kill in the traditional sense. She mercifully puts Cato out of his misery rather than have him continue to be painfully mauled to death by the mutts. Although Cato's death is what allows Peeta and Katniss to be the Victors, it is also out of kindness and a sense of human decency that she shoots him. Granted, it is also her arrow that sends the Career flying into the muttations' mouths at all, but she does *that* to save Peeta, whom the reader is also rooting for. As far as kills go, then, Collins (2008) allows us to root at least for an ethical killer. Peeta, of course, only has one "real" kill under his belt, and we're meant to understand that he did so reluctantly and only as a ploy to stay allied with the pack of Careers (p. 160). Our heroes have limited blood on their hands.

Collins (2008) also makes sure that other potentially ethically confusing murders and deaths are dealt with in the safest manner possible. Thresh, the male tribute from District 11, viciously murders Clove with a rock to the skull, but he does it because he overheard her bragging about Rue's death (p. 287). His choice also saves Katniss, whom Clove was about to enjoy slicing open. After he lets Katniss go as payback for treating Rue with dignity, both Katniss and the reader are nervous about the possibility of her having to kill him in order to win. However, Collins handles it deftly—his death is "off stage" and by Cato's hand, exactly what Peeta was grimly hoping for (p. 293). Foxface, the wily redhead who seems to elude all of the other tributes and whom Katniss admires for her cunning, dies a rather quiet offstage death by eating the (unknowingly) poisonous nightlock berries Peeta gathered while Katniss hunted. After the hovercraft extracts Foxface's body from the arena, Katniss praises her cleverness and Peeta even offers up that it was *unfair* that she died that way (p. 320). The tributes the reader likes the most are then also treated with as much ethical fairness as possible as Collins kills them off in order for District 12 to emerge collectively victorious.

Although discussed in the section above on mimesis, the ethics of the "almost-suicide" is worth mentioning here, too. For a 21st century Western audience, especially a teenaged one, suicide is seen as a wholly selfish act, one that *must* have an alternative. And yet, as I argued earlier, though the authorial audience certainly understands that neither tribute will die, this same audience would also not necessarily be averse to the nightlock working, either. The narrative audience would be distraught—our heroes are dead!—but the authorial audience, who is primed to hate the Capitol, the Gamemakers, and their sick Games, at least understands the positive political and ethical ramifications of this suicide stunt: it would upend the system we want upended, because Katniss's and Peeta's death would be politically motivated, not romantically.[7] Though certainly not the first set of teenagers to commit suicide in literature—*Romeo and Juliet* comes instantly to mind—this is a case in which the audience is, even in the smallest way, not wholly opposed to the idea given how we have been positioned by the implied author. Would their deaths satisfy reader desires? Of course not. But Collins has, at least somewhat, created a storyworld in which the audience is put in a tiny ethical conundrum by not being fully opposed to suicide as a choice.

WE'RE NOT AS BAD AS THE CAPITOL, I PROMISE: ETHICALLY VIEWING THE FILM

If Collins (2008) uses a single focalizer character-narrator as her primary ethical spokesperson, what happens when the narrative shifts to another medium and the possibility of narration and homodiegetic focalization is (mostly, almost entirely) eliminated? Much like novels with "first person" narrators who die during the course of the story are rare, so are films with homodiegetic focalizers. *Cloverfield* (Reeves, 2008), *The Lady in the Lake* (Montgomery, 1947), and *The Blair Witch Project* (Myrick & Sanchez, 1999) are examples, and the latter uses alternating focalizers, not singular. Typically speaking, filmmakers utilize external or "zero" focalization (Genette, 1980): even though we have a main character or characters, the viewing audience is privy to information they cannot possibly have. Though films with voice-over narration are far more common—whether or not this technique is used satisfactorily is another conversation—*The Hunger Games* (Ross, 2012) is not one of them.

It is not my intent in this section to argue whether or not the film adaptation of the novel is "good" or "bad" according to issues of formal fidelity, or whether fidelity should be the sole arbiter of an adaptation's aesthetic success.[8] Instead, I want to use the tools of rhetorical narrative theory to articulate the ways in which the affordances of film impact the audience, specifically with regard to positioning us ethically. I argue that scenes and dialogue created solely for the movie—most of which Katniss cannot be privy to—are what ultimately guide the audience to their ethical conclusions.

The movie opens with screen text giving a brief history of the previous rebellion and the subsequent Dark Days and Treaty of Treason, which stipulate the requirements for the annual Hunger Games. Yet instead of immediately cutting to

District 12, which is where the novel starts, we are instead introduced to Caesar Flickerman, a television personality sporting a blue bouffant hairdo, talking with Seneca Crane, the Head Gamemaker, in a live interview. Seneca states that the Games are "part of our tradition," "serve as a reminder of the rebellion," and are "the price the districts had to pay," but he also asserts that they now are what "knits us all together," a phrase that garners cheering from the audience (Ross, 2012). Before answering another question from Flickerman about his "personal style" in arena-making, we cut away to a mountain road, a small wooden shack of a house, the words "District 12" in the far right corner, and the sound of horrific screaming. The next scene is of a young blonde girl—we learn quickly her name is Prim—shrieking in her sleep at the thought of being "reaped" for the Games and being comforted by her older sister, who assures her that her selection is unlikely, as it is Prim's first year of eligibility, and her name is only entered in the pool once. Katniss then sings her a lullaby—the one which she sang to Rue in the novel, though audience members unfamiliar with the source text won't know that—to try to calm her before heading out. It is only then that we get many, many shots of District 12 that are meant to signal poverty—dilapidated houses, hordes of skinny, dirty children in the street or on falling-down porches, men in overalls carrying metal lunch buckets as they walk to work, etc.

For the next 25 minutes, the film follows Katniss to the Meadow where she meets Gale, to the reaping where she volunteers to take the place of her sister, and on the train to the Capitol. Although some details are altered, they are not so dramatic that it changes much. Prim being the one to give Katniss her soon-to-be-famous mockingjay pin actually makes more symbolic sense than how it is handled in the novel, albeit somewhat heavy-handedly. That Katniss is somewhat unlikeable—something that will not help her in the Games—is accentuated in the film, since we are not solely in her head. She nearly stabs her and Peeta's mentor, Haymitch, in the hand with a knife prior to him revealing that the way to stay alive in the Games is "to get people to like you" (Ross, 2012). Though she does readily admit in the novel that she is stubborn and unfriendly, we are primed to brush this off because we are already on her side.

After the pre-Games skills scores are announced—for which Katniss earns an eleven out of twelve for shooting an arrow through an apple on the Gamemakers' buffet—we once again cut to President Snow talking to Seneca about the insidious purpose of the Games and needing a winner to intimidate the districts, rather than just rounding up 24 kids and executing them on the spot, which would be "faster." The President explains that the possibility of winning the Games, which results in the Victor living in luxury and bringing his or her district honor, gives the people "hope. It is the only thing stronger than fear. A little hope is effective. A lot of hope is dangerous. Spark is fine, as long as it's contained" (Ross, 2012). When Seneca responds with confusion, Snow demands that he "contain it." This declaration, in addition to linguistically continuing the series' theme of fire and rebellion, makes clear that Katniss and Peeta, both poor and from an outlying district that has not had a Victor in over two decades,[9] should not have a chance. Not "do not," but *should* not.

It is only after Katniss, Peeta, and the other tributes enter the arena that the external focalization really begins to impact the storytelling ethics. Horrific scenes of the murderous bloodbath at the Cornucopia are included; about half the tributes are eliminated in the first few minutes, which we "get" to watch, even though Katniss is not actually present for this in the novel. Yet rather than remaining focused solely on Katniss and the immediate danger of the Games themselves, once "the show" begins, we get cut away scenes to people watching with glee (in the Capitol) or reluctance (in District 12), and even a shot of Gale actively not watching—though it is required viewing—as his small act of resistance and repugnance.

While the actual audience is undoubtedly horrified at the outset by the depiction of teenagers killing each other, it is not until 75 minutes into the film that we are clued into the perverse power the Gamemakers enjoy wielding. Katniss has wandered far, far out of the main area as a means of conflict-avoidance, and is, unbeknownst to her, actually nearing the edge of the arena itself, two kilometers away from the nearest person. We cut away to shots of the Gamemakers in the control room, where an unnamed technician mentions Katniss's location to Seneca, who tells him to get her to turn around. After shots of Katniss resting in a tree interspersed with the technician playing with his interface, a wildfire starts. As she is sprinting through the woods for her life, fireballs coming at her from every direction, the technician says in a near joyful tone, "killing another, on my count" (Ross, 2012), and he fiddles with his high-tech screen simulator gadget to shoot several more balls of fire at her, all of which she narrowly escapes. Since they are watching her in real time, Seneca calls for a tree to come crashing down in her path. She trips, avoids another fireball but gets burned, and then, naturally, runs to the lake to ease her pain. Another technician tells Seneca that she is "almost there," to which he replies, "Lucia, get another cannon ready" (Ross, 2012). Since the fire did not kill her, they have led her to Cato and the pack of Careers who are after her instead, assuming that they will finish the job.

Although we were likely suspicious as a result of Seneca's conversations with President Snow, the audience now understands the secret underbelly of the Games: the Gamemakers have control over the arena, can influence the outcome, and find pleasure in the "plot" devices they provide for their audience, not caring, of course, that everyone except those in the Capitol are watching children from their community be hunted. Seneca seems especially susceptible to this desire to pander to the audience—and perhaps rightfully so, as his job depends on the show's inherent entertainment value—as even Haymitch, the notoriously drunk and laughable District 12 mentor, can convince him that people want to "root for young love" (Ross, 2012). Seneca's conversation with Haymitch is immediately followed by another interaction with President Snow in which he warns Seneca to "be careful" in allowing too many people to root for an underdog.

President Snow's earlier warnings about hope might seem like political paranoia to an audience unfamiliar with the novel. The filmmakers, therefore, have to find a way to clue the audience in to just how right he is and how even the seemingly smallest acts can result in rebellion. After Katniss sings Rue to her death and places a bouquet of wildflowers in her resting corpse hands, she presses three fingers of her left hand to her mouth and raises them toward the sky, in full view of the arena cameras. This is the gesture of solidarity from District 12, shown to Katniss herself after she took Prim's place, which she now shares with District 11 upon losing a tribute. We cut away to a shot of a crowd of people—we are told it is District 11 with a caption—watching in a town square, responding to her in kind. The injustice of the Games and the recognition that at least one tribute is aware of it, plus having just watched a child member of their community die, sparks an outburst. One man strides toward a uniformed Peacekeeper—the obviously ironically named guards trained by the Capitol to maintain order in each district—and strikes him, after which people begin stampeding the staging area with the screens, toppling over and knocking down towers used for transmitting the television signal and trashing property. It is almost exactly what President Snow predicted: mayhem.

In the novel, Katniss understands, at least somewhat, that her participation in the Games has an air of performance, and how the Gamemakers "have to" operate; therefore, the reader knows, too. She knows, for instance, that the cameras won't be able to edit out flower-covered Rue because they will have to show the hovercraft collecting her body. She knows that the Gamemakers call a "feast" at the Cornucopia in order to bring the last remaining tributes into physical proximity of one another. She understands that the Gamemakers—even more than she and the other tributes—are responsible for providing entertainment to the eager crowd. She also understands how President Snow uses the Games to continually pit the districts against one another as a means to control them and ensure they don't attempt another uprising. But this point has to be hammered home a bit harder for the movie audience, given that we are not privy to Katniss's thoughts. Therefore, showing District 11 in utter chaos as a result of Katniss's kindness ensures that the audience understands the significance of her act as one that sparks rebellion and positions Katniss as a threat to President Snow.

The last scene in the film that I want to discuss in detail is not a moment of cut-away external focalization, but rather a piece of dialogue included solely in the movie that assists in the ethical positioning of the audience. As we know from my earlier discussion of Katniss and Peeta's near-suicide, they and Cato are the last remaining tributes. In order to kill Cato, but not Peeta, Katniss shoots an arrow into the hand that grips her district ally, causing Cato to release Peeta before plunging off the metal Cornucopia into the waiting, savage maw of several mutts. In the novel, this scene has almost no dialogue, save Cato almost laughing at his (erroneous) realization that Katniss cannot get rid of him without losing Peeta, too. Yet in the movie, as Cato grips Peeta and they both hover precariously near the edge of the metal contraption, he says to her, with blood literally dripping out of his mouth:

Go on shoot. And we both go down and you win. Go on. I'm dead anyway. I always was, right? I didn't know that till now … how's that? Is that what they want? No … I can still do this. *I* can still do this. One. More. Kill. It's the only thing I know how to do. Bring "pride" to my district. Not that it matters. (Ross, 2012)

Seconds later, Katniss fires an arrow through his hand, he releases Peeta, who knees him in the stomach, and down he goes.

Throughout the entire film, Cato has been portrayed as the most vicious, bloodthirsty, self-assured tribute. The product of District 2, where they train Careers who usually win the Hunger Games, Cato is big, strong, and unrelenting. He snaps the neck of the tribute guarding the food Katniss destroys and is shown stabbing and killing many of the tributes murdered in the opening sequence. He explicitly enjoys hunting Katniss, does not (or cannot) come to Clove's aid when Thresh is about to smash her head in, and is the one responsible for Thresh's death—no easy feat given how large of a person the latter is, either. Yet the screenwriters (including Collins) chose to give him a powerful line of dialogue that is not from the source text right before his death. In this moment, too, he is emotionally vulnerable, perhaps for the first—and obviously the last—time. Why? What does this do for us as viewers?

We get to see that Cato, like Katniss, Peeta, and the others (especially Rue and the boy from District 4) are children. Even though Cato has had the "privilege" of being trained for the Games in a way that only the tributes from Districts 1 and 2 are, he is a teenager who recognizes that his entire existence, his *whole purpose for living,* is to be used as a murderous pawn. The scene described above shows that even for him, killing other kids is emotionally taxing and soul wrenching, even though the Capitol (and his district?) see the Games as "fun" and think he does, too. He recognizes that surviving the arena is not a reflection on him, but on his community; without it, he has failed them, even though of course, it is the other way around. Namely, it shows that Cato is human, just like Katniss and Peeta: which is exactly what President Snow wants to avoid. Although it alters his previous characterization to some degree, this invented dialogue is, in my opinion, one of the best ethical choices in the entirety of the film. Cato is no longer just a vicious enemy, but a scared, emotionally distraught teenager without much of an identity reflecting on his mortality moments before his imminent demise. This is not how District 2 tributes (or any of them, really) are "supposed" to feel according to President Snow's plan. Cato's death speech not only humanizes him, it humanizes the viewer. Given the events we have just witnessed, especially with Cato, the audience may have forgotten that *we should not be rooting for him to die, either.* He is a kid forced to fight for his life because a corrupt dictator says so, and for punishment of "crimes" even his grandparents were not alive for. We should be loath to forget that—though we probably have—and we need a reminder. Even more than reading present tense narration, the moviegoer is a voyeur—a willing voyeur—in the sick reality of the Games.[10]

CONCLUSION

Although texts like *The Hunger Games and Philosophy: A Critique of Pure Treason* (Dunn, Michaud, & Irwin, 2012) and other essays, including those in this particular volume, do a fine job of discussing issues of ethics, gender identity, and social class in Collin's (2008) wildly popular books and subsequent film adaptations, rhetorical narrative theory works "inside out" rather than "outside in" and ties the ethics of a text to its aesthetics (Phelan, 2005a) rather than applying a preconceived framework to a reading. The narration and focalization, especially, highlight the ways in which the novel and film are constructed to position the reader/viewer ethically and illuminate how the narrative and authorial audiences are constructed for each. If we consider texts as means by which authors communicate with audiences, and the methods afforded to each medium, we move away from viewing the film adaptation as "good" depending on its fidelity to the source text, or the first person present tense narration as "preferred" or "fashionable." Rather, rhetorical narrative theory provides us with a set of tools to consider how we are being positioned and for what purpose and how those positions and purposes shift as both a consideration and indication of audience.

But why does this matter? As English teachers and scholars routinely ask their students, so what? I think that most importantly, the analysis and interpretation of Collins's novels reveals the trilogy, or at least the inaugural installment, to be sophisticated and complex, two words not always associated with novels marketed toward teenagers. To be sure, many young adult novels and series—even best-selling ones—are, at best, examples of awful writing and simplistic plot, or at worst, trendy, insufferable fluff. Yet this reputation unfairly precedes any addition to the YA genre, especially to those in the ivory tower of academia. In marked contrast to the stereotype, Collins has created not only a riveting dystopian storyworld that has gone on to become a multi-media powerhouse franchise, but written a text that is technically and thematically interesting, nuanced, and rich. In the on-going debate among educators and literary scholars, analyses like mine and others demonstrate that *The Hunger Games* can hold its own against the canon despite its oft-maligned status as being "merely" young adult.

NOTES

[1] Present tense narration got a bit of media attention in 2010 when three of the six nominees for the Man Booker Prize were written in this mode, much to the chagrin of authors like Philip Hensher—a one-time Booker judge who declared the choice "fashionable"—and Phillip Pullman (Miller, 2010).

[2] To be fair, Katniss's name is used on the dust jacket of the novel. However, while the paratext is certainly important to our initial narrative interpretations, it is not the narrative itself; therefore, for the purpose of this particular argument, I am focusing on what the implied Collins created for her implied reader.

[3] Narrating once already dead, like Susie of Alice Sebold's *Lovely Bones* (2002), is an example of unnatural narration (in which an entity without the capability of speech is narrating), and therefore in a somewhat different category, even though the narration is homodiegetic with a single focalizer. Other examples of "ghostly" narrators exist.

[4] John Gardner's 1971 novel *Grendel*, a reimagining of the Anglo epic poem Beowulf, is possibly the only example, and this speaks to an issue of audience, surely: the marketed audience of Collins's novel has probably not read this.

[5] The film adaptation is even less suspenseful—Claudius interrupts Katniss and Peeta while the berries are still in their hands.

[6] Not using this terminology exactly, book critic Laura Miller (2010) notes "the breathless, life-or-death action in [Collins's] young-adult novels would lose much of its suspense if the first-person narrator, Katniss, was apparently relating the events at a later date" (para. 5).

[7] Or at least not solely romantic—Peeta's motivations are, at least in part, romantic, though we're also meant to believe he understands Katniss's larger ploy when she whispers "trust me" and holds his gaze (p. 344).

[8] Though I do think this particular adaptation is a "good" one, for a much more in depth argument about the history of adaptation theory and why we should not pit "cinematic apples against prose oranges" see Bolton (2013, pp. 23-25).

[9] For a larger discussion of this voyeurism, with a particular focus on audience engagement with reality television and its inspiration for and impact on Collins's series, see Mortimore-Smith (2012) and Henthorne (2012, pp. 95-107).

REFERENCES

Alexi, S. (2007). *The absolutely true diary of a part-time Indian.* New York: Little, Brown, and Company.

Anderson, L. H. (1999). *Speak.* New York: Farrar, Strauss, Giroux.

Anderson, M. T. (2002). *Feed.* Cambridge, MA: Candlewick.

Baker, D. (2011, December 29). Present tensions, or it's all happening now. *The Horn Book.* Retrieved from: http://www.hbook.com/2011/12/opinion/present-tensions-or-its-all-happening-now/

Bolton, M. (2013). The rhetoric of intermediality: Adapting means, ends, and ethics in *Atonement. Diegesis. 2*(1), 23-53.

Booth, W. C. (1961/1983). *The rhetoric of fiction* (2nd ed.). Chicago: University of Chicago Press.

Chatman, S. (1978). *Story and discourse: Narrative structure in fiction and film.* Ithaca, NY: Cornell University Press.

Chobsky, S. (1999). *The perks of being a wallflower.* New York: Pocket Books.

Collins, S. (2008). *The hunger games.* New York: Scholastic.

DelConte, M. (2007). A further study of present-tense narration: The absentee narratee and four-wall present tense in Coetzee's *Waiting for the Barbarians* and *Disgrace. Journal of Narrative Theory. 37*(3), 427-446.

Dunn, G. A., Michaud, N., & Irwin, W. (Eds.). (2012). *The Hunger Games and philosophy: A critique of pure treason.* Hoboken, NJ: John Wiley & Sons.

Gardner, J. (1971). *Grendel.* New York: Knopf.

Genette, G. (1980). *Narrative discourse: An essay in method.* Ithaca, NY: Cornell University Press.

Henthorne, T. (2012). *Approaching The Hunger Games trilogy: A literary and cultural analysis.* Jefferson, NC: McFarland.

Lloyd, S. (2009). *The carbon diaries: 2015.* London: Holiday House.

Miller, L. (2010, September 22). The fierce fight over the present tense. *Salon.* Retrieved from: http://www.salon.com/2010/09/22/present_tense/

Montgomery, R. (Director). (1947). *The lady in the lake* (Motion picture). USA: MGM.

Mortimore-Smith, S. R. (2012). Fueling the spectacle: Audience as "Gamemaker." In M. F. Pharr & L. A. Clark (Eds.), *Of bread, blood and The Hunger Games: Critical essays on the Suzanne Collins trilogy* (pp. 158-166). Jefferson, NC: McFarland & Company.

Myrick, D., & Sanchez, E. (Directors). (1999). *The Blair witch project* (Motion picture.) USA: Artisan.

Phelan, J. (1994). Present tense narration, mimesis, the narrative norm, and the positioning of the reader in *Waiting for the Barbarians.* In J. Phelan & P. J. Rabinowitz (Eds.), *Understanding narrative* (pp. 222-245). Columbus, OH: Ohio State University Press.

Nünning, A. (2005). Implied author. In D. Herman, M. Jahn, & M. L. Ryan (Eds.), *Routledge encyclopedia of narrative theory* (pp. 239-240). New York: Routledge.

Phelan, J. (2005a). *Living to tell about it: A rhetoric and ethics of character narration.* Ithaca, NY: Cornell University Press.

Phelan, J. (2005b). Rhetorical approaches to narrative. In D. Herman, M. Jahn, & M. L. Ryan (Eds.), *Routledge encyclopedia of narrative theory* (pp. 500-504). New York: Routledge.

Phelan, J. (2007). *Experiencing fiction: Judgments, progressions, and the rhetorical theory of narrative.* Columbus, OH: The Ohio State University Press.

Rabinowitz, P. J. (1977). Truth in fiction: A reexamination of audiences. *Critical Inquiry, 4*(1), 121-141.

Rabinowitz, P. J. (1987). *Before reading: Narrative conventions and the politics of interpretation.* Ithaca, NY: Cornell University Press.

Reeves, M. (Director). (2008). *Cloverfield* (motion picture). USA: Paramount.

Ross, G. (Director). (2012). *The hunger games.* USA: Lionsgate.

Salinger, J. D. (1951). *The catcher in the rye.* New York: Little, Brown, & Company.

Schuhmann, E. (1999). Shift out of first: Third-person narration has advantages. In P. P. Kelly & R. C. Small, Jr. (Eds.), *Two decades of the ALAN review* (pp. 314-319). Urbana, IL: NCTE.

Sebold, A. (2002). *Lovely bones.* New York: Little, Brown, & Company.

IRIS SHEPARD AND IAN WOJCIK-ANDREWS

11. ARE THE -ISMS EVER IN YOUR FAVOR?

Children's Film Theory and The Hunger Games

Analyzing film adaptations of young adult novels through the lens of critical theory reveals valuable information about each genre and provides insight into the culture in which the texts were created and the shaping influence of market forces in the production and distribution of the texts. Connors and Shepard (2013) state, "When one adopts a critical stance in relationship to young adult novels, it is possible to appreciate them as sophisticated, multi-layered works of literature that are open to myriad interpretations and that are capable of challenging students" (p. 10). The same is true for film adaptations of young adult texts.[1] Using critical theory—and ultimately teaching critical theory to young adult viewers—uncovers the complexity of books and their film adaptations and unmasks what our society values. Additionally, engaging texts critically and encouraging young viewers to do the same helps create an awareness of troubling moral positions of voyeuristic spectatorship in films like *The Hunger Games* (Ross, 2012) where kids killing kids is at the heart of the story.

The Hunger Games series constitutes for First World Cinema[2] a financially lucrative enterprise designed to fill the economic void produced by the Harry Potter and Twilight franchises. As Susan Shau Ming Tan (2013) states, "*The Hunger Games* is the American response to *Harry Potter*. As *Harry Potter* draws on traditional British structures to create its world, so too does *The Hunger Games* trilogy draw upon specifically American traditions as it envisions a future" (p. 70). Investigating the interplay of American consumer capitalism and gender in children's and young adult films is essential for a complete understanding of the series. To these historical materialist and feminist-oriented approaches to children's and young adult films we add a third: a discussion of *The Hunger Games* (Ross, 2012) through what Shohat and Stam (1994) call "the grid of multiculturalism" (p. 347). At issue is not the movie's superficial lip service to the politics of diversity—this is to be expected from Hollywood-centric movies, or what New Zealand filmmaker and writer Barry Barclay (2003) calls "Cinemas of the Modern Nation State" (p. 7)—but the death of the African American characters, especially Rue, as a necessary consequence for Katniss's Caucasian quest. As blogger Snarkycake (2013) bluntly states in a post titled "Straw Feminism," "Killing off a black girl to service the story of a white girl, [sic] is no better than killing a woman to service the story of a man … An ism is still an ism" (p. 3).

S. P. Connors (ed.), The Politics of Panem, 189–202.

IRIS SHEPARD AND IAN WOJCIK-ANDREWS

MARX, HISTORICAL MATERIALISM AND *THE HUNGER GAMES*

Adapted from the book of the same name, Ross's (2012) blockbuster movie version of *The Hunger Games*, which at the time of this writing has grossed $408 million domestically and $691 million worldwide ("Hunger Games," 2014), is set in the fictional country of Panem. In Collins's (2008) novel, a brief "history of Panem" (p. 18) is narrated by Katniss herself. In the opening scenes of the movie, which establishes a general level of poverty among the people of Panem primarily by showing specific images of elderly people as disheveled, hungry, and worn out, President Coriolanus Snow informs viewers of Panem's history. As is well known by readers and viewers alike, Panem, from the Latin phrase *panem et circenses*, "bread and circuses," was divided into 12 districts after the apocalyptic war. Each provides the centralized government in the Capitol with specific commodities that perpetuate the Capitol residents' lavish lifestyle whilst the people in the districts live at (or below) subsistence level. For example, District 4 serves the Capitol by providing seafood, agriculturally based District 11 provides produce (we'll discuss the ramifications of this later), and District 12, which produces coal, is home to Katniss, her sister, their mother, and the "world's ugliest cat" (Collins, 2008, p. 3). An impoverished mining district in what appears to reference the Appalachian Mountains, District 12's socio-economic structure mirrors the broader political structure of Panem. It contains two distinct economic and social classes—the extremely poor coal mining families who live and work in an area nicknamed the Seam, and a few families such as the Mayor's who live and work in better off neighborhoods.

Under the dictatorship of President Snow and his ironically named Peacekeepers, a privileged and powerful media maintains rigid control over Panem's inhabitants in part through the nationally televised Hunger Games and the annual reaping from which the Games' young tributes are drawn. Vividly depicted in the movie, and the cause of much concern among film critics and parents,[3] the gladiatorial-like Games in which kids must kill other kids or be killed themselves are shown as the central means by which the media, on behalf of and in collusion with President Snow, manipulate the people of Panem into accepting that any uprisings they may envision are futile. Fans of the Hunger Games trilogy know that as a consequence of its earlier rebellion, District 13 was ostensibly "obliterated" (Collins, 2008, p. 18), after which both the Games and the annual ritual of the reaping were established.

Katniss's transformative role over the course of the four movies so far planned is to defy the authorities and liberate the people. Her journey begins when she volunteers for the Games in place of her younger, more fragile sister Primrose, affectionately known as Prim and described in the book as being as "fresh as a raindrop, as lovely as the primrose for which she was named" (Collins, 2008, p. 3). Katniss's journey ends, at the conclusion of the first movie at least, with her and Peeta playing the role of star-crossed lovers. In the epilogue to *Mockingjay* (Collins, 2010), as in that of Rowling's (2007) *Harry Potter and the Deathly Hallows*, it is revealed that the series' protagonists, Katniss and Peeta, have stayed together: they have two children. It remains to be seen how Hollywood, no stranger to the comingling of politicians and movie stars, adapts that ending.[4]

In *The German Ideology* (1924/1972), Marx argues that "the ruling material force of society is at the same time its ruling intellectual force" (p. 44). The privileged political and cultural elite who reside in the Capitol are, in Marx's (1924/1972) terms, Panem's ruling material and intellectual class (p. 44). It is they who rose to power in the aftermath of a war that led to the destruction of North America and the emergence of Panem as a country divided into two distinct social classes, the haves and the have nots. The latter constitute a pool of cheap labor—a permanent underclass—structured into Panem's economy in order to service its governing elite. Marx further argued, and the storyworld of the film constructs seems to agree, that class division in the final instance is economically determined. Near the beginning of Ross's (2012) adaptation, we see not only images of impoverished elderly people, but also downtrodden mine workers entering and leaving the mines. From a materialist point of view, these workers are clearly alienated from their labor and, given the grim expressions on their faces, from themselves as well. They are presented not only as lacking any control over the coal they produce, but also, as in the case of Katniss's father, dying as a result of deplorable working conditions. Meanwhile, the affluent inhabitants of the Capitol live comfortably and safely.

These economically determined inequalities force Panem's population to make difficult moral choices. For example, Katniss, a far more politically savvy heroine in the book than in the movie adaptation, a point to which we will return momentarily, recognizes that despite the unfairness of these imposed economic hardships, they can be partially mitigated if parents have their children's names entered multiple times in the lottery of the Games. Parents are thus confronted with a profound moral choice, a "Sophie's Choice"[5] whereby entering their child's name in the reaping can ensure the family enough food to survive but also, quite possibly, result in their child's death. Tan's (2013) point that the economic system in Panem turns "children into agents of their families' survival [and that] Childhood is stripped away as families and adults offer up their children as potential sacrifice" (p. 56) is well made. It is clear that many of Panem's parents are constantly making unimaginably difficult moral choices brought on by an inhumanely exploitative economic system.

One of the most important aspects of *The German Ideology* is not just Marx's (1924/1972) assertion that ruling class ideas emerge from an unequal division of labor grounded in the forces of production, but his observation about how those ideas remain the ruling ideas. This is of utmost importance to Marxist theory. Marx argued that to maintain its dominant position, the ruling class of any given historical period must not only spread their economic interests around the world—in *The Communist Manifesto* Marx (1848/1972) writes that the bourgeoisie must "nestle everywhere, settle everywhere" (p. 87)—but also make ideas such as the global spread of democracy, capitalism, privatization, and so on appear as "the common interest of all the members of society, that is, expressed in ideal form: it has to give its ideas the form of universality" (p. 45). The historical moment of any revolutionary class, even as it assumes and consolidates its power through "political centralization" (p. 88), must be accompanied by a system that makes its ideas appear to be the ideas of the "whole mass of society" (p. 45). Capitalism, a system that benefits a minority at the expense of the majority, must nonetheless appear beneficial to all. For this to happen, Marx further argues, the dominant ideas of any given historical moment must be divorced from their political and ideological context. Capitalism, for example, must be seen as divorced from the petty squabbles among Republican or Democrat, Labor or Conservative, management or workers. It must be seen as universal, timeless, transcendent, beyond the specifics of history and social change.

From the point of view of Panem's ruling elite, the reaping, the accompanying festivities, and the televised Hunger Games themselves largely fulfill the role of making a specific, unwanted idea accepted by the majority of the people. Early in the movie when Seneca Crane, the Head Gamemaker, is interviewed by Caesar Flickerman, the television host who also interviews Katniss and Peeta before and after the Games, Seneca, whose name alludes to Lucius Annaeus Seneca, one of the men thought responsible for the Roman games, remarks that the Hunger Games are part of a "tradition ... [that] ... comes out of a particularly painful part of our history. But it's been the way we've been able to heal" (Ross, 2012). Seneca's use of key words such as "tradition," "our," "history," and "heal" are telling. For him, placing the Games within a tradition, albeit a painful one that led to the nation's healing, obfuscates their presence as an oppressive political strategy imposed by the victorious political party over a revolutionary group of disgruntled workers. If the Hunger Games are presented as the symbol of a nation's healing, they can hardly be seen as oppressive, especially if festivities accompany their actual violence and the victims, re-presented as victors, achieve either wealth for themselves and their families and/or recognition and status for their districts. As Seneca's interview with the obsequious Flickerman ends, Seneca slowly and dramatically raises his hands, locks his fingers together in an image of unity, and icily comments that the Games are now "something that knits us together" (Ross, 2012).

With these words and with this gesture, the Hunger Games are presented as having transcended their original punitive purpose to become the means by which a particular idea regarding the survival of the few (only one child survives the arena) is seen and internalized as ultimately worth the death of many (most die). This idea is then again internalized as representative of a broader set of relationships between the Capitol (the survival of a few) and the people of Panem at large (the death of many). In short, from a classic Marxian point of view, one that emphasizes *The German Ideology* (1924/1972) and *The Communist Manifesto* (1848/1972) as its founding texts, the movie's premise, the building block that underpins everything else, is a futuristic, post-apocalyptic world in which the masses are enslaved by a political and cultural minority who count among their armory not just the physically repressive Peacekeepers, but also the media's skillful production and manipulation of words and images related to self-sacrifice, wealth, and privilege. If the Hunger Games are "games," with all of the connotations of childish play the latter word evokes, and since they are televised and thus experienced only vicariously by all of Panem's viewers, the ruling class questions whether the Games are really harmful.

In the literary and filmic worlds that Collins (2008) and Ross (2012) construct, the Games, their status as entertainment, and their reception by Panem's audiences are ultimately a not so subtle criticism of contemporary American audience's relationship to mass entertainment and the apathy such entertainment breeds. In an interview with Rick Margolis (2008), Collins commented that the inspiration for *The Hunger Games* came whilst she was surfing television one night. As she flicked from images of young people competing for a prize on a reality show to equally young people fighting real wars, she became concerned that American audiences as a whole were becoming increasingly desensitized to the plight of others (Margolis, 2008). Collins imagines the book and the movie, given her involvement as Executive Producer, as a warning to audiences about the mind numbing apathy that contemporary mass media generates as images from utterly trivial reality shows compete for ratings alongside profoundly disturbing images of children suffering around the world. Further, the movie also functions as a warning about what might subsequently happen as that apathy grows: the end of democracy and the beginning of an autocracy, a political system in which one ruler maintains absolute power through the manipulation of images and ideas by an equally powerful and corrupt media, precisely what we find in *The Hunger Games* (Ross, 2012), and not unlike what we find in the United States today.

The question thus arises: to what extent does the movie adaptation of Collins's (2008) novel effectively model the dangers of an autocracy?[6] To what extent is the United States actually heading toward the kind of dystopia imagined in *The Hunger Games*? The evidence that 21st century American society is inexorably moving in the direction of the kind of world that Collins envisions is compelling. In the United States, as in Panem, there is an ever-widening division between the rich and the poor as Hope Yen (2013) reported recently in *The Huffington Post.* In both worlds, youth and beauty appear valued above everything else. Before the release of the second film, *Catching Fire* (Lawrence, 2013), magazines such as *Covergirl* started a make-up line based on the fashions of the Capitol. By replicating the fictional Panem's fashions in this way, and by asking audiences literally to buy into the cultural life of Panem, there is a strong argument to be made that Panem and the contemporary United States are frighteningly similar, especially with regards to the media's ability to breed apathy in the face of real human tragedy and thus slowly but surely blur the distinction between "reel" and real world violence. Instead of successfully critiquing the excesses of capitalism and fulfilling Collins's goal of increasing awareness about the dangers of violence, the film's emphasis on the glamor of the Capitol and the accompanying co-marketing of make-up and accessories—the economic realm in other words—may become the most durable aspect of the film. Sadly, no one is dressing as the poor miners from District 12. Instead, our privileged media and marketing corporations encourage consumers to re-make themselves in the image of Panem's elite. To be sure, from a media literacy perspective, issues of replication and identification might prove a rich area to unpack with young viewers. Encouraging them to question the ultimate effects of *Covergirl's* marketing strategies and, in turn, the machine of capitalism itself could yield positive results for our society as a whole. But if we do not ask young viewers these difficult questions, the adaptation remains part of the problem, not the solution.

It doesn't help that the young protagonists of the movie, Katniss and Peeta, themselves seem inured to the violence that would otherwise define them. We recall that the Games have purportedly been running for seventy-four years. The second film, *Catching Fire* (Lawrence, 2013), focuses on the seventy-fifth Hunger Game where the tributes are reaped from a pool of victors. Thus, by the seventy-fifth competition, 1,776 children have been subjected to the horror of the Games, and 1,151 have died at the hands of other children. To prepare for their second Hunger Games, Peeta and Katniss watch recordings of previous Games. Katniss states, "Peeta puts in the tape, and I curl up next to him on the sofa with my milk which is really delicious with honey and spices, and lose myself in the Fiftieth Hunger Games" (Collins, 2009, p. 235). The protagonists themselves have become alienated from the violence of the Games. Consequently, it is reasonable to question the extent to which they themselves have become as culpable as the Capitol's privileged audience for the death of others in the film and, by association, blunting our experience of violence in real life. Wouldn't the film adaptation of the novel offer a more effective warning, pedagogically speaking, if Katniss and Peeta refused to watch the Games on television, thus modeling for young adults in the real world their rejection of mass media's tendency to trivialize human suffering, in this instance the death of children? For *The Hunger Games* adaptation to function effectively, audiences, young and old, should see heroes and heroines such as Peeta and Katniss reject the instruments of their torture, the societal chains by which they are physically enslaved. Watching Katniss and Peeta enjoying television shows provided by Panem's equivalent to what *The Nation* in 2006 referred to as the National Entertainment State[7] does nothing to resolve the class divisions that structure North American social life. Thought-provoking though it may be, Ross's (2012) *The Hunger Games* adaptation merely "reproduces the conditions of production" (Althusser, 1971, p. 127) that perpetuate divisive social formations and class divisions.

FROM REVOLUTIONARY TO BEAUTY QUEEN: FEMINISM AND *THE HUNGER GAMES*

Feminist film theory has undergone numerous developments since the 1960s, a point that Patricia White (2000) makes in her chapter on "Feminism and Film" in *Film Studies: Critical Approaches*. White charts the history of feminism and film studies from the early days of "images of women" criticism, initiated by critics such as Molly Haskell and Marjorie Rosen in the 1960 and 1970s, to semiotic, ideological, psychoanalytic, and reception studies, the latter occurring in the 1990s. Other collections of essays such as *Multiple Voices in Feminist Film Criticism* (Carson, Dittmar, & Welsch, 1994) chart similar histories and include extensive discussions regarding films starring women of color. Specifically in relation to children's and young adult film criticism, critics such as D. Soyini Madison (1995) in *From Mouse to Mermaid: The Politics of Film, Gender, and Culture* use black feminist theory to discuss movies for young adult audiences such as *Pretty Woman* (Marshall, 1990). In doing so, Madison and others in the anthology see class, gender, and race as interconnected categories appropriate for analysis of films for young adults, especially those produced, marketed, and distributed by Hollywood.

Following the release of Ross's (2012) adaptation of *The Hunger Games*, there has been a range of reactions among feminist film critics. Katha Pollitt (2012), for example, commends the character of Katniss. Noting that Hollywood rarely does justice to a book, Pollitt argues that Katniss Everdeen "is a rare thing in pop-fiction: a complex female character with courage, brains, and a quest of her own" (para. 4). Lex (2012), a contributor to *Fan Girl: The Blog*, agrees, arguing in "Journey of a Strong Female Heroine: Katniss Everdeen" that Katniss's quest to an extent mirrors Campbell's journey of the hero, but ultimately differs markedly from that structure. Campbell's model looks back in history to predominantly male heroes whose masculinist journeys to identity inevitably involve their struggling and eventually succeeding alone. Lex points out that contemporary heroines draw upon fundamentally feminine qualities such as nurturing and relationships to achieve their quest. Unlike their male counterparts, heroines do not go it alone. They actively seek help from others. For Lex and other similar minded bloggers, Katniss perfectly reflects these liberal feminist approaches to the journey of the heroine. However, more politically-minded and left-oriented feminist critics see Katniss as less heroic. Snarkycake's blog post (2013), for example, critiques Katniss as just another heroine who plays a supporting role, arguing that Katniss is a "fascinating example of the much heralded 'strong female character' [that] is actually a very disturbing sexist trope, a straw feminist, whose story doesn't teach [women] to be courageous, and self-reliant, but instead to be better than other women, by being more like men" (para. 30).

While these differences of opinion among feminist critics are welcomed, we want to return here to the issue of adaptation and consider how specific changes made between book and film have a crucial impact on our understanding of Katniss and her role as heroine. Overall, with the changes that Ross (2012) makes in his adaptation, the young adult novel written as a warning for American teenagers morphs into an entertaining film sold around the world to a general audience. Consequently, the movie ceases to be a warning. Instead it functions as a commodity designed to reap profits for Lions Gate Productions. Unsurprisingly, Katniss's role in the book as a political critic and agitator is downplayed in the movie, and her presence as a star is highlighted. In the novel, Collins (2008) gives Katniss a political consciousness. She knows the brutal history of Panem, "the country that rose up out of the ashes of a place that was once called North America" (p. 18). She knows about the play of language, recognizing that "in District 12 ... the word tribute is pretty much synonymous with the word corpse" (p. 22). She knows that regardless of how the Games are presented, underneath all the glitz and glamor "the real message is clear" (p. 19): rebel against the authorities and, like District 13, you will be destroyed. Yet in Ross's (2012) adaptation, Katniss's political consciousness is conspicuously absent.

In keeping with most young adult fiction's narrative style, Collins's (2008) book is written from Katniss's point of view. We see what she sees. Unfortunately it is precisely her matter-of-fact narrative that the film takes away and turns into dazzlingly visual effects. Images replace words. More emphasis is placed on Katniss' wardrobe than her potential as a leader. Her dresses, instead of being seen as a reflection of her disgust at the "Capitol and its hideous fashions" (p. 63), instead come across as a stunningly beautiful expression of a girl on fire. On Facebook, the official Hunger Games site (2014) posted a place for fans to vote on which dress was the most beautiful called "Which of Cinna's Creations do you Admire Most?" Noticeably absent from the film and from all of the marketing are lessons and Facebook surveys about becoming a revolutionary figure, starting a grassroots rebellion, or simply challenging Panem's political and cultural authorities in ways that do not involve further bloodshed. In short, Katniss's sense of herself as an agent of revolutionary political and moral change is drastically undercut over the course of the movie. In Collins's (2008) novel, her understanding of history, class, and the possibilities for social change is suggestive of what Antonio Gramsci (1971) calls an organic intellectual, one who directs "the ideas and aspirations of the class to which they belong" (p. 3). In the movie she is a violent beauty queen. Of course, there are several reasons for this change. Fast-paced action sequences and special effects attract more viewers. From Hollywood's point of view, a young adult movie that features thoughtful, reasoned inner monologues from a smart sixteen year-old about the possibilities of a classless society is not as commercially viable as seeing an attractive female ride into the Capitol on a chariot of fire. But then, arguably, one of the cinematic strategies that Hollywood-centrist companies employ to eschew radical change is to value movie heroines for their looks rather than their political voices, perpetuating the objectification of women. Not surprisingly, this stance is frequently replicated in the real world.

THE POLITICS OF WHITENESS: MULTICULTURALISM AND
THE HUNGER GAMES

We think it important to critique First World movies such as *The Hunger Games* (Ross, 2012) using a lens of multiculturalism in order to highlight how films can appear progressive on the one hand yet be reactionary on the other hand because of the racially charged colonialist tropes they—First World film companies such as MGM and Warner Brothers—have typically used since the beginning of the twentieth century. The premise of *The Hunger Games*—that the horrors of a dystopian world such as Panem are unsettlingly similar to the horrors of American life today—is thought provoking and pedagogically enlightening for younger audiences perhaps unaware of how film, including children's and young adult fantasy films, point to real life situations, trends, and movements. Indeed, there are relevant lesson plans that could explore the politics of adaptation and the power of the media. Likewise the role of American audiences flicking through thousands of television channels could be compared to Panem's cultural and political elite viewing the Games. Which is the more dangerous scenario?

A progressive pedagogy of young adult film should also explore issues of race inscribed in films since *The Birth of a Nation* (Griffith, 1915). The issue then in 1915 is the same now almost a hundred years later: the representation of race in First World movies such as *The Hunger Games* (Ross, 2012). The aspect of multiculturalism, or race studies, that we are interested in here is what Shohat and Stam (1994) call the "racial politics of casting" (p. 189). Shohat and Stam argue, "Within Hollywood cinema, Euro-Americans have historically enjoyed the unilateral prerogative of acting in 'blackface,' 'redface,' 'brownface,' and 'yellowface,' while the reverse has rarely been the case" (p. 189). In other words, Hollywood-centric movies typically employ white actors and actresses to play non-Caucasian roles. *The Birth of a Nation* (Griffith, 1915) and *The Jazz Singer* (Crosland, 1926) are often cited as early examples of the intersections of race, politics, and casting and we would argue that the practice remains in place today in films like Ross's (2012) *The Hunger Games*. A case in point would be the casting of Jennifer Lawrence to play Katniss Everdeen. In Collins's (2008) novel, Katniss is described as having "straight black hair ... [and] ... olive skin" (p. 8). Like Gale, she has "gray eyes" (p. 8). In Ross's (2012) film, however, the character is played by white, blue-eyed Jennifer Lawrence. To its credit, Lions Gate makes gestures toward accuracy, sensitivity and authenticity in *The Hunger Games*. African American actors play Rue (Amandla Stenberg), Thresh (Dayo Okenlyl), and Cinna (Lenny Kravitz). Even so, whilst Ross's use of African American actors to play characters described as dark-skinned is appropriate, many viewers vehemently disliked the ethnically correct casting of Rue and Thresh. Rosen (2012), in "*Hunger Games* Racist Tweets," quoted multiple fans as stating that the casting of Amandla Stenberg as Rue completely ruined the movie for them. Beyond these personal responses to the movie's racial casting, the underlying, structural issue lies with the remaining characters being cast as white without any particular narrative justification. Blogger Alexiel (2011) states, "If Collins intended this as a metaphor to Third World struggles and wars, and Katniss is a woman of color—then I love the trilogy because it allows women and people of color to envision their struggles differently. They could see themselves as heroes and agents of change" (para. 21). But, Alexiel goes on to state, if Collins intended Katniss to be white then she "is deliberately appropriating the struggles of millions and placing white protagonists in places where people of color should be (and in reality, are)" (para. 22). Despite Collins's own representation of Panem as multiracial,[8] the movie's default position remains white.

In Ross's (2012) adaptation, Rue's death is a perfect example of what Donald Bogle (2001), in *Toms, Coons, Mulattoes, Mammies, and Bucks: An Interpretative History of Blacks in American Films*, calls the image of the "ebony saint" (qtd. in Shohat & Stam, p. 203). A variation on the Uncle Tom and pick ninny figure, the trope of the "ebony saint," whereby a black character dies, literally or symbolically, so that a white character can live (surely an extreme form of blackface) has existed since the silent era and continues today in movies as different as *The Help* (2011), *The Blind Side* (2009), *Captain Phillips* (2013) and, we argue, *The Hunger Games* (2012). Thus, in her first Games, Katniss joins forces with Rue in order to protect her, in part because Rue reminds Katniss of her sister Prim. Unfortunately, Katniss's presence only endangers Rue as it draws the more vicious tributes to them. Rue potentially would have survived the Games hidden in the trees while the other tributes battled it out, much like Mags and Beetee survived their respective Games, if Katniss had not intervened. Consequently, Rue becomes a stepping-stone in Katniss's survival, and her death serves as a beginning for Katniss's career as a rebel. Tan (2013) argues that Katniss's alliance with Rue results in her becoming a revolutionary symbol: "Even moments after she honors Rue, this contact with an 'other' expands exponentially as Rue's district sends Katniss bread, an unheard-of gesture of solidarity, an unprecedented moment of communication between the districts" (p. 59). Nonetheless, Katniss's life is predicated upon the death of the African American, "ebony saint" character, Rue. When Katniss honored Rue's death by surrounding her body with flowers, she showed human tenderness and a respect for the sanctity of human life. But that is not the last time viewers see Rue's body. She appears again towards the end of the Games as a genetically modified mutt. Tan (2013) comments, "With the dismemberment of Rue, the Capitol undermines Katniss's earlier reclamation of Rue, a demonstration that Rue is still a 'piece in their Games.' Rue's body is vulnerable even in death, still subject to power and punishment" (p. 64). Meanwhile, Katniss lives on, fought over by two handsome princes and the darling of the Capitol in much the same way that Lawrence became the darling of Hollywood. For all its criticism of government and the media, *The Hunger Games* (Ross, 2012) is at heart simply another First World, Hollywood blockbuster extravaganza whose choice of actors points to the "intrication of economics and racism" (Shohat & Stam, 1994, p. 190). As such, it glosses over the historical realities of American race relations, a history that structurally privileges a white majority at the expense of a black minority.

Blackface, or the overall politics of whiteness, is privileged in other ways in Ross's (2012) film. The relationship between race and region also defaults to cultural stereotyping. Several articles have explored the parallels between District 12 and Appalachia. For example, Lana Whited (2012) states that Katniss has "deep Appalachian roots and that her odyssey illustrates several key themes associated with that region" (p. 327). Other districts are rooted in far more disturbing historical soil. District 11, Rue's district, is an agricultural district. As in the other districts, a tyrannical government enslaves the people of District 11. However, District 11 is the only non-white district, and its inhabitants are all African American. First, why are the districts segregated? Second, why are African Americans put in an agricultural district? With America's bloody history of slavery, the echoes are disturbing and, given Collins's (2008) heart-felt gestures toward multiculturalism, this choice points to the worst kind of cultural stereotyping. In this aspect, *The Hunger Games* (Ross, 2012), like *The Help*

(Taylor, 2011), is a dangerous movie: what it perpetuates is the myth of white supremacy and black subservience.

CONCLUSION

Historical materialist approaches to children's and young adult films have a useful application today. Historical materialist readings of dystopian movies such as *The Hunger Games* (Ross, 2012) make important contributions to discussions about the representation of history and social class in film. They show how class in First World movies is typically a framing device that permits the emergence of the individual. Historical materialist readings are also powerfully self-reflexive. We question not just the extent to which the socially and economically stratified fictional world of *The Hunger Games* reflects the real world economic inequalities and social and cultural contradictions of the modern global economy, but also the degree to which, like the uncaring spectators in the Capitol who merely want to be entertained and couldn't care less about a few child-like tributes, we are equally complicit in the exploitation of children today.

Additionally, historical materialism is obviously interested in economic issues, especially in relation to First World production companies and their franchises. The Harry Potter, Twilight, and Hunger Games series adaptations earn billions of dollars for film studios such as MGM, Warner Bros., and others. But the historical materialist tradition is also fundamentally concerned with moral issues: profit margins shouldn't be the only concern in the production of a film. This is especially relevant to dystopian movies featuring young people. What is the moral, rather than the economic, cost of producing movies for young audiences in which teenagers kill teenagers? The movie adaptation of *The Hunger Games* (Ross, 2012) perpetuates, rather than solves, the problems it raises, including those of socio-economic, political and cultural inequality, mindless marketing and crass consumerism, adaptation and spectatorship and the totality of their intersections to history, class, gender, and race.

By acquainting adolescent (and adult) viewers with critical theory, much can be gained by reading against the ideological grain of the film. Helping students acquire an understanding of relevant critical theories encourages them to ask difficult questions, interpret complex films like *The Hunger Games* (2012), and decide for themselves what is really 'reel.' Thus, classroom projects grow out of applying critical theory to young adult films, including presentations, creative writing, essays, dramatic interpretations, and other forms of arts-integration. Whatever form these learning experiences take, it is essential that, as educators, we critically engage popular adaptations of young adult films in much the same way we would literature while encouraging our students to do the same.

NOTES

[1] For a straightforward discussion of the relationship between film adaptation and the young adult novel, see Foster (1994).

2   Contemporary film studies typically distinguish between First, Second, Third and Fourth World cinemas. First World Cinema is synonymous with blockbuster, Hollywood type movies designed to maximize profits for companies such as MGM, Warner Brothers, Columbia, and so forth. Hollywoodcentric movies are narratively and ideologically conservative. Second World Cinema is often equated with independent, art-house kinds of movies produced within and without the United States. Politically charged Third Cinema, or Thirdist films, emerged from Latin America during the 1960s and 1970s. Third World films employ unconventional cinematic strategies and unknown actors to articulate their anti-colonial, anti-capitalist narratives. According to Maori director Barry Barclay, Fourth World cinema emphasizes the self-representation of indigenous or tribal groups such as the Inuits and Aboriginal Australians.

3   According to *Time Magazine's* "The Hunger Games reaches another milestone: Top 10 Most Censored Books," there were several objections to the series, named third most challenged, including concerns that the books are "anti-ethnic," "anti-family," and "occult/satanic." The film version faced more international criticism than in the U.S. According to McQuinn (2014), *The Hunger Games* received more complaints in Ireland than any other film within the past two years. Several parental complaints about gratuitous violence were filed in England as well according to the *BBC* and *The Guardian*.

4   For a fuller discussion of the relationship between Hollywood and politics see, for example, Ross (2011).

5   The phrase 'Sophie's Choice' is derived from Alan J. Pakula's 1982 movie adaptation of William Styron's novel of the same name. Specifically, it refers to the moment in the movie when one of Hitler's high-ranking soldiers tells a Jewish mother, Sophie, that she must choose one of her children to stay behind (and face certain death) whilst she and the other child escape to freedom on the train that she is trying to board. Even though the choice is impossible, the anguished, heart-broken mother, movingly played by Meryl Streep, leaves her son and takes her daughter with her. It is considered one of the most powerfully haunting scenes in movie history. The phrase "Sophie's Choice" remains relevant today, especially in movies such as *The Hunger Games* whereby parents must make horribly difficult moral choices brought on by exploitative economic forces.

6   See Bandura (1977). As part of the broader developments in the field of social learning theory, in the 1970s, Albert Bandura developed the concept of symbolic modeling by which a movie, for example, models an outcome to which that movie's audiences may (or may not) respond either positively or negatively. This concept, and others from social learning theory, has an interesting application to certain film genres, especially the dystopian genre that implicitly teaches a lesson: apocalyptic conditions are bad for everyone and thus should be avoided at all costs. The question for *The Hunger Games* as a movie is whether it effectively shows what those dangers are—lots of violence—and thus convinces audiences to avoid them or whether it glorifies or romanticizes those dangers and thus further blurs the distinctions between the real and the reel, precisely what Collins was trying to avoid.

7   See The National Entertainment State, 2006 (2006).

8   In April of 2011, Suzanne Collins told Entertainment Weekly that her characters "were not particularly intended to be biracial. It is a time period where hundreds of years have passed from now. There's been a lot of ethnic mixing. But I think I describe them as having dark hair, grey eyes, and sort of olive skin ... But then there are some characters in the book who are more specifically described" (Valby, 2011, para. 24). For instance, Thresh and Rue. Collins went on to say, "They're African-American" (para. 26). Director Gary Ross added: "Thresh and Rue will be [played by actors who are] African-American. It's a multi-racial culture and the film will reflect that. But I think Suzanne didn't see a particular ethnicity to Gale and Katniss when she wrote it, and that's something we've talked about a lot" (para. 28).

REFERENCES

Alexiel. (2011). *Why Katniss Everdeen is a woman of color* [Blog post]. Retrieved from http://xalexiel.blogspot.com/2011/03/why-katniss-everdeen-is-woman-of-color.html

Althuser, L. (1971). *Lenin and philosophy and other essays* (B. Brewster, Trans.). New York: Monthly Review Press.

Bandura, A. (1977). *Social learning theory.* Englewood Cliffs: Prentice Hall.

Barclay, B. (2003). Celebrating fourth cinema. *Illusions Magazine, 35*(7), 7-11.

Bogle, D. (2001). *Toms, coons, mulattoes, mammies, and bucks* (4th ed.). New York: Bloomsbury Academic.

Carson, D., Dittmar, L., & Welsch, J. (1994). *Multiple voices in feminist film criticism.* Minneapolis, MN: University of Minneapolis Press.

Collins, S. (2008). *The hunger games.* New York: Scholastic.

Collins, S. (2009). *Catching fire.* New York: Scholastic.

Collins, S. (2010). *Mockingjay.* New York: Scholastic.

Connors, S.P., & Shepard, I. (2013). The case for young adult literature. *Signal Journal, 35*(3), 6-10.

Crosland, A. (Director). (1926). *The jazz singer* [Motion picture]. USA.

Foster, M. H. (1994). Film and the young adult novel. *The ALAN Review, 21*(3).

Gramsci, A. (1971). *Selections from the prison notebooks.* (G. Hinton and G.N. Nowell, Trans.). New York: International Publishers.

Griffith, D.W. (Director). (1915). *The birth of a nation* [Motion picture]. USA.

Hunger Games. (2014). *Box office mojo.* Retrieved May 15, 2014 from http://boxofficemojo.com/movies/?id=hungergames.html

Hunger Games facebook. (2014). *Which of Cinna's #CatchingFire creations do you admire the most?* [Facebook post]. Retrieved from https://www.facebook.com/TheHungerGamesMovie

Larrick, N. (1965, September). The all white world of children's literature. *Saturday Review*, 63-65.

Lawrence, F. (Director). (2013). *Catching fire* [Motion picture]. USA.

Lex. (2012). Journey of a strong female heroine: Katniss Everdeen. *Fan girl: The blog* [Blog post]. Retrieved from http://fangirlblog.com/2012/03/journey-of-strong-female-heroine-katniss-everdeen/

Madison, S. D. (1995). Pretty Woman through the triple lens of black feminist scholarship. In E. Bell, L. Haas, & L. Sells (Eds.), *From mouse to mermaid: The politics of film, gender, and culture* (pp. 224-235). Bloomington: Indiana University Press.

Margolis, R. (2008, September). A killer story: An interview with Suzanne Collins, author of *The Hunger Games. School Library Journal.* Retrieved from http://www.slj.com/2008/09/authors-illustrators/a-killer-story-an-interview-with-suzanne-collins

Marshall, D. (Director). (1990). *Pretty woman* [Motion picture]. USA.

Marx, K. (1924/1972). The German ideology. *On historical materialism* (pp. 14-76). New York: International Publishers.

Marx, K. (1848/1972). The communist manifesto. *On historical materialism* (pp. 84-102). New York: International Publishers.

Marx, K. (1888/1972). Theses on Feuerbach. *On historical materialism* (pp. 10-13). New York: International Publishers.

McQuinn, C. (2014). 'The Hunger Games' topped complaints to film censor. *Independent.ie.* Retrieved from http://www.independent.ie/entertainment/movies/the-hunger-games-topped-complaints-to-film-censor-29887295.html

Pakula, A. J. (Director). (1982). *Sophie's choice* [Motion picture]. USA.

Pollitt, K. (2012). The Hunger Games' feral feminism. *The Nation.* Retrieved from http://www.thenation.com/article/167182/hunger-games-feral-feminism#

Rosen, C. (2012). 'Hunger Games' racist tweets: Fans upset because of Rue's race. *Huffington Post.* Retrieved from http://www.huffingtonpost.com/2012/03/26/hunger-games-racist-tweets-rue_n_1380377.html

Ross, G. (Director). (2012). *The hunger games* [Motion picture]. USA.

Ross, S. J. (2011). *Hollywood left and right: How movie stars shaped American politics.* Oxford: Oxford University Press.

Rountree, W. (2008). *Just us girls: The contemporary African American young adult novel.* New York: Peter Lang International Academic Publisher.

Rowling, J. K. (2007). *Harry Potter and the deathly hallows.* New York: Scholastic.

Shohat, E., & Stam. R. (1994). *Unthinking Eurocentrism: Multiculturalism and the media.* London: Routledge.

Snarkycake. (2013). *Straw feminism: The problem with Katniss Everdeen and the 'better girl' trope* [Blog post]. Retrieved from http://snarkycake.blogspot.com/2013/12/straw-feminism-problem-with-katniss.html

Tan, S. S. M. (2013). Burn with us: Sacrificing childhood in *The Hunger Games. The Lion and the Unicorn, 37*(1), 54-73.

Taylor, T. (Director). (2011). *The help* [Motion picture]. USA.

The Hunger Games reaches another milestone: Top 10 censored books. (2012). *Time Magazine.* Retrieved from http://entertainment.time.com/2011/01/06/removing-the-n-word-from-huck-finn-top-10-censored-books/

The National Entertainment State, 2006. (2006). *The Nation.* Retrieved from http://www.thenation.com/article/national-entertainment-state-2006#

Valby, K. (2011). Team Hunger Games talks: Author Suzanne Collins and director Gary Ross on their allegiance to each other, and their actors. *Entertainment Weekly.* Retrieved from http://insidemovies.ew.com/2011/04/07/hunger-games-suzanne-collins-gary-ross-exclusive/

White, P. (2000). Feminism and film. In J. Hill & P. C. Gibson (Eds.), *Film studies: Critical approaches* (pp. 115-132). Oxford: Oxford University Press.

Whited, L. (2012). The hunger games. *Journal of Appalachian* Studies, *18*(1/2), 326-331.

Yen, H. (2013). 80 percent of U.S. adults face near-poverty, unemployment: Survey. *The Huffington Post.* Retrieved from http://www.huffingtonpost.com/2013/07/08/poverty-unemployment-rates_n_3666594.html

12. THE REVOLUTION STARTS WITH RUE

Online Fandom and the Racial Politics of The Hunger Games

Thresh brings the rock down hard against Clove's temple. It's not bleeding, but I can see the dent in her skull and I know that she's a goner. There's still life in her now though, in the rapid rise and fall of her chest, the low moan escaping her lips.

When Thresh whirls around on me, the rock raised, I know it's not good to run. And my bow is empty, the last loaded arrow having gone in Clove's direction. I'm trapped in the glare of his strange golden brown eyes. "What'd she mean? About Rue being your ally?"

"I–I–we teamed up. Blew up the supplies. I tried to save her, I did. But he got there first. District One," I say. Maybe if he knows I helped Rue, he won't choose some slow sadistic end for me.

"And you killed him?" he demands.

"Yes. I killed him. And buried her in flowers," I say. "And I sang her to sleep."

Tears spring to my eyes. The tension, the fight goes out of me at the memory. And I'm overwhelmed by Rue, and the pain in my head, and my fear of Thresh, and the moaning of the dying girl a few feet away.

"To sleep?" Thresh says gruffly.

"To death. I sang until she died," I say. "Your district … they sent me bread." My hand reaches up but not for an arrow that I know I'll never reach. Just to wipe my nose. "Do it fast, okay, Thresh?"

Conflicting emotions cross Thresh's face. He lowers the rock and points at me, almost accusingly. "Just this one time, I let you go. For the little girl. You and me, we're even then. No more owed. You understand?"

I nod because I do understand. About owing. About hating it. I understand that if Thresh wins, he'll have to go back and face a district that has already broken all the rules to thank me, and he is breaking the rules to thank me, too. And I understand that, for the moment, Thresh is not going to smash in my skull. (Collins, 2008, pp. 287-288)

INTRODUCTION

The excerpt above highlights how the protagonist of Suzanne Collins' (2008) *The Hunger Games*—our revolutionary hero—Katniss Everdeen escapes the throes of death to live and lead and change the dystopic future that is at the heart of the trilogy. The climactic moment of mercy and of tribute to a fallen comrade for Thresh, a fallen sister for Katniss, is but one of many pivotal moments in Collins' opening volume. A traditional reading of this scene would suggest that it is Katniss's likeability, her empathic relationship with Rue that saves her. Her sense of justice and loyalty also appear to allow her to save her District 12 partner, Peeta, at the novel's conclusion and to act as mascot for an oppressed working class's revolutionary uprising.

However, we would argue that this simply isn't the case.

Katniss is not the revolutionary matriarch we are led to believe across the Hunger Games trilogy.

Rue is.

And while we will ground our reading of the Hunger Games trilogy throughout this chapter in how media responds to and expands texts in an era of "participatory culture" (Jenkins et al., 2009), we also want to spend time highlighting that we are not alone in our belief that the first volume in Collins' trilogy casts the most revolutionary character of the series as martyr for a mounting revolution. Rue's death sparks social change; Katniss is simply there to stand witness as Rue's disciple. What's more, this chapter attempts to problematize hegemonic readings of the Hunger Games and, in particular, highlight how racialized political life beyond the confines of this work clouds how mass media interpret and respond to youth of color in young adult literature. As we look at how fans responded to casting black actors in the film adaptation of the novel as well as how online fan communities explore the revolutionary impact of Rue, we emphasize that public imagination often cannot see racialized life in young adult literature and how this genre can incite critically conscious identity formation for readers. Ultimately, we see Collins' (2008) *The Hunger Games* as a book that informs civic identity for its readers. In particular, a critical reading of this book can define powerful civic lessons for youth of color.

This chapter looks at two very different dialogues that are spurred largely through online fan communities and public social networks like Twitter. In doing so, we uncover racial identities constructed in readers' interpretations of the Hunger Games. Like the fans and their dialogue, our analysis moves messily between Collins' (2008) novel and director Gary Ross' (2012) film adaptation. Often, fans will use images and quotes from the film to develop larger thematic arguments tied to the Hunger Games as a franchise—a film, book series, and imaginative world ripe for exploration and remix.

THE RUE-VOLUTIONARIES: YOUTH READING, RESPONDING, AND
RECIRCULATING ONLINE

As critical scholars of color, it is important to note that we do not own nor did we originate the notion of Rue as the revolutionary crux of the Hunger Games. We want to first clarify that our understanding of Rue as a powerful, necessary revolutionary comes from our own fomenting scholarship related to critical readings of race, class, and gender in young adult literature (Garcia, 2013). Further, such conceptual readings are shaped by social dialogue across communities and peer networks both online and in person. In fact, we will describe below several ways online fandom communities help challenge hegemonic readings of Collins's (2008) *The Hunger Games* and how our participation within these spaces helps amplify our own critical dialogue with other scholars and young adult literature fans.

One of us, Marcelle, wrote a blog post in which she described the powerful role Rue had in her viewing and understanding of the world Collins (2008) constructs in *The Hunger Games*. In her post, she wrote:

When I first read *The Hunger Games* (no spoilers for those who haven't read the series. But, if you haven't, read it!), I instantly related to the character Rue, a 12-year old girl from District 11 selected to participate in the 74th Hunger Games. From the author's description of District 11 and of Rue, I pictured her to be a little brown-skinned, naturally curly haired Black girl. And, apparently, when I saw the first film, so did a lot of other people. Yet, there was a social media frenzy about people's upset and disappointment that the role of Rue was acted by a young Black actress, Amandla Stenberg. For me, this role was cast perfectly–Ms. Stenberg embodied everything I imagined Rue to be. But, also, how wonderful for young Black girls and for the little Black girl in me to read about and see representations of ourselves even in an imagined world. (Haddix, 2013)

We will return to the "social media frenzy" caused by Stenberg's casting later in this chapter. For now, we want to focus on the powerful role Rue, the actress Amandla Stenberg, and race played in readings and viewings of both Collin's (2008) novel and the subsequent film adaptation for fans across the world. Such work does not fit merely within the academic setting of journals and conference presentations but spills more broadly into the vast landscape of young adult literature fandom.

In looking at online fan spaces like blogs and Tumblr pages, we want to foreground some basic information on youth fandom and memes. Scientist Richard Dawkins (1976) coined the term "meme" to illustrate ways ideas and organisms replicate and spread. He writes:

Examples of memes are tunes, ideas, catch-phrases, clothes fashions, ways of making pots or of building arches. Just as genes propagate themselves in the gene pool by leaping from body to body via sperms or eggs, so memes propagate themselves in the meme pool by leaping from brain to brain, via a process which, in the broad sense, can be called *imitation*. (p. 192)

Dawkins' work is foundational in offering a definition of memes that persists today; it is a definition that is meme-like in its own right, propagating itself in literature and popular discourse. While there is little research about which memes are successful in their virality (see Garcia-Herranz et al., 2014), memes are important cultural literacy performances for youth engagement. Building on Dawkins' (1976) definition, literacy research has explored how memes can offer powerful spaces for the growth of sociocultural development. Knobel and Lankshear (2007) have highlighted memes as "a new literacy practice" with significance for "enacting active/activist literacies" (p. 203). In this context, the writing, reading, and circulation of memes (primarily in online environments) is a powerful literacy practice that allows youth to comment on and engage with their sociocultural world.

As both fans and scholars of young adult literature, we engage with memes from a stance of pedagogical possibility and extracurricular fandom. Our own work writing about young adult texts like Collins' (2008) *The Hunger Games* on personal blogs helps us engage in this world of fandom and production (perhaps in more limited ways than the large cohort of Tumblr-users we will look at below). In writing in the non-academic spaces of online blogs, contributions like Marcelle's help engage in larger dialogue around works that we may be passionate about. The comments that the blog post received illustrate the varied spaces in which we carry our scholarship and critical reading of literature and media. From university and literacy-focused colleagues to online peers to friends and family, the hybrid "extra space" (Kirkland, 2009) of Marcelle's blog highlights how discourse and engagement reaches across audiences.

Recognizing the ephemeral nature of memes—one day a sensation and, perhaps, the next gone—we want to look at a momentary dialogue about *The Hunger Games* book and film in an online fan community. That this meme persists for two years beyond its original creation (as of this writing) attests to its ability to reach and connect with a wide readership. And though intended as a multimodal, online product, we attempt to recreate the primary content of what has been shared. Looking at the same moment Katniss' life is spared that opens this chapter, one online meme uses animated GIF images (Graphic Interface Format) to depict the film-version of the scene in comic-like panels (see Figure 1).

Each of the images above is a looped 2 to 4 second snippet of video from the film and the captions recreate the dialogue of the scene. In doing so, this user (and many who adopt a similar use of this genre) allow viewers to *read* and re-read the film as text, reminding us of the ways we can do the same with the printed source material.

Figure 1. GIF images enact the lasting influence of Rue.

Though the origins of such memes are difficult to pinpoint, the emerging conversation and its most prominent authors is not. While one Tumblr account— http://taylor-swift.tumblr.com/—is credited for first posting this six-GIF narrative, the conversation it provoked is more telling.[1] The first response that is largely contained in the reshared narrative is a short exposition that reframes this scene and also the *entire* premise of revolutionary identity within the book. It is important to note that the images above are not the meme in full. Instead, it is the images *and* the following dialogue that were circulated. As such, below is a description of the three textual components that were a part of the meme. Tumblr member prismatic-bell (2013) writes:

Can we just stop and talk about this for a minute?

Thresh doesn't make an alliance. Thresh doesn't waste time liking her. Thresh knows that either he must kill her or she must kill him for one of them to win.

But this is the only way he can repay her for protecting Rue when he couldn't. It's the only way he can repay her for honoring Rue when he couldn't. He honors her by sparing her friend, the girl who would have died for her.

The revolution really doesn't start with Katniss.

It starts with Rue.

In the hundreds of thousands of repostings of this post, a new commenter, mockingatlas, follows the above explanation with a four word, all capitalized, bolded response: "***SOMEBODY FINALLY SAID IT.***"

The meme concludes with a third commenter that provides a much lengthier, 505-word explanation of how readers misinterpret *The Hunger Games*. 2srooky begins by writing:

This is exactly the point I've been trying to make for years. Okay, so the revolution gets it's [sic] kindling with Katniss. She volunteers, well that's new, she rebels in the display of talents by shooting the apple. This triggers her perfect score, okay. These aren't really "Revolutionary" though.

What follows is a nuanced understanding of how Katniss plays the 74th annual Hunger Games competition just as any other competitor would. She utilizes the "Star Crossed Lovers" motif to her advantage. 2srooky explains that Katniss' acute media savvy is life-saving, but not necessarily revolutionary in nature. Ultimately, the comment makes clear that "*what changes the game is Rue.*" The argument that is developed concludes with two sentences that build upon the first commenter, 2srooky's, claim: "*So the revolution never started with Katniss, she was just the tinder for Rue's ignition. Rue was the real Mockingjay.*"

Looking over this narrative, notice that the intent of the original poster of the six images may not have been in concert with this critical retelling of *The Hunger Games* story. He or she (or they) could have been simply reinforcing the sheer, good-natured-personality of Katniss as the reason she is able to lead a class-based revolution in the future installments of the book and film franchise. However, in the collective discourse around this image, the meme that develops is one that states otherwise; it challenges the central premise that Katniss is the revolutionary leader in Panem and posits, instead, Rue as the instigator of social revolution.

Measuring the scale of memes and this kind of fandom is difficult. However a few numbers reveal the power of this narrative within online fandom's community. As of March 2014, this dialogue, and the original six-panels of GIFs, had over 300,000 "notes" on Tumblr. To better explain what these notes *mean*, here is a screenshot of 10 of these notes from one Tumblr user, Prismatic-Bell, that shared the dialogue (see Figure 2).

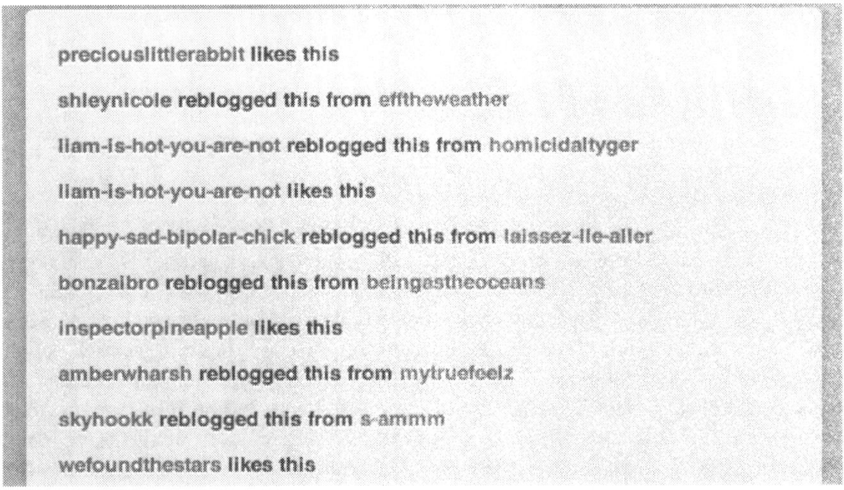

preciouslittlerabbit **likes** this

shleynicole **reblogged** this from efftheweather

liam-is-hot-you-are-not **reblogged** this from homicidaltyger

liam-is-hot-you-are-not **likes** this

happy-sad-bipolar-chick **reblogged** this from laissez-lle-aller

bonzaibro **reblogged** this from beingastheoceans

inspectorpineapple **likes** this

amberwharsh **reblogged** this from mytruefeelz

skyhookk **reblogged** this from s-ammm

wefoundthestars **likes** this

Figure 2. A sample of how a popular meme is distributed and amplified on Tumblr (http://prismatic-bell.tumblr.com/post/69343374028/can-we-just-stop-and-talk-about-this-for-a)

Though there are occasionally comments sprinkled into these notes, the list above highlights how notes on Tumblr act primarily as a log of who "likes" the content on a page, if they share it (by reblogging it and hosting the content on their own Tumblr page), and how they found it. For example, the second line of the above content indicates that user shleynicole posted the dialogue and GIFs to his or her own Tumblr page and originally found it from a page called efftheweather. We can extrapolate that across the 300,000 notes, the dialogue of revolution was shared hundreds of thousands of times. Each "reblog" of this content brings it to a new Tumblr audience. This does not include users that may post this content on non-Tumblr pages or share it in other ways. For instance, Antero first saw this post when it was shared via Twitter, which then sent him to a prominent Tumblr account focused on young adult literature, http://mitaukano.tumblr.com/. The traffic around these memes is *active*: to "read" memes often means viewers *do* something with them; they get shared, "liked," and discussed on other digital mediums. The scale of a single meme extends beyond its originator. As the example here depicts, memes are not only multimodal but also multi-authored.

How memes are constructed today has implications for literacy production and civic engagement of youth, as we discuss below.

LITERACY PRODUCTION OF MEMES

In framing their edited collection *The Fan Fiction Studies Reader,* Hellekson and Busse (2014) outline six key directions in which scholarship of fanfiction and fan studies can be understood:
– Fan fiction as interpretation of source text.
– Fan fiction as a communal gesture.
– Fan fiction as a sociopolitical argument.
– Fan fiction as individual engagement and identificatory practice.
– Fan fiction as one element of audience response.
– Fan fiction as a pedagogical tool. (pp. 8-9)
Looking at this list, one can imagine the Rue-focused meme as one that can be interpreted across these different lenses. In particular, readers of *The Hunger Games* (Collins, 2008) as well as educators can recognize the powerful, pedagogical potential in recasting and re-understanding the main tensions at work near the end of the book. Perhaps more importantly, we see the transgressive nature of memes as a liberatory literacy practice for youth. The intersection of "sociopolitical argument" and "pedagogical tool" illustrates the robust nature that memes like the one above play in defining value for readers of the novel (and viewers of the film adaptation). In her own analysis of a popular meme—the Confession Bear—Jacqueline Vickery (2013) argues that "anonymity and remix allow users to transgress social boundaries (p. 23). Couching this work within the cultural landscape of participatory media (Jenkins et al., 2009), Vickery (2013) notes that "[p]articipatory and remix culture allow users to challenge forms, transgress boundaries, and appropriate space" (p. 23).

The Rue-focused meme explored in this chapter highlights how a young adult text like Collins' (2008) can function as more than merely a site for consumption. By allowing critical voices to share and explore the meaning making of this book for different audiences, *The Hunger Games* acts as a locus of literacy production. In her concluding chapter in Knobel and Lankshear's *A New Literacies Sampler,* Lewis (2007) writes:

> They [memes] circulate widely and change—get parodied, modified and so forth. Also, "reading" the memes involves knowledge of how they have circulated—a deep understanding of cross-references and intertextuality— where the memes have come from, what they refer to, and where the language or images have been before they became this particular meme. (p. 253)

The Hunger Games fans that created, circulated, and "liked" this meme demonstrate the powerful possibilities of "participatory culture" (Jenkins et al., 2009). Further, the chained responses of "liking" and "reblogging" that have occurred more than a quarter-million times highlight the civic power of teen-focused "networked publics" (boyd, 2014). And while, in this light, memes can be understood as powerful and positive tools for youth to identify with and find recognition in popular texts, online viral responses can also swing the other way. In the next part of this chapter, we want to look at another viral response to *The Hunger Games* novel and film adaptation as a means to contrast fan response and understand the cultural hegemony that underpins cultural production and interpretation today.

CONFRONTING THE UNIMAGINABLE: INVISIBLE RACIAL REPRESENTATION IN YOUNG ADULT LITERATURE

In her TEDtalk "The Danger of a Single Story" (2009), award winning Nigerian writer and author Chimamanda Ngozi Adichie begins by talking about how, in her early writing and illustrations as a child, she developed characters that looked and sounded like the characters in the stories she read—her characters were all white and blue eyed, she describes. From her immersion in British books with white characters, she only imagined characters in her writing who were foreign and unknown to her and her own lived experience. Of her introduction to African writers, she says:

> ... because of writers like Chinua Achebe and Camara Laye I went through a mental shift in my perception of literature. I realized that people like me, girls with skin the color of chocolate, whose kinky hair could not form ponytails, could also exist in literature. I started to write about things I recognized. Now, I loved those American and British books I read. They stirred my imagination. They opened up new worlds for me. But the unintended consequence was that I did not know that people like me could exist in literature. So what the discovery of African writers did for me was this: It saved me from having a single story of what books are.

This admission is a powerful one—Adichie did not know that non-white people with diverse backgrounds and experiences could exist in literature in legitimated ways. The omission of diverse characters and histories from literature is significant, especially given the growing diversity of readers. There remains a lack of diverse representation in young adult literature, despite authors making efforts to diversify their characters and storylines. Yet the landscape of young adult fiction does not reflect the diversity in our society. So, what then for dystopian societies? What then for societies that are unreal and imagined?

The social media uproar with the casting of young African American actress Amandla Stenberg as the character Rue for Ross's (2012) film adaptation was indicative of a resistance toward the diversification of young adult literature and of readers' inability to imagine a raced dystopian world. Even in an imagined world, a character can only be white and blue-eyed. As hinted at in Marcelle's blog post shared earlier in the chapter, many Hunger Games fans were surprised and angry with the movie portrayal of Rue as a black girl, despite Collins' (2008) description of her as having "dark eyes and satiny brown skin" (p. 98). Indeed, many fans used

Twitter as a space to unleash their emotional responses and racist reactions. Jezebel blogger Dodai Stewart (2012) archived several of these tweets in her post, "Racist *Hunger Games* Fans Are Very Disappointed." Are there racial limits to the imagination? Does not being able to imagine Rue as a black girl make a person racist? In the tweet below, the Twitterer calls out racism and admits how the representation of Rue as a black girl made him less empathetic and "sad" about her death (see Figure 3).

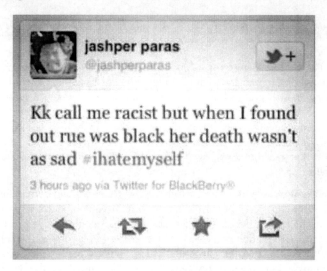

Figure 3. Twitter response to the casting of Amandla Stenberg for the Hunger Games film.

Yet, despite being racist, Twitterers expressed great outrage about characters who were central to *The Hunger Games* (Collins, 2008) plot, like Rue, Thresh, and Cinna, being played by African American actors (see Figure 4).

This anger and media "boycott" of the film may not have been as significant had persons of color only been included to support and bolster the understanding of the other main characters, marginalizing race and diversity. Had the Hunger Games franchise gone the typical route of having characters of color in ancillary roles that were tangential to the actual plot, such outrage would have been foisted. Instead, it is *because* Rue is such a central character for readers that they reject her skin color as anything but white.

In looking at the responses to casting decisions made for the film adaptation of Suzanne Collins' (2008) novel, we want to emphasize that the "racist rage" exhibited by book readers can be understood in terms of hegemonic culture. Antonio Gramsci (1971) describes "social hegemony" as social structures that develop "consent ... caused by the prestige (and consequent confidence) which the dominant group enjoys because of its position and function in the world of production" (p. 12). Broadly, we can understand this as the notion that individuals are not "ruled by force alone, but also by ideas" (Bates, 1975). In concert with

Adichie's (2009) discussion of the "single story" and its dangers, we can imagine hegemony as a means of dictating social expectations and beliefs within young adult literature. Because of the prevalence of white, hegemonic characters in texts like Collins (2008) *The Hunger Games*, it is *literally* unimaginable for some readers to see depictions of characters other than white. That the text dictates characters like Rue and Thresh as non-white in the book does little to change the hegemonic climate in which many people read.

Figure 4. Additional Twitter responses to the casting of black actors in The Hunger Games.

It is striking to consider the ways the two meme-like online literacy practices discussed in this chapter propel or push against hegemony. While the Tumblr image and subsequent fan dialogue discussed above highlight a necessary retelling of hegemonic discourse around the Hunger Games franchise, the Twitter responses to Rue's casting reinforce hegemonic social conventions. Vickery (2013), in discussing the Confession Bear meme, notes that the role of "normative assumptions and hegemonic culture ... work to bind the meme" (p. 23). The Twitter responses shared here function similarly: they deracinate literal interpretations of the novel as a means to inflating racist, social discourse. In contrast to the Confession Bear meme, the Rue-volution is one that directly challenges hegemonic culture. As Bates (1975) writes:

> an old order cannot be made to vanish simply by pointing out its evils, any more than a new order can be brought into existence by pointing out its virtues. A social order, no matter how exploitative, cannot be understood simply as a conspiracy of wicked rulers. (p. 365)

As we challenge and confront power structures that reinforce racist readings of texts like Collins' (2008) *The Hunger Games*, we must consider the pedagogic responsibility for educators to address wider conditions of the state and society that produce, negotiate, transform, and bear down on the conditions of teaching so as to either enable or disable teachers from acting in a critical and transformative way (Giroux, 1987, pp. 14–15). The teacher education classroom must operate as a space where beginning and practicing teachers can openly dialogue about underlying assumptions and color-blind ideologies that they too have when engaging with texts like *The Hunger Games* (Collins, 2008). When readers say that they do not see race when reading young adult literature, they are perpetuating a whiteness by default standpoint. The "polite" and "politically correct" response is to assert that race, gender, class, sexuality, and other identity markers are not factors that impact one's ability to relate to and understand characters in literature. Declaring that a character's racial identity does not affect one's reading of a text maintains the hegemonic culture, where whiteness is the norm.

Not seeing and naming race in novels such as Collins' (2008) *The Hunger Games* also limits readers' comprehension of the text. From a critical literacy framework, the text beckons readers to consider who is included and excluded from the dominant center; it calls to question issues of power, who is in control and who is controlled. Dismissing a racialized reading of *The Hunger Games* glances over Collins' description of the citizens of District 11 as darker skinned individuals. If not people of color, who did readers imagine? Would readers have been more willing to accept a casting of Rue or Thresh as Latino or Asian or Native American? Or, would the film have received the same Twitter backlash? Denying a critically raced analysis omits significant aspects of the text's plot and presumably the author's intent. The Hunger Games Twitter response is not anomalous. Similarly, people took to Twitter to lament the representation of Marvel superhero Spiderman as a Latino male character in the popular comic book series, the casting of African American actor Michael B. Jordan as the Human Torch in the upcoming *Fantastic Four* film, and most recently, the casting of African American actress Quvenzhané Wallis as the lead role in the remake of the film *Annie*. Casting the Oscar-nominated actress as 'Annie' caused a stir among Twitter racists who ironically could not imagine a narrative with a young black child, growing up poor with no parents, singing and dancing. In seeing this cycle of unimaginative proclivity play out again and again, we acknowledge the irony of Thresh claiming forgiveness, "Just this one time," for the singular "little girl," Rue (see Figure 5).

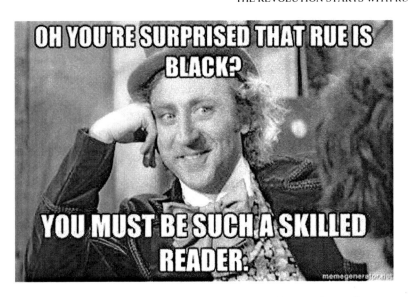

Figure 5. Meme responses challenge assumptions of Hunger Games fans
(http://hungergamestweets.tumblr.com/).

CONCLUSION: CONFRONTING THE IMAGINATION

In her collection of essays, *Releasing the Imagination*, Maxine Greene (2000) writes of "imagination as a means through which we can assemble a coherent world" (p. 3). In looking at the various responses to the Hunger Games franchise in online spaces, we can see young adult fiction as a textual space that coalesces, builds, and—often—rejects the social world. That an imaginary, dystopic environment can function as a litmus test for how we see contemporary, Western society is powerful. Greene extends her explanation by noting that:

> imagination is what, above all, makes empathy possible. It is what enables us to cross the empty spaces between ourselves and those we teachers have called "other" over the years. If those others are willing to give us clues, we can look in some manner through strangers' eyes and hear through their ears. That is because, of all our cognitive capacities, imagination is the one that permits us to give credence to alternative realities. It allows us to break with the taken for granted, to set aside familiar distinctions and definitions. (p. 3)

Agreeing with Greene's explanation of imagination as the provocation for understanding difference, we also see hegemony clouding interpretations of race, *even when the author notes such explanations*. As we consider the pedagogical implications of how readers perceive and understand race in Collins's (2008) *The Hunger Games*, we want to acknowledge the stifling room for revolutionary action by characters that are not white. More broadly, we wonder if youth of color can be

215

considered revolutionary or, in actuality, if this is a role reserved primarily for white protagonists?

While we applaud the strong feminist role that Katniss can be seen embodying, the racial politics in which *The Hunger Games* is read, viewed, and marketed mean that Rue's identity as a non-white, powerful woman are ignored by most readers and film goers. In looking at the tension *between* the voices of the Rue-volutionaries online and the Twitter-deniers, we are reminded that hegemony can be iteratively, slowly rebuilt to reflect the re-imagination of critical readers. As Bates (1975) notes in discussing Gramsci's development of a definition of social hegemony, "for Gramsci, civil society is a sphere of potent historical action" (p. 357). In considering the puissant role young adult texts like those in the Hunger Games trilogy play in today's society, educators, librarians, parents, and enthusiastic readers must challenge and question how we interpret or under-represent race in popular culture. Unlike Thresh's singular moment of mercy—*"Just this one time, I let you go. For the little girl"* (Collins, 2008, p. 288)—it is not enough for us to acknowledge the revolutionary potential of one female of color in one young adult text. We must attest to, speak up for, and challenge the absence of revolutionary images of youth of color.

NOTES

[1] The "about" section of this Tumblr account asserts that the page is a fan's work and not the pop singer, Taylor Swift.

REFERENCES

Adichie, C. (2009). *Chimamanda Adichie: The danger of a single story*. Retrieved March 23, 2013 from, http://www.ted.com/talks/chimamanda_adichie_the_danger_of_a_single_story.html

Bates, T. R. (1975). Gramsci and the theory of hegemony. *Journal of the History of Ideas, 36*(2), 351-366.

boyd, d. (2014). *It's complicated: The social lives of networks teens*. New Haven: Yale University Press.

Collins, S. (2008). *The hunger games*. New York: Scholastic.

Dawkins, R. (1976). *The selfish gene*. Oxford: Oxford University Press.

Garcia, A. (2013). *Critical foundations in young adult literature: Challenging genres*. Rotterdam: Sense.

Garcia-Herranz, M., Moro, E., Cebrian, M., Christakis, N. A., & Fowler, J. H. (2014). Using friends as sensors to detect global-scale contagious outbreaks. *PLoS ONE, 9*(4), e92413. doi:10.1371/journal.pone.0092413

Giroux, H. (1987). Introduction: Literacy and the pedagogy of political empowerment. In P. Freire & D. Macedo (Eds.), *Literacy: Reading the word and the world* (pp. 1-28). London: Routledge.

Gramsci, A. (1971). *Selections from the prison notebooks*. New York: International Publishers.

Greene, M. (2000). *Releasing the imagination: Essays on education, the arts, and social change*. New York: Routledge.

Haddix, M. (2013). Searching for the girl in me [Blog post]. Retrieved from http://zengangstastyle.wordpress.com/2013/12/30/searching-for-the-girl-in-me/

Hellekson, K., & Busse, K. (2014). *The fan fiction studies reader*. Iowa City: University of Iowa Press.

hungergamestweets. (2012). *I've been waiting forever for Willy Wonka to weigh in on this ...* [Blog post]. Retrieved from http://hungergamestweets.tumblr.com/

Jenkins, H., Clinton, K., Purushotma, R., Robison, A. J., & Weigel, M. (2009). *Confronting the challenges of participatory culture: Media education for the 21st century.* MacArthur Foundation.

Kirkland, D. E. (2009). Researching and teaching English in the digital dimension. *Research in the Teaching of English, 44*(1), 8-22.

Knobel, M., & Lankshear, C. (2007). Online memes, affinities, and cultural production. In M. Knobel & C. Lankshear (Eds.), *A new literacies sampler* (pp. 199-227). New York: Peter Lang.

Lewis, C. (2007). New literacies. In M. Knobel & C. Lankshear (Eds.), *A new literacies sampler* (pp. 229-237). New York: Peter Lang.

mitaukano. (2013). *Can we just stop and talk about this for a minute?* [Blog post]. Retrieved from http://mitaukano.tumblr.com/post/69614145038/2srooky-mockingatlas-prismatic-bell-can.

Prismatic Bell. (2013). *Can we just stop and talk about this for a minute?* [Blog post]. Retrieved from http://prismatic-bell.tumblr.com/post/69343374028/can-we-just-stop-and-talk-about-this-for-a

Ross, G. (Director). (2012). *The hunger games.* USA: Lionsgate.

Stewart, D. (2012, March 26). *Racist Hunger Games fans are very disappointed* [Blog post]. Retrieved from http://jezebel.com/5896408/racist-hunger-games-fans-dont-care-how-much-money-the-movie-made/all

Vickery, J. R. (2013). The curious case of Confession Bear: The reappropriation of online macro-image memes. *Information, Communication & Society, 17*(3).

P. L. THOMAS

AFTERWORD: WHY ARE STRONG FEMALE CHARACTERS NOT ENOUGH?

Katniss Everdeen and Lisbeth Salander, from Novel to Film

The covers of Stieg Larsson's Millennium Trilogy (*The Girl with the Dragon Tattoo, The Girl Who Played with Fire*, and *The Girl Who Kicked the Hornet's Nest*) had caught my eye often during my many visits to the bookstore. But I always disregarded the novels as "popular" until something compelled me to consider the works further. Simultaneously, a buzz rose around the coming U.S. film version of the first novel (although the entire trilogy had already been adapted to film in Larsson's native Sweden).

Once I started reading *The Girl with the Dragon Tattoo*, I began to reconsider my assumptions about genre (the publisher identifies the novels as "crime") as I fell in love with Larsson as a writer, the novels themselves, and most importantly, the character Lisbeth Salander. Larsson offers a powerful dramatization of a disturbing and too often ignored truth about our contemporary world: The world remains a very violent and unfair place for women.

I have written (Thomas, 2014) about Salander as an "other," reduced to criminal by the very judicial and social systems designed to protect the innocent. In the final book (so far) of the trilogy, *The Girl Who Kicked the Hornet's Nest*, Salander's status as "other" is detailed:

> "Our client on principle does not speak to the police or to other persons of authority, and least of all to psychiatrists. The reason is simple. From the time she was a child she tried time and again to talk to police and social workers to explain that her mother was being abused by Alexander Zalachenko. *The result in every instance was that she was punished* [emphasis added] because government civil servants had decided that Zalachenko was more important than she was." (Larsson, 2009a, p. 733)

Despite her exceptional qualities, and despite the abuse she and her mother suffered in their home, Salander is the repeated victim of *systemic* inequity. Nonetheless, as a reader, I continue to consider Salander one of the most powerful characters in literature as well as one of the most well drawn female characters.

When I ventured into Suzanne Collins's the Hunger Games trilogy (*The Hunger Games, Catching Fire*, and *Mockingjay*), I was struck by the parallels—both trilogies, both with "fire" in the second volume, and both with notably strong female main characters. The young adult dystopian trilogy by Collins, I believe, falls short of Larsson's accomplishments, but there is much in Collins that rises—

as do Larsson's novels—above common criticisms of science fiction and young adult literature, most significantly, Katniss Everdeen.

But the trilogies from Larsson and Collins offer another parallel that sits in the film adaptations of the works, raising an important question: Why are strong female characters not enough?

KATNISS EVERDEEN AND LISBETH SALANDER, FROM NOVEL TO FILM

After I had read both trilogies, I saw the 2011 U.S. film adaptation of *The Girl with the Dragon Tattoo* with Daniel Craig and Rooney Mara in the two leads. I thought the film was quite strong, considering that most films as novel adaptations fall well short of the originals. But my greatest concerns did lie with the portrayal of Salander.

When the Hunger Games trilogy became popular and film adaptations began dominating the public discourse around the works (arguments about who was being cast in the roles and controversy over the white-washing of the novel-as-film), I was struck by the first movie posters I saw for the second film (see Figure 1).

Figure 1. Film posters for Catching Fire.

The representation of Katniss in these posters triggered two thoughts immediately: first, Katniss has been stylized as a superhero, and second, this transformation of a strong female character into a superhero reminded me of the

U.S. film version of Salander, who was treated differently in the film posters for that film (see Figure 2).

Figure 2. Film posters for 2011 U.S. film version of The Girl with the Dragon Tattoo.

While the posters of Katniss mask her strong persona behind the trappings of a superhero, the posters of Salander position her *behind* (and thus lesser) than the male lead. However, in the film itself, particularly when Salander is riding her motorcycle, Salander too is masked as superhero, spurring for me images of the recent rebooting of the Batman films directed by Christopher Nolan and starring Christian Bale.

Art is an act of recreation, and adaptation (Thomas, 2012) is yet another layer of recreation. But art also serves as both a reflection of the so-called "real" world and an influence on that real world. In the film versions of Katniss's and Salander's stories, we are confronted with some troubling questions:

- Broadly, why are strong female characters not enough? The novel versions of Katniss and Salander are incredibly compelling as strong female characters; their strengths also are more realistic than the unreal contexts drawn by the genres of the two narratives. I often suspended belief for the narratives, but held fast to the characters Katniss and Salander.
- What messages are sent by rendering both characters as superheroes—to society, to men, and to women?
- Are medium/genre messages embedded in the adaptations? Also, are readers of novels (by the nature of readers or print-only text) more capable or willing to embrace strong female characters than viewers of films (also by the nature of film viewers or video)?
- What happens to the imagined character in print-only text once that character is embodied in real-life actors?

It is here, among the problems and questions raised by texts of all sort among genre, medium, and form, that I believe we must bring students. Our texts do not have to be pure or perfect—as is often the case with how women, minorities, and many "others" are portrayed—but nearly all texts can serve well our critical purposes to unpack art as it unpacks the real world captured in that imagined world.

When we discover that a character or a work such as Katniss Everdeen and the Hunger Games trilogy has spoken to our students, we must allow their invitation to stand, and then we must offer them safe spaces to challenge the texts that challenge us. With Katniss Everdeen, I want my students to answer for me, why are strong female characters not enough?

REFERENCES

Collins, S. (2008). *The hunger games*. New York: Scholastic Inc.
Collins, S. (2009). *Catching fire*. New York: Scholastic Press.
Collins, S. (2010). *Mockingjay*. New York: Scholastic Press.
Larsson, S. (2009a). *The girl who kicked the hornet's nest* (R. Keeland, Trans.). New York, NY: Vintage Crime/Black Lizard.
Larsson, S. (2009b). *The girl who played with fire* (R. Keeland, Trans.). New York, NY: Vintage Crime/Black Lizard.
Larsson, S. (2009c). *The girl with the dragon tattoo* (R. Keeland, Trans.). New York, NY: Vintage Crime/Black Lizard.
Thomas, P. L. (2014). Schools as prisons: Normative youth pedagogies. In A. Ibrahim & S. Steinberg (Eds.), *Critical youth studies reader*. New York, NY: Peter Lang USA.
Thomas, P. L. (2012, Fall). Lost in adaptation: Kurt Vonnegut's radical humor in film and print. *Studies in American Humor, 3*(26), 85-101.

AUTHOR BIOGRAPHIES

Hilary Brewster is an Assistant Professor of English at Marshall University, where she teaches young adult literature, literary theory, and English education methods. Her publications with Palgrave Macmillan and *Bookbird Journal* focus on rhetorical analyses of young adult literature, including Harry Potter.

Sean P. Connors is an Assistant Professor of English education in the College of Education and Health Professions at the University of Arkansas. His scholarship and teaching focuses on the application of diverse critical perspectives to young adult literature. Sean's publications are featured in *The ALAN Review* and *English Journal*. He is the incoming editor of *SIGNAL Journal*.

Antero Garcia is an Assistant Professor in the English Department at Colorado State University. His research focuses on developing critical literacies and civic identity through the use of participatory media and gameplay in formal learning environments. Among Antero's publications are the recent books *Critical Foundations in Young Adult Literature: Challenging Genres* (Sense, 2013) and *Teaching in the Connected Learning Classroom* (Digital Media Hub, 2014).

Marcelle Haddix is a Dean's associate professor and program director of English education at Syracuse University. She also directs *Writing Our Lives*, a program geared toward supporting the writing practices of urban youth. Her publications are featured in *Research in the Teaching of English, English Education*, and *Journal of Adolescent and Adult Literacy*.

Michael Macaluso is a doctoral student and Graduate Instructor in the College of Education's Curriculum, Instruction, and Teacher Education Program at Michigan State University. Michael's scholarship focuses on critical perspectives in English Education.

Brian McDonald, M.A., M. Div., is a Senior Lecturer in literature for the English Department of Indiana/Purdue University, Indianapolis Campus (IUPUI). His teaching and scholarship focus on both literary and philosophical interpretation of the works he teaches, and is informed by the thought of Rene Girard, Phillip Rieff, and philosophers of early and late antiquity.

Cori McKenzie is a doctoral student and Graduate Instructor in the College of Education's Curriculum, Instruction, and Teacher Education Program at Michigan State University. Cori's scholarship focuses on English Education and critical theory.

Meghann Meeusen is a doctoral candidate at Illinois State University, where she teaches children's literature and acts as the associate editor of the *Grassroots Writing Research Journal*. Her research focuses on adaptation studies, children's fantasy and visual culture, gender studies, and cultural-historical activity theory.

Rodrigo Joseph Rodríguez is an Assistant Professor of English Education in the Department of English at The University of Texas at El Paso. His scholarship focuses on classroom and social contexts that inform students' learning gains through culturally and socially responsible literacies, including the teaching of children's and young adult literatures. He lives in El Paso and Austin, Texas.

Iris Shepard completed her PhD in English Literature at the University of Arkansas. Her scholarly and research interests have led her to focus on the representation of the child in children's film and young adult literature. Iris has presented her work at a number of national conferences. Her work has been published in a range of journals and essay collections, including *JAELP* and *Blue Collar Pop Culture*.

Anna O. Soter is Professor Emerita, College of Education and Human Ecology at The Ohio State University. Dr. Soter's research and scholarship has focused on literary theory applied to young adult literature, discourse analysis and critical thinking, and language study in educational settings. In addition, she has expanded her scholarship to explore the relationship of poetry and writing well-being, language as a field of energy, the role of language in the lives we live, and transforming language pedagogy.

Susan S. M. Tan is a final year PhD student at the University of Cambridge. Her dissertation focuses on historical initiation in young adult dystopian literature.

P. L. Thomas is an Associate Professor of Education at Furman University in Greenville, South Carolina. He taught high school English in South Carolina before becoming a teacher educator. He is a column editor for *English Journal* (National Council of Teachers of English) and author of *Ignoring Poverty in the U.S.* (IAP, 2012). He has written volumes on several authors, including Barbara Kingsolver, Kurt Vonnegut, Margaret Atwood, and Ralph Ellison. He edited *Science Fiction and Speculative Fiction: Challenging Genres* (Sense, 2013) and co-edited with A. Scott Henderson *James Baldwin: Challenging Authors* (Sense 2014), which are also part of the series in which the current volume appears. His scholarship and commentary are located at http://radicalscholarship.wordpress.com and can be followed at @plthomasEdD.

Roberta Seelinger Trites holds the rank of Distinguished Professor at Illinois State University, where she teaches children's and adolescent literature in the Department of English. Her scholarly interests in adolescent literature include narrative theory, feminism, and cognitive linguistics.

Ian Wojcik-Andrews is a professor of children's literature at Eastern Michigan University. His current scholarship involves looking at children's and young adult films from various critical perspectives.

CPSIA information can be obtained at www.ICGtesting.com
Printed in the USA
LVOW09s2138280814

401421LV00005B/42/P